AGING [barcode D0958934] HEALTH

"I think this manual is an essential guide to aging for the elderly and anyone concerned about an elderly person. It translates confusing medical terminology into simple language, explaining everything from what normal aging really is to medical problems such as Alzheimer's. This wonderful book will improve health care for the elderly by teaching the public what questions to ask health care providers."
—Liebe Kravitz, M.S.W.,
Harvard Medical School

"*[AGING IN GOOD HEALTH]* simultaneously provides information about the important health issues while maintaining a warm and personal tone. Indeed, Dr. Beers is talking to all readers as though they were his own patients, friends, and family."
—Leslie Libow, M.D.,
The Mount Sinai School of Medicine

"Dr. Beers's kindness and clinical acumen come through, throughout. But, to me, the key characteristic of this book compared to so many others is its honesty and scientific rigor. If you want to know about yourself as you age—then read this book."
—Arlene Fink, Ph.D.,
UCLA Department of Medicine

"This is a wonderful book which will be greatly appreciated by young and old alike who strive to understand the changes in aging and the ways in which each person can enhance later life."
—Terrie Fulmer, R.N., Ph.D.,
Geriatric Nursing, Yale University

"This is a turn-of-the-century book that could well be found in the hands of every mature and older adult."
—James E. Birren, Director,
Borun Center for Gerontological Research, UCLA

AGING IN GOOD HEALTH

A Complete, Essential Medical Guide for Older Men and Women and Their Families

MARK H. BEERS, M.D.,

AND

STEPHEN K. URICE, PH.D., J.D.

POCKET BOOKS

New York   London   Toronto   Sydney   Tokyo   Singapore

For our parents
Who gave us the chance to grow old
and
For Liebe

The ideas, procedures and suggestions in this book are intended to supplement, not replace, the medical and legal advice of trained professionals. Laws vary from state to state, and if legal advice is required, the services of a competent professional should be sought. In addition, all matters regarding your health require medical supervision. Consult your physician before adopting the medical suggestions in this book, as well as about any condition that may require diagnosis or medical attention.

The authors and publishers disclaim any liability arising directly or indirectly from the use of this book.

An *Original* publication of Pocket Books

POCKET BOOKS, a division of Simon & Schuster Inc.
1230 Avenue of the Americas, New York, NY 10020

Copyright © 1992 by Trustees of the Beers/Urice Revocable Trust
Interior illustrations copyright © 1992 by Beth Weadon Massari

Front cover photo: Ron Chapple/FPG International

Beers, Mark H.
    Aging in good health : a complete, essential medical guide for older men and women and their families / Mark H. Beers and Stephen K. Urice.
      p. cm.
    Includes index.
    ISBN: 0-671-72822-9 : $10.00
    1. Aged—Health and hygiene. I. Urice, Stephen K. II. Title.
RA777.6.B44 1992
613'.0438—dc20
                                     91-28682
                                        CIP

First Pocket Books trade paperback printing January 1992

10 9 8 7 6 5 4 3 2 1

POCKET and colophon are registered trademarks of
Simon & Schuster Inc.

Printed in the U.S.A.

ACKNOWLEDGMENTS

We are indebted to many people who assisted us in preparing this book. First, we thank our many teachers, in particular the late Dr. George Wolf, Dr. William Alan Tisdale, Dr. Richard Besdine, Dr. John Rowe, and Liebe Kravitz, MSW. We are also grateful to colleagues—Dr. David Reuben, Professor Jesse Dukeminier, Charles A. Collier, Jr., Esq., Michael McCarthy, Esq., and Paul N. Frimmer, Esq.—who read portions of the manuscript and corrected our errors. We also thank Donna Smith, Babette Rogers, and Eleanor Mac-Dougal, who emerged from retirement to read the manuscript and to tell us where it could be made clearer for our audience. Their recommendations, almost all of which we adopted, should make this book easier for you to use.

We were especially fortunate in finding our illustrator, Beth Weadon Massari. Beth chose a career in medical illustration as a means of helping educate others about their bodies and themselves. Although she had not previously prepared drawings of older people, when asked, she took up the challenge with gusto. Showing exceptional sensitivity to the subject matter and to the readers of this book, Beth has created accurate and beautiful illustrations, and we thank her.

We also thank Thomas A. Cox for a week of solitude at his summer cottage on Sutton's Island, Maine, during which several chapters of this book were written. Professor William Kelly Simpson generously extended the use of his house for our working trips to New York.

Michael Sanders and Claire Zion, our editors at Pocket Books, were remarkably insightful in their suggestions, and we cannot thank them enough for their efforts, advice, and reassurance.

We must thank the midwives who saw to it that this book went from good idea to actual print. We benefitted from the wise counsel of our good friend John A. Silberman, Esq., and of our agent, Mel Berger.

Finally, it is no understatement to say that we would not have written *Aging in Good Health* were it not for the encouragement and advice of Professors Sylvan Barnet, Mort Berman, and Bill Burto. These nominally retired scholars provided us with the incentive to produce the book, read the manuscript at various stages of its development, and offered many more good ideas than we chose to adopt. We trust they forgive our obstinacy.

Of course, the final responsibility for what is written here rests with us. Any errors that remain are ours alone.

—MHB, SKU
Santa Monica, California
June 1991

FOREWORD

Although we have many interests in common profession-
ally, Mark Beers, Stephen Urice, and I did not meet because
of them. We were introduced by a mutual friend, a well-
known photographer whose work I admire and with whom I
had shared many good, even hedonistic, meals. The pleasures
of the table proved to be a common bond among all of us.

In the north of England, where I grew up, people who enjoy
eating are viewed with great approval, being generally re-
garded as healthier and perhaps even more virtuous than
people who don't. My perception, therefore, may be skewed in
this regard. But the appreciation for the joy of life that has
imbued our meals together, the relish for living in all its
aspects, seems to me to inform Mark's work. He is anxious
that people should be able to enjoy their lives as fully and for
as long as possible and wants to help them do so.

Aging, unfortunately, frightens many of us; fatalism and
lack of knowledge compound this fear, and consequently the
years when we should be enjoying ourselves can too often be
marred by uncertainty and anxiety. In this book the authors
confront many of these anxieties and give easily comprehen-
sible, sympathetic advice on what to do about them. If there
is one overriding quality in their approach that I admire more
than others, it is this clarity, this carefully worked-for simpli-
city. My years in journalism have taught me that such simplici-
ty is one of the hardest things for any writer to achieve, and
there is a certain amount of envy mixed with my admiration.
Forty years ago, when I was at school, biology and chemistry
were the subjects that made me feel most inadequate intellec-
tually. Finding my way through this book with such ease made
me feel cleverer, as well as more knowledgeable. (Is aging
actually good for the brain?) Above all, I felt astonished that
never once did the mass of information bog me down. And
they're not even professional writers. How dare they!

In my fifties, I appreciate being forwarded—and forearmed—about the potential developments of the next few decades. And I appreciate the calm, sensible way in which the book places its information in context, weighing the pros and cons of different approaches, never losing sight of the main objective—maintaining the quality of one's life. We all have our different concerns and priorities. I turned first to the chapter on prevention, reading it out of sequence for some quick reassurance. It led to some new resolutions and a glad recognition of the chapter's message: "You can take advantage of the present to preserve your future."

Every married man has probably been accused at some point in the marriage of cultivating deafness, and after fifty the charge can carry an extra helping of poison on its tip. The chapter on hearing came second for me after the chapter on prevention. It helped me consider the possibility rationally rather than dismissing it as one of the canards women use against men.

One of the more irritating and all-pervasive unpleasant-nesses of ill health is the humiliating descent one takes from being a person to being a patient. In outlining the care and maintenance of the body, the writers never lose sight of the whole person to whom those mechanical parts belong. Over and over throughout the book the reader is grateful for the way in which the information is kept in the context of living. The final chapter on the legal issues surrounding health care carries this concern a crucial step further, with invaluable advice on keeping control of one's life.

They are frank, too, about the limitations of current knowledge. As they state, theories of aging are "like the mythology of ancient societies. They attempt to explain something we desperately want to understand and which we would like to control. The truth is, though our knowledge is growing every day, we understand aging very little and can do almost nothing to control it." Beers and Urice guide us caringly through the mysteries, helping us live as well as we can with the knowledge that is available.

—J. HENRY FENWICK
Editor, *Modern Maturity*

CONTENTS

LIST OF FIGURES   *xii*

LIST OF TABLES   *xiv*

INTRODUCTION   *3*

∼ **1**
NORMAL AGING   *9*

∼ **2**
MEDICATIONS   *23*

∼ **3**
HEART   *44*

∼ **4**
BLOOD   *72*

~ **5**
BONES   *87*

~ **6**
SKIN   *109*

~ **7**
MOUTH AND TEETH   *125*

~ **8**
VISION AND EYES   *132*

~ **9**
HEARING AND EARS   *150*

~ **10**
CONSTIPATION AND THE
GASTROINTESTINAL SYSTEM   *161*

~ **11**
CANCER   *184*

~ **12**
DIABETES   *204*

13
STROKE 217

14
TREMOR AND PARKINSON'S DISEASE 230

15
DEMENTIA AND ALZHEIMER'S
DISEASE 243

16
URINARY INCONTINENCE 260

17
SEXUALITY, GYNECOLOGY, AND
REPRODUCTIVE ORGANS 273

18
PREVENTION 288

19
LEGAL ISSUES 301

GLOSSARY 324

INDEX 335

LIST OF FIGURES

FIGURE 1   THE HEART—VIEW SHOWING
            CHAMBERS OF THE HEART   45

FIGURE 2   THE HEART—VIEW SHOWING
            SURFACE OF THE HEART   46

FIGURE 3   A HEALTHY CORONARY ARTERY
            AND ONE WITH CORONARY
            ARTERY DISEASE   51

FIGURE 4   HOW AN ANGIOPLASTY WORKS   62

FIGURE 5   THE HIP AND TYPES OF HIP
            FRACTURES   101

FIGURE 6   THE SKIN   111

FIGURE 7   THE EYE—FRONTAL VIEW   133

FIGURE 8   THE EYE—CROSS-SECTIONAL
            VIEW   133

FIGURE 9   THE EAR—CROSS-SECTIONAL
               VIEW   *152*

FIGURE 10   THE GASTROINTESTINAL
               SYSTEM   *162*

FIGURE 11   FEMALE URINARY TRACT   *261*

FIGURE 12   MALE URINARY TRACT   *261*

LIST OF TABLES

TABLE 1   NORMAL PHYSIOLOGICAL
CHANGES OF AGING   *18*

TABLE 2   MEDICATIONS WITH SPECIAL RISK
FOR THE ELDERLY   *27*

TABLE 3   MEDICAL CONDITIONS AND THE
MEDICATIONS THAT CAN MAKE
THEM WORSE   *34*

TABLE 4   BETTER AND WORSE SLEEPING
AND ANXIETY PILLS   *38*

TABLE 5   TYPES OF LAXATIVES   *174*

TABLE 6   CAUSES OF DEMENTIA   *250*

TABLE 7   MEDICATIONS THAT CAN CAUSE
URINARY INCONTINENCE   *269*

TABLE 8   MEDICATIONS THAT CAN CAUSE
SEXUAL IMPOTENCE   *279*

xiv

AGING IN GOOD HEALTH

INTRODUCTION

I wrote *Aging in Good Health* for people who want to take an active role in their health care. To receive the best medical care, particularly if you are old, you must be well informed and be your own advocate.

As a geriatrician—a doctor who specializes in the medical needs of the elderly—I came to realize that most of my patients, and their families, arrive at my office woefully underinformed or misinformed about the medical effects of aging. I decided to write this book after discovering that I was repeating to each of my patients, and to concerned members of their families, the same basic information. It was not only my patients who had questions: my own parents, my parents' friends, and my friends who had parents, all called from time to time for answers. What became clear was the need for a reliable medical handbook written specifically for people who are old and for people who care about someone who is old. *Aging in Good Health* is that book. I hope it will serve as your introduction to geriatric medicine and become your first reference whenever you have questions about your health, your medications, or the quality of medical care you are receiving.

3

This book explains the normal changes of aging; describes many of the abnormal conditions and diseases common in later life; tells you what you can do to prevent disease; and discusses the treatments you may need if you do suffer illness or injury. Accordingly, this book will allow you and your family to hold more meaningful and productive discussions with your doctor. The better informed you are, the better prepared you will be to ask the right questions. *Aging in Good Health* will help you to get more out of your visits to the doctor by teaching you about your special medical needs, by leading you through the questions you are likely to be asked, and by suggesting the questions that *you* should be asking.

WHAT IS GERIATRIC MEDICINE?

Aging in Good Health is about *geriatric* medicine, the medical specialty that delivers health care to older people. As you get older, your medical needs change; they differ substantially from the needs you had twenty years ago. Just as your parents saw to it that you were examined by a pediatrician when you were an infant, today you need a specialist's care to address the many physical and mental changes you are experiencing in old age.

Geriatricians, the doctors who practice geriatric medicine, are specialists in the unique conditions and diseases of old age. Most geriatricians trained first in internal medicine or family practice. They then studied for additional years, learning about the particular medical needs of the elderly. All geriatricians have one thing in common: they like working with the elderly and their families.

Many elders do not routinely need the care of a geriatrician. You may find that most of your health care needs are adequately handled by a good internist or family practitioner. However, not all doctors understand your special medical requirements. One goal of this book is to help you determine whether your doctor's care is effective for you. If you are fortunate enough to have a doctor who provides you with good care, special situations may still make it prudent or necessary for you to consult a geriatrician. For example, if you experience a sudden change in your medical or mental condition, are hospitalized, require an operation, or suffer a fall or complications from medications, you should have the advantage of a geriatrician's expertise.

About This Book

For Whom Is This Book Written?

Although this book is addressed to you, the person who has reached old age, it is intended equally for your children, family, and other loved ones who want or need to interact more effectively with you, your doctors, and your other caregivers. Often, it is someone close to you who may first recognize the signs of an impending medical problem, who may need to share the task of maintaining your good health, or who may participate in discussions about your health. This book has also been written for them. They can use it now, to help you, and later, as they grow older, to help themselves.

How This Book Is Organized

Aging in Good Health covers many topics in geriatric medicine. You can read it from cover to cover, learning generally about the many normal changes and abnormal conditions that occur with aging. Or you can use it as a reference to understand more fully the specific conditions or changes that are of concern to you. If you are interested in a specific term or topic, check the Index to see where in the book it is discussed. There are twelve illustrations prepared especially for this book; they will give you a visual guide to specific parts of the body that commonly experience medical problems late in life. Refer to them as you read the text. The Glossary at the end of the book provides definitions of technical terms.

Aging in Good Health has two kinds of chapters. The first describes a specific organ system—the eye, the heart, the skin, for example—and discusses the normal changes and abnormal conditions that can occur with age. The second kind

describes a particular medical problem—dementia, incontinence, and diabetes, among them—and tries to give you a
good understanding of what it is, how it is evaluated, and what
can be done either to prevent or to treat it. Also, in the first
chapter on normal aging, I try to teach you what doctors
mean by the terms *normal, aging,* and *old.* I describe the
many physiological changes that you are experiencing and
explain how those changes affect your health. The medical
portion of the book closes with a chapter on prevention,
which describes how you can avoid many medical difficulties.
The final chapter discusses legal issues that affect how you
can plan to make health care decisions and manage your
property in case illness or injury makes it impossible for you
to communicate your wishes.

Your Health Care Team

Throughout this book, I will introduce you to the many
people who may play a role in delivering health care to you.
The most important of these is your primary-care physician.
This person may be a geriatrician, internist, or family practitioner.

The role of your primary-care physician—whether a geriatrician or not—is crucial. He or she is the one person who
oversees and coordinates all of your medical care. For reasons
you'll see later, you must keep your primary-care physician
informed about *all* of your medical conditions and about
every drug you are taking. For example, as you will learn in
the chapter on medications, even over-the-counter drugs can
have a profound effect on how you feel and can interact badly
with other medicines you may be taking or with a medical
condition you may have.

A particular medical condition or illness may require that
you be seen by any of a number of specialists—an ophthalmologist for cataracts, a gastroenterologist for a problem with
your colon, or an oncologist for cancer treatment, for example. These individuals are introduced in the appropriate sections of the book.

There are other professionals whose expertise directly affects your health and how quickly you recuperate from an illness or an accident. For example, your pharmacist plays an important role in your health care. He or she can assist you in understanding the purpose of your medicines, can offer advice on products to lessen the challenge of incontinence, and can provide suggestions if you must have an over-the-counter medicine and can't reach your doctor. Your physical and occupational therapists directly contribute to your recovery from a stroke and can make the difference between a long period of rehabilitation and a shorter one. Finally, and perhaps most important, at some time you and your family are likely to need the advice of a medical social worker.

Do not confuse medical social workers with government officials who administer welfare programs. Rather, these highly trained professionals are expert in counseling you and your family on the health care system and how it can work for—rather than against—you. They form a very important part of your health care team, helping you to understand the kinds of facilities and services that are available in your community, assisting in arranging for services, and giving insights into the emotional difficulties that often accompany poor health or injury. Your primary-care physician or hospital should be able to put you in touch with a medical social worker trained specifically to work with older people. Take advantage of this resource: social workers often work wonders.

TERMS USED IN THIS BOOK

Too often, doctors and nurses use complex medical terminology that they rarely explain. Although I have steered away from such jargon whenever possible, when it is necessary, you will find the terms defined in context and usually also in the Glossary. After reading this book, you should be able to follow discussions with your medical professionals more easily. However, if you ever find yourself unable to understand your doctor or other health care provider, don't wait until you get home to look up the meaning of a new term or concept! Insist that your doctor, nurse, or therapist explain what he is saying in plain language.

Throughout the book, I use the words *old, older, elderly, senior,* and *aged.* Some people may take offense at one or more of these terms, feeling that another one is more respectful, but I feel that each carries equal regard. This book strives to be honest about the health problems of late life; it does not enter the debate over whether older people prefer to be called elders, elderly persons, senior citizens, the aged, or the old.

It is not easy to grow old in our country today. Ageism—prejudice against the elderly—exists everywhere in our culture, including the medical profession. Your age alone is never a valid reason for any health care practitioner to provide you with any but the highest quality care. To assure yourself that you are receiving the best of care, you need to learn about the changes you are experiencing, about the new medical challenges that you will confront as you get older, and about the many steps that you can take to help yourself. One goal of this book is to give you the information you need to determine if you are getting good care and, if not, to lead you to ask the questions that will put you on the track of getting better care. Another equally important goal is to raise your awareness of what you must do to stay or to get healthy. There is little that even the best doctors, nurses, therapists, and social workers can do for you if you are reckless with your health—if you misuse medications, follow a bad diet, or refuse to recognize warning signs of cancer, diabetes, or glaucoma.

In short, I have written this book based on one premise: the more you know, the easier it will be for you to work with your doctors and other caregivers and the more likely it is that you will receive the best possible health care.

—MHB
Santa Monica, California
May, 1991

1

NORMAL AGING

W ho is old and what is old age? Do you suddenly become old on your sixty-fifth birthday when you were "middle-aged" the year before? Are the changes you experience in your health related simply to getting older or to a specific illness? Does it matter if the changes are normal or abnormal? These questions are not easy to answer. Yet, the answers often tell you a great deal about what you can expect, what you can prevent, what you can correct, and what you must accept. Understanding what normal aging is and how it is likely to affect you is both helpful and fascinating.

WHAT IS OLD AGE?

A young boy is walking his old, arthritic dog. A man comes up and asks the boy how old his dog is. The boy replies, "Rex is very old—he's eleven." "And how old are you, young fellow?" the man asks. "I'm twelve," the boy replies.

"Old age" is not a state of mind or a state of health. There are, however, many definitions of old age, each based on a different set of priorities. For example, by one definition, old age starts when you are no longer essential to your community. In industrialized societies, you traditionally leave the work force at age 65, so, many people consider old age to begin then. In more primitive societies where war, defense, and hunting were the necessary activities of society, old age began when you could no longer carry on these tasks. A warrior/hunter might retire at 40, like one of today's pro football stars. If continuing the species is the goal of society, old age can be defined as beginning when a woman can no longer bear children. You might be old at 50, then.

Prejudices against older people, called *ageism,* are often based on these kinds of definitions and the notion that older people are not valuable and productive members of society. These biases ignore the contributions that old persons continue to make, and the obligations of society to care for and respect those people who made our present comforts possible through their contributions in the past.

In an attempt to reconcile various definitions of *old age,* some gerontologists—the scientists who study aging—speak of chronological aging, biological aging, and psychosocial aging.

Chronological aging is purely objective, with the passage of years marking the transition into chronological old age, often set arbitrarily at 65 years. *Biological old age* occurs when your physiology reflects changes usually associated with growing old. Some people will become biologically aged in their fifties while others will remain biologically young into their eighties. This is a functional definition, independent of the calendar. The third definition, *psychosocial aging,* includes psychological and social changes. An 80-year-old, confined to a wheelchair with a broken hip, might still be considered young by this definition if she were actively raising her grandchildren, creating and selling works of art, and planning future events for herself and her family. On the other hand, a healthy 55-year-old man who was not working toward any goals, had no responsibilities, or was not producing anything useful or creative, would be considered old.

Aging is a continuous process. It begins at the moment of birth and continues through all stages of development. We grow from infancy to childhood, gaining our independence and learning to control our bodies; we move from childhood to adolescence, during which we become sexually mature and physically our most fit; we progress into adulthood and perfect our skills and build our careers and families, putting to use our sexual, physical, and mental development. Finally, we proceed to old age, the concern of this book.

THEORIES OF AGING

Regardless of the definition we use, we are generally able to recognize when someone is old. In fact, we can recognize when a dog, cat, or horse is old. Although dogs do not live as long as humans, all dogs begin to get old at approximately the same age. And, although human beings can die at any age, there is a maximum age beyond which no one lives.

With good nutrition, hygiene, and medical care, the *average human life span* has increased dramatically over the centuries. In 1900 a newborn could be expected to live until age 47; today, a newborn can be expected to live to age 75. But the *maximum human life span,* the age to which the oldest persons live (about 110 years old), has not increased for as long as recorded history. (If we count Methuselah who was said to have lived for 10,000 years, the human life span has decreased dramatically since biblical times.)

How is it that a dog can be old at 11 years of age while a person has not yet reached maturity at 12 years? Why is it that despite our ability to prolong the average life span by almost thirty years in less than a century, our maximum life span has remained the same for thousands of years? Why does every form of life grow old and then die? Why can't we live forever? Scientists have developed several *theories of aging* to attempt to answer these questions. Since we do not yet know with any certainty why all living things age, these theories are merely attempts to explain what scientists do not yet understand. Nevertheless, the theories are useful to researchers, because they provide a way to organize thinking and discussion about these questions. I will describe two of these theories as examples.

The Free-Radical Theory

The free-radical theory of aging asserts that animals grow old because of particular chemical processes. Chemicals produced as by-products of biological activity in turn harm the very cells that made them. One such kind of chemical, called a *free radical,* is particularly destructive, attacking the basic building blocks of cells. As we age, more and more destruction occurs, until cells can no longer function properly. When enough cells do not function, whole organ systems—the kidneys, the brain, and the heart—begin to shut down, eventually leading to death. Even bacteria, which do not have complex organ systems, may be harmed and killed by free radicals.

The free-radical theory recognizes that there are many factors that govern the speed of the chemical destruction, including toxic elements in the environment. Additionally, each species produces and resists free radicals differently, which is why some animals live longer than others. Genetics make individuals and families more susceptible or less, which explains why some people live longer than others.

Programmed Senescence

In another theory of aging, *programmed senescence,* the rate at which we age and grow old is predetermined. (*Senescence* means "old age.") The genetic material that controls virtually every function of our cells, the theory says, also controls how fast they age and when they die. After enough cells die, our organs fail; eventually we die.

This theory also implies that there is a benefit to growing old; aging, growing old, and dying are good processes because they prevent overpopulation and allow the young to strengthen society. As one group of people ages, younger and stronger persons take on their roles in the community, bringing new strengths, better genes, and novel ideas. According to this theory, then, the rate of aging for each species, including humans, evolved because it was the best one for the survival of that species.

There are other theories of why we age and many variations

of the two presented here. But in one way, all these theories are like the mythology of ancient societies. They attempt to explain something we desperately want to understand and would like to control. The truth is, although our knowledge is growing every day, we understand aging very little and can do almost nothing to control it.

NORMAL VERSUS ABNORMAL AGING

Normal does not necessarily mean good or healthy. Normal is not even necessarily better than abnormal. Normal aging may, at times, be distinctly less desirable than abnormal aging. For example, it is not normal to be able to run a marathon at age 95, but many people would be happy to be so abnormally physically fit. It is not normal to write symphonies at age 11, but many people would love to have a grandchild as abnormal as Mozart, who had already written several by that age. In the world's longest-running musical comedy, *The Fantasticks,* a teenage woman prays, "Please, God, please. Don't let me be normal!" On the other hand, when you call your doctor for the results of a test, what you hope to hear is the news that your results were "normal."

In science, normal is usually defined statistically. Normal is what most people are, normal is what is average. When your doctor says that your laboratory values are normal, what does that mean? The normal laboratory value for every test is determined by performing it on large numbers of people who have no apparent disease. Using statistical analysis, scientists determine what the average result is and establish a range of values that they call "normal." Say, for example, you go for a checkup, and your doctor discovers that one of your liver tests is abnormally high. The abnormal value does not necessarily mean that something is wrong with your liver. However, because the laboratory value is outside the normal range, there is an increased likelihood that you are ill. Statistically, a small number of healthy people will have abnormal laboratory values on any given test. Thus, if you hear that you have a result that is not normal, do not immediately worry; talk to your doctor to determine just what the laboratory test means. Remember too that the opposite is also true: a normal test value does not prove that you don't have disease. A certain percentage of people with disease will produce normal test results. Thus, a normal test result is not necessarily a guarantee of good health any more than an abnormal result is a certain indicator of disease.

An abnormal value does suggest that statistically you are more likely to have a medical problem. Some tests reveal the presence or absence of disease very accurately, and so the report of an abnormal value on one of those tests is worrisome; other tests are less reliable indicators, and an abnormal value causes less concern. Nevertheless, in general, but not always, the more your test result diverges from the normal value, the more likely you are to have a problem.

Just as with laboratory tests, in talking of normal aging, "normal" does not necessarily indicate the best and "abnormal" does not necessarily mean the worst. An 85-year-old woman with several chronic diseases, some difficulty in walking, and who has been widowed for five years may be normal, but you may desire to be healthier. The 95-year-old marathon runner is abnormal but may be a model for what you hope to be.

In aging, as with laboratory values, what is normal can cover a very wide range. Should you fall outside the range of normal, it means only that you are not average. "Normal" and "abnormal" are also not the same as "curable" and "incurable." There are normal aging changes whose negative effects can be treated, ameliorated, or cured, and there are abnormal changes that can't be helped. Nonetheless, you must realize that you are likely to experience the changes described in this book as changes of *normal* aging, even though you may strive to prevent them or seek treatment to cure or control them.

Since "normal" doesn't say much about what is better or worse, some gerontologists have suggested the term *successful aging* to describe the best way to age. Successful aging implies that all is as well as it possibly can be. Rather than hope to age normally and thus to be average, we should strive to age successfully.

NORMAL AGING CHANGES

There are many other factors besides age that researchers must consider when they try to determine the changes that indicate normal aging. These other factors include diet, exercise, pollution, activity, occupation, and heredity. For example, if scientists tried to determine whether normal aging leads to a decrease in the flexibility of muscles and joints, they would get very different results studying retired dancers rather than retired bankers. To determine whether weight gain is a normal part of aging, the results would differ dramatically if the study included only older Chinese women or only Eastern European men. If scientists studied a large group of retired mail carriers, they might conclude that arthritis of the shoulder (where they carry the heavy mailbag) occurs normally with age.

To discover which changes relate to aging and which are controlled more by some factor other than age, scientists must study large groups of people and examine many issues. These studies are complex, and much of the information doctors have about aging is still incomplete. Many of the changes that we think are related to aging, may in fact be related to other things. The environment in which you live, your lifestyle, and your genetics will affect your health in many ways, and throughout this book I will describe how. Yet, many of the changes you are experiencing and will experience as you get older are directly related to your age; you will experience them even if you live the healthiest of lifestyles.

Cellular and Chemical Changes

Cells are the basic building blocks of your body. They make proteins, convert food sources to energy, contract so that muscles can pull and push, produce electrical signals so that nerves can communicate, and produce chemicals that help fight infections, to name just a few of their myriad functions. Virtually all of your cells change as you age.

When scientists measure the activity of cells in the laboratory, they find that cells from older animals are less active in several ways. For example, older cells multiply more slowly and stop multiplying sooner than younger cells. They use up food supplies more slowly and often have lower levels of enzymes, the chemicals that allow cells to carry out diverse functions. In essence, older cells slow down.

As you age, you also have fewer numbers of certain types of cells—fewer brain cells, white blood cells, and muscle cells. You still have many more of each type of cell than you actually need, but fewer than you once had.

Many cells produce chemicals that act to communicate with other cells, fight infections, build skin, and stop bleeding. As you age, many of your cells change the amount of chemicals they produce. Brain cells produce less acetylcholine and dopamine, two of the chemicals that the brain uses in its complex functions. In women, the ovaries stop producing estrogen and progesterone, the female hormones; and in men, the testicles produce less testosterone, the male hormone. White blood cells produce fewer antibodies, the chemicals that help fight infection. Cells in your stomach produce less histamine, a chemical that stimulates other cells in your stomach to produce acid, and so, ultimately, your stomach produces less acid.

On the other hand, the levels of some other chemicals increase. Your adrenal glands produce larger amounts of epinephrine, a chemical that stimulates the speed and force of your heart and opens the breathing passages of your lungs. However, your heart and lungs become less sensitive to the effects of this chemical as you age.

Some proteins change in character as well: collagen, a protein that is a major structural support in skin and cartilage, becomes less elastic and less soluble as you age. In your brain, certain cells produce a protein called amyloid, which is not found in younger persons.

These changes in cells and in the levels of chemicals and proteins are interesting, but are they important to anyone but scientists? In some ways, yes. They probably explain why older people get sick more often, why the functions of organ systems decline, and why, ultimately, everyone dies.

Changes in Organ Systems

What really counts, however, is how aging makes you feel. It is of little importance to most people that blood flow to the brain decreases with age. But if you know that a decrease in blood flow may make you faint, then the change in function is much more important. You may not care about changes in the level of acetylcholine or changes in your brain's ability to respond to it, but when you learn that these changes cause many medications to produce confusion in older people, you may care a great deal.

Scientists have learned that the physiological functions of many organ systems change with age, independent of disease and environmental influences. That is not to say that nutrition, environmental exposure, stress, and many other factors play no role but rather that any major physiological change is related to aging more than to any other discernible factor. We call such changes "normal changes of aging." Some of these often cause unwanted symptoms and as such are certainly not beneficial. However, they are considered normal because they occur in most people.

Table 1 describes some of the organ systems that are known to undergo changes with aging. An examination of some of these may help you understand just how much your body is affected by advancing age.

Later, in the appropriate chapters, I will discuss in detail many of these physiological changes, but a few examples here will show you the importance of the normal changes in organ function.

Your kidneys excrete excess water, certain waste products, and toxic substances including medications, control the amount of salt in your blood, and assist in regulating your blood pressure. By age 85, your two kidneys will weigh one-third less than when you were 25 and have about half as much blood flow through them. They cannot excrete as much salt nor concentrate your urine as they once could. Thus, if your kidneys are stressed or damaged from medications, trauma, or very high or very low blood pressure, your body will feel the effects more dramatically. The salt level in your blood can

T A B L E 1
NORMAL PHYSIOLOGICAL CHANGES OF AGING

Organ System	Normal Age-Related Changes	Consequences
BRAIN	Blood flow decreases Levels of many chemicals change	Fainting (syncope) occurs more often Confusion occurs more often
EYES	Lens stiffens Retina is less sensitive to light	Difficulty focusing on close objects Difficulty seeing in dim light
EARS	Less able to hear high frequencies	Difficulty in understanding voices
MOUTH	Fewer taste buds	Many foods taste bitter or lack taste
SMELL	Less able to detect odors	Many foods taste bland
HEART	Lowered acceleration of pulse Decreased maximal output of blood Heart muscle stiffens Lower response to certain stimulants	Fainting (syncope) occurs more often Less able to perform strenuous sports Congestive heart failure is more common Less increase in heart rate
LUNGS	Less air movement with each breath Less oxygen transferred to blood	Strenuous exercise is more difficult Difficulty breathing at high altitudes

LIVER	Liver shrinks	None
	Decreased blood flow	Medications reach higher levels in body
	Less active enzyme system	Medications reach higher levels in body and last longer
KIDNEYS	Kidneys shrink	None
	Decreased blood flow	Effects of medications last longer
	Urine is less concentrated	Dehydration is more common
	Decreased ability to excrete salt	Abnormal salt levels occur commonly
BLADDER	Muscles of wall weaken	Becomes more difficult to urinate
	Less ability to delay urination	Incontinence is more common
PROSTATE	Enlarges	Urinary retention is more common
SKIN	Underlying fat begins to thin	Wrinkles are more prominent
		Skin tears more easily
		Hypothermia is more common
IMMUNE SYSTEM	Less antibody produced	Infections occur more commonly and spread more quickly
METABOLISM	Blood sugar levels rise after eating	Probably none

more easily become abnormal; you can get dehydrated easily; many medications will remain in your body for a very long time; and your kidneys can become permanently damaged.

With age, your liver also gets smaller, and the blood flow through it decreases. Additionally, the enzyme system that works with your kidneys to break down many medications is considerably less active than it once was. Thus, as with the kidneys, your liver is more easily damaged and is less able to inactivate medications and other toxins. These changes mean that any drug you take can have a prolonged action and can build up to higher levels in your body than when you were younger.

Much less blood flows to your brain now than when you were young. Under most conditions, you still have ample blood flow for your brain to function normally. However, if your blood pressure falls suddenly, or if the oxygen level in your blood falls, your normal brain functioning may be affected. That is one reason why you may faint more often than a younger person. Also, the levels of many neurotransmitters—the chemicals that nerves use to communicate with one another—are lower and the cells of your brain are less responsive to many of their effects. Because of these normal changes, confusion occurs more commonly from medication, fever, and other illnesses.

The immune system is not located in any one organ, so you might not think of it in the same way as you do the kidneys, liver, and brain. However, the function of the immune system is essential; it protects you from foreign substances such as bacteria, viruses, and fungi, and even from illnesses caused by something as simple as a splinter. With aging, many changes occur in the immune system. For example, the cells that recognize foreign particles seem to be less able to do so. The cells that fight infection by directly destroying foreign substances are less responsive, and the levels of the chemicals that help destroy foreign organisms are lower. These changes mean that you are less able to ward off infection. Thus, you are likely to become sicker from a viral infection, such as influenza, than is a younger person. You are more likely to develop herpes zoster than a middle-aged adult and are more susceptible to pneumonia. If you do get pneumonia, it may make you much sicker. In fact, many infections are more common and more severe in older people and therefore require fast attention and optimal treatment.

Age Versus Other Factors

There is a story about an 85-year-old man who complains to his doctor that his right knee is bothering him. The doctor answers, "What do you expect? That knee has taken you up and down stairs for eighty-five years; it has walked for you for eighty-five years. It has danced for you, kicked for you, stood for you, and jumped for you for eighty-five years. After eighty-five years of service, you should expect that it will bother you!" As the man gets up to leave, he turns and says to the doctor, "So why does my left knee feel fine?"

Obviously, there are factors other than years that affect our health and the way we age. Some of these come from the environment. What we have eaten and drunk, the air we have breathed, and the work we have done all play a role in how our bodies grow older. The genes that we inherit also influence our aging. In some families, many members live into their nineties, remaining vigorous and healthy. In others, many people die young or seem frail and sick by the time they reach their sixties. Some families are cursed with heart disease or cancer, and others are blessed with good health.

There are so many influences on the way we age that it is impossible to define normal aging within narrow limits. In fact, the range of "normal" grows wider as we age. We can all recognize when a newborn baby is normal. We can describe a normal weight within several pounds and a normal height within several inches. We know what things a normal newborn can and cannot do and we can predict what the infant will be able to do a few weeks or months later. But recognizing when an older person is normal is much more difficult. The normal weight of an 85-year-old man is dependent on so many things; his weight may be normal at 165 pounds if he is 5 feet 10 inches tall, but he may be seriously overweight at 150 pounds if he is only 4 feet 11 inches. What a normal 85-year-old can and cannot do physically is impossible to say, and what he might be able to do in several weeks or months is not within our ability to predict.

Being normal is not the goal of getting older; normal is simply the average. It is important, however, to recognize which changes are normal, because most people can expect to experience them. Nonetheless, many undesirable normal changes can be prevented or treated. Throughout this book I will explain, whenever possible, which changes are considered normal; but remember that normal means neither "best" nor "untreatable."

2

MEDICATIONS

Americans love medicines. When we're sick, even with a minor complaint, we want to be made better with a pill or tablet. Forty percent of all visits to the doctor include the writing of a prescription, and more than half the time that someone over age 65 goes to an emergency room he or she is given a medication. Although people over age 65 constitute only about 11 percent of our population, they consume more than a quarter of all the medications sold in this country. The average older person fills more than fifteen prescriptions each year, and as a nation we spend more than $10 billion annually on medication for people over age 65. All this drug use might be justified if we were certain that you needed and were helped by it. But the proof is lacking. Researchers estimate that more than one-third of the medications prescribed for the elderly are unnecessary. And, essential or not, *no* medicine—not even an over-the-counter drug—is without the risk of side effects.

The older you are, the more likely you are to have adverse reactions to drugs; if a side effect does occur, it is more likely to be severe. Such side effects as confusion, oversedation, stomach upset, light-headedness, impotence, dry mouth, blurry vision, constipation, urinary retention and incontinence, fainting, and falls and fractures can appear. In short, medication side effects can lead to serious medical problems.

You are likely to develop side effects from medications for three main reasons:

- Certain age-related physiological changes alter the way your body responds to and eliminates medication.
- Elders use more medications.
- Elders sometimes take medications improperly.

The physiological changes of aging that affect medication use, the overuse of medicines, the improper use of medicines, and the medications posing particular risks to the elderly are the topics discussed in this chapter.

AGING AND YOUR BODY'S CHANGING RESPONSE TO MEDICATION

The physiological changes that occur normally with aging affect the way you respond to many medications. This is to be expected. Just as you would not even think of giving a child the same medicine in the same dose as that for a young adult, so too in late life, the medicines that can be safely taken, and their dosages, differ from those that were appropriate in middle age. As compared to younger persons, in you, the same drug may last longer, reach a higher level in your body, or act more strongly (or weakly) at the same dosage.

Changes in How Your Body Metabolizes and Excretes Medicine

Age alters your body's ability to neutralize (metabolize) and to get rid of (excrete) medicine. Every medication, whether taken orally or by injection, is eventually converted to an inactive form or is excreted from your body, or both. These processes take place in your liver and kidneys, whose functions decrease with age, causing many drugs to remain active and stay in your body longer. That is why the effects of certain drugs may continue for a much longer period and why their levels may become too high to be safe.

For example, flurazepam (Dalmane) has long been a popular sleeping pill. In young people, its effects last just long enough for a good night's rest—about twelve hours. But this medication can remain in *your* blood for as long as three days. During that time, it continues to cause sleepiness and, sometimes, confusion and light-headedness. If you take the medicine nightly, within a few days the level of the drug can become high enough to cause grave side effects, including serious confusion and falls.

Increased Sensitivity

The longer duration and higher levels of medications are not the only concerns: you are now more sensitive to many drugs. For example, your body is more sensitive to the effects of narcotics—codeine (in Tylenol #3), propoxyphene (in Darvon and Wygesic), pentazocine (Talwin), oxycodone (in Percocet and Percodan), and morphine—all of which are used to control serious pain. The appropriate dose of any of these drugs to control pain in a younger person may be too strong for you, making you confused or sleepy, slowing down your breathing, and perhaps leading to urinary incontinence and to falls. If you are in pain, one of these medications may be necessary, but it should be used cautiously and, generally, at a lower dosage. When narcotics are used, you, your family, and your doctor must be vigilant in watching for side effects. I almost always recommend that my patients who must use a narcotic also take a stimulant laxative (such as cascara or Dulcolax) at the same time, because constipation is virtually a universal side effect for older persons taking a narcotic. (See chapter 10 for more information on constipation.)

Anticholinergic Effects

One part of the nervous system functions largely with the help of a chemical transmitter called acetylcholine; medications that block the effects of acetylcholine are called "anti-cholinergic." You are particularly sensitive to anticholinergic medications, which alter the effect of this chemical, because of age-related changes in your level of acetylcholine and your body's ability to use it. Acetylcholine is necessary for many organs, most importantly the brain, to function properly. For unknown reasons, your body produces less of this critical chemical as you age, and your body's ability to use it also decreases. It is not surprising, therefore, that anticholinergic medications can make any elderly person confused and are most problematic in persons with Alzheimer's disease.

Anticholinergic medications can disrupt the proper functioning of the bladder, colon, heart, blood vessels, eyes, and mouth; their use often leads to urinary retention, constipation, light-headedness, fainting, blurred vision, and dry mouth. Many commonly prescribed and over-the-counter medications have anticholinergic effects. Several of these medications are set out in Table 2. When possible, avoid them. If you must use one, be alert for side effects.

Other Physiological Changes

Two other age-related physiological changes particularly affect the way your body responds to medications. As you get older, your body's ability to maintain its vital functions within normal limits (called "homeostasis") decreases, and your organs lose their excess capacity to work—that is, they lose their functional reserve.

Homeostasis is the ability of the body to respond to change and to correct for it. Take, for example, body temperaure. If it's forty-six degrees outside and you go outside, your body temperature, without homeostasis, would tend to fall to the temperature around you. Instead, your body burns glucose, generates heat through muscle activity (like shivering), and decreases blood flow to the extremities to conserve heat. Your body adapts; your temperature remains normal. That's what homeostasis is. As you get older, however, your ability to adapt is slower and less effective. It may take you longer to warm up, and you might feel the cold more quickly and

T A B L E   2

MEDICATIONS WITH SPECIAL RISK FOR THE ELDERLY

MEDICATION	PROBLEM

SLEEPING AND ANTIANXIETY MEDICATIONS	
ALL	All sleeping medications can be habit-forming, and in most people they lose their effectiveness if used every night. They can make you feel tired during the day and in some cases cause confusion.
LONG-ACTING flurazepam (Dalmane) chlordiazepoxide (Librium) diazepam (Valium)	The effects of these medications last much longer in you than in younger people. They are more likely to cause you to feel tired during the day or to become confused. They have been shown to increase the risk of falling and fracturing a hip. If you must use a sleeping pill or an antianxiety medication, avoid these.
DIPHENHYDRAMINE (Benadryl)	This is the active ingredient in many over-the-counter sleeping pills. It is the only sleeping medication that has anticholinergic side effects; it can lead to constipation, inability to pass urine, light-headedness, confusion, blurred vision, and dry mouth. Do not use it.

ANTICHOLINERGIC MEDICATIONS	
MANY ANTIHISTAMINES such as: diphenhydramine (Benadryl) chlorpheniramine (Chlor- Trimeton)	

MEDICATION	PROBLEM
SOME ANTIDEPRESSANTS, especially amitriptyline (Elavil)	

MANY ANTIPSYCHOTIC MEDICATIONS, for example:
  chlorpromazine (Thorazine)
  thioridazine (Mellaril)
  thiothixene (Navane)
	These medications can lead to constipation, inability to pass urine, blurred vision, dry mouth, light-headedness, and confusion. They are especially problematic for people with memory problems or dementia and those with trouble urinating due to an enlarged prostate. Avoid them.

MOST GASTROINTESTINAL ANTISPASMODICS, such as:
  belladonna
  dicyclomine (Bentyl)
  propantheline (Pro-Banthine)
  clinidium (Librax)
  hyoscyamine (Donnatal)	

MANY MUSCLE RELAXANTS, such as: cyclobenzaprine (Flexeril)	

NARCOTIC PAINKILLERS

ALL	All narcotic pain killers can cause sedation, urinary retention, and constipation. Take a stimulant laxative when using narcotics. These medications can sometimes cause confusion.
PENTAZOCINE (Talwin)	Pentazocine is more likely than many narcotics to cause confusion, and it interacts with all other narcotic pain killers, making them less effective.

MEDICATION	PROBLEM

PROPOXYPHENE (Darvon, Darvocet, Wygesic)

Propoxyphene is no more potent than aspirin or acetaminophen (Tylenol) in controlling pain but has all the side effects of the other narcotics. Avoid it.

DIABETES PILLS

CHLORPROPAMIDE (Diabenese)

Chlorpropamide is very long-acting and can cause prolonged low blood sugar. This medication also affects the kidneys' ability to excrete water and can lead to electrolyte abnormalities. Safer diabetes medications are available.

ANTIPSYCHOTIC MEDICATIONS

ALL
  e.g. haloperidol (Haldol)
  thioridazine (Mellaril)
  thiothixene (Navane)
  chlorpromazine
    (Thorazine)

All of these medications sedate, and can cause confusion, light-headedness, constipation, urinary retention, and blurred vision. They can lead to Parkinson's syndrome with tremor, stiffness, and a shuffling gait, and they sometimes cause abnormal body movements, especially of the muscles of the face. Frequently they are inappropriately used, especially in nursing homes.

intensely. Suddenly, you understand why your friends winter in the south!

When you were young, your body's major organ systems had the capacity to perform beyond what your body demanded of them. They had what doctors call a *functional reserve*. With age, that reserve diminishes. Thus, if you take a medicine that demands increased function of one organ, that organ may not be able to meet the need.

Medications you might be given to lower your blood pressure present a good example of how these two normal physiological changes affect your response to even the most widely used medications. A younger person who takes a medication that rapidly lowers blood pressure is able to compensate for the lower pressure by speeding up her heart and constricting her blood vessels, assuring that an adequate amount of blood continues to reach her body's tissues. Furthermore, the younger person's brain is receiving so much more blood and oxygen than necessary that a temporary reduction in blood flow probably would not make her faint or confused. You, however, cannot speed up your heart or constrict your blood vessels as quickly as you once could, and your circulatory system provides your brain with very little above the necessary blood flow and oxygen. Thus, even a minor decrease in the blood supply to your brain may cause you to faint.

Particular Medication Risks

Although the federal Food and Drug Administration (FDA) tests new drugs extensively before approving them for general use, trials with the elderly are usually very limited. Be wary of using a newly released medication, as it may cause a side effect not found during the FDA tests. I generally do not prescribe a newly marketed medication for my patients until it has been in general use for a year, by which time side effects not discovered in trial testing should have become known through medical journals and professional networks. If your doctor recommends a newly released medication, ask if the drug is really better than medications that have been available longer and with which there is experience in the elderly. If there is some advantage to the new medication, it may be worth the extra risk; if not, why take a chance?

Newly released medications are only one source of trouble. Many widely used drugs that have long been available pose extra risks for the elderly. Table 2 describes some of these medications; *avoid them, if possible.* If you are using one of these medications, ask your doctor if there is an alternative that would be safer.

OVERUSE OF MEDICATION: HOW MUCH IS TOO MUCH?

Sir William Osler, the father of modern medicine, reportedly said that one of the duties of a physician was to teach patients not to take medicines—a lesson we seem not yet to have learned very well. Today, if you are an average American over age 65, you are currently using at least four different medications.

The overuse of medicine is a serious health problem of national scope. Nearly one-seventh of all of the hospitalizations of elders is due to a medication problem. One in a thousand hospitalized elderly persons dies from a medication side effect. The statistics are worrisome: when you are 65, you are twice as likely to have an unwanted side effect from a drug than when you were 35, and four times more likely when you reach age 80. *In short, there are times when the benefit of taking a medication is simply not worth the risk.*

The Use of Many Medications

There are several reasons why using many medications at the same time ("polypharmacy") can lead to trouble.

First, simply being exposed to several different chemicals increases the chance that one of them will cause a side effect. For example, if you are taking four drugs at the same time, the risk of having a serious side effect is about one in twenty; if you take more than ten drugs (not uncommon), your chance is about one in four.

Second, drugs tend to interact with one another, and the risk of an interaction increases geometrically as the number of medications you take increases. Drugs interact in many different ways. For example, one drug can prevent another from being absorbed by the stomach and intestines; can increase or decrease the level of another drug; can accentuate the effects of another drug or block its actions; can make another drug more toxic. Just because drugs interact, of course, is no reason to insist on taking only one medicine if you actually need two or more. If your doctor is aware of a potential interaction, he or she can consider how best for you to use the essential but interacting medications together.

If your doctor does not know of *all* the medicines you are taking, drug problems are especially likely to occur. How can your doctor plan for possible drug interactions if he or she doesn't know about every medicine you take? *Always tell each of your doctors about all the medicines you use, including over-the-counter preparations.* Bring a list of your current medications with you whenever you go to any doctor or hospital.

Not only can a medication alter the effects of other medications, it also can have a profound effect on a medical condition other than the one for which it was prescribed. For example, if you are a man with a prostate problem who has difficulty starting your stream of urine, you may find it impossible to urinate at all if you take a medication like an over-the-counter sleeping pill containing Benadryl (diphenhydramine). This difficulty occurs because Benadryl weakens the bladder's ability to squeeze. If you have glaucoma, Benadryl will worsen that condition, too. And if you suffer from dementia, the medicine can cause you to become terribly confused. Thus, while the sleep medication may help you get rest, it may also make your prostate, vision, and mental problems worse. Take another example: certain eye drops, such as timolol (Timoptic), given to treat glaucoma, can worsen congestive heart failure and heart conduction problems such as "sick-sinus syndrome." Most older persons have more than one medical condition at any one time. Thus, whenever you consider taking an additional medicine to treat a problem, consider carefully the effects that the new drug may have on your other medical conditions.

Table 3 describes some medical conditions that can be made worse by medications. If you have one of the medical conditions listed in Table 3 and are taking a medication that is listed with it, ask your doctor if the medication is correct for you. Sometimes it is necessary to take a medication even when it is known to affect a medical condition you have, but under those circumstances, you and your doctor will want to be particularly careful to watch for unwanted side effects.

Most doctors are cautious when prescribing medications to people who have complex medical conditions, but sometimes doctors make mistakes. To compound the risk, you may go to a specialist who will prescribe a medication for one specific problem. The specialist may not communicate regularly with your primary-care doctor and thus may not know about the other medicines you are taking or your other medical problems. That is why one doctor, your primary-care doctor, must know about *all* the medications you take. If you are referred to a specialist, be certain that you tell the specialist about all your medications and medical conditions. If the specialist prescribes a medicine, speak with your primary-care physician to be certain that the medicine is safe for you, before you take it.

UNDERUSE OF MEDICATION

While the overuse of medicine and the use of multiple medicines pose the greater risks, certain medications are in fact *underused*. There is no reason to suffer a readily preventable or treatable illness.

Although influenza usually only inconveniences younger people, it can cause very serious illness and death in older people. Unfortunately, only 10 to 20 percent of older Americans get vaccinated against the flu annually even though the vaccine has been shown to be safe and very successful in

T A B L E   3

MEDICAL CONDITIONS AND THE MEDICATIONS THAT CAN MAKE THEM WORSE

Medical Condition	*Medication*
GLAUCOMA	amitriptyline (Elavil) diphenhydramine (Benadryl) and most other antihistamines most antipsychotics most gastrointestinal antispasmodics disopyramide (Norpace)
DEMENTIA	amitriptyline (Elavil) diphenhydramine (Benadryl) and most other antihistamines most antipsychotics most gastrointestinal antispasmodics narcotic painkillers disopyramide (Norpace)
INCONTINENCE	diuretics (water pills) sleeping pills
ENLARGED PROSTATE	amitriptyline (Elavil) diphenhydramine (Benadryl) and most other antihistamines most gastrointestinal antispasmodics narcotic painkillers disopyramide (Norpace)

SYNCOPE (fainting)	nitroglycerin
	hydralazine
	prazocin
	beta blockers (*e.g.,* propranolol
	   [Inderal], atenolol [Tenormin],
	   nadolol [Corgard], metoprolol
	   [Lopressor])
	verapamil (Calan, Isoptin)
	timolol (Timoptic) eye drops

BREATHING PROBLEMS	beta blockers (*e.g.,* propranolol
	   [Inderal], atenolol [Tenormin],
	   nadolol [Corgard], metoprolol
	   [Lopressor])
	sleeping pills

Medical Condition	Medication
CONGESTIVE HEART FAILURE	beta blockers (e.g., propranolol [Inderal], atenolol [Tenormin], nadolol [Corgard], metoprolol [Lopressor]) disopyramide (Norpace) verapamil (Calan, Isoptin) timolol (Timoptic) eye drops
GASTRIC ULCERS	aspirin nonsteroidal antiinflammatory agents prednisone
KIDNEY FAILURE	nonsteroidal antiinflammatory agents captopril (Capoten) enalapril (Vasotec)
IMPOTENCE	many of the medications used to treat hypertension (See Table 8)
CLAUDICATION (leg cramps when walking)	beta blockers (e.g., propranolol [Inderal], atenolol [Tenormin], nadolol [Corgard], metoprolol [Lopressor])
DEPRESSION	beta blockers (e.g., propranolol [Inderal], atenolol [Tenormin], nadolol [Corgard], metoprolol [Lopressor]) reserpine

preventing the disease. Another example is the pneumonia vaccine. Although it does not prevent all cases of pneumonia, the vaccine can decrease the likelihood of your contracting the disease and may decrease its severity if you do get it. Yet, only 10 percent of Americans over age 65 have been vaccinated against pneumonia.

Vaccines are not the only underused medications. As discussed in chapter 16, which focuses on urinary incontinence, doctors routinely fail to prescribe the medications that have been shown to alleviate this embarrassing and sometimes serious problem. Similarly, many doctors do not prescribe a medication, pentoxifylline (Trentyl) to treat leg cramps and pain caused by inadequate blood circulation (claudication). Although the drug is not always successful, it helps many people, has few side effects, and is easier to try than the only alternative treatment—a major operation that poses considerable risk. I generally recommend a trial period with the drug when claudication interferes with my patients' ability to walk or exercise.

In short, while the emphasis here is on the dangers of using too much and too many medicines, certain medications are not used enough. Using any drug or treatment appropriately can be an important key to a long and healthy life.

TAKE AS DIRECTED—AND THIS MEANS YOU!

Even if your doctor carefully and cautiously prescribes medicine for you, if you don't take it correctly—in the right amount at the right time and following all other directions—you can develop serious medical problems. There are many kinds of mistakes. You may confuse the schedule of one drug for another, take the wrong dose of the right drug, stop a medication too soon, or continue a medication too long. If you take several medications (and you probably do), these errors are easy to make. Several simple precautions may help:

- Understand how to take your medications properly. Your doctor, your doctor's nurse, and your pharmacist can help you. Know when to take each medicine, how often, and for how long. Ask if it should be taken around-the-clock, only at mealtimes, or never at mealtimes. Be certain to know when to stop taking the medicine.
- Ask about possible side effects and be certain that you understand and watch for them.
- If you have a memory problem, ask a family member, neighbor, or friend to leave out pills, set a timer, or call you to remind you to take your medication. Sometimes it is necessary to hire a visiting nurse or other assistant to be certain that you take your medications properly.
- If your medication schedule is too complicated, ask your

doctor if it can be changed. If not, ask about alternative medicines whose schedules are easier to follow.

■ Know which over-the-counter medications are generally not recommended for older people, and consult your doctor or pharmacist before using any of them.

■ Whenever you see a new doctor, and whenever any doctor prescribes a new medication or stops an old one, review all of your medication use with your primary-care doctor.

■ Of course, if you do not feel well after starting a new medicine, call your doctor at once.

A final word of caution: I have seen patients who thought they could take a medication prescribed for a friend or relative because their problems seemed similar. This is a foolish and an extremely dangerous assumption. *Never take a medicine unless your own doctor prescribes it for you.* You wouldn't ask a family member or friend to set your broken arm; don't rely on their advice when it comes to taking medicines.

YOUR PHARMACIST

When you purchase a medicine, you are paying for a pharmacy service, which includes more than just putting the medication into a container; you are paying for the experience and knowledge of your pharmacist. He or she can be an important source of reliable information and good advice.

For example, your pharmacist can explain how to take your medicine correctly, can describe the side effects that might occur, and can tell you about interactions between the medicine you are about to take and other medicines you are taking or other medical conditions you may have. If you need to, ask your pharmacist to package the medicine in a way that is best for you. If you have trouble reading small print, ask the pharmacist to use a label in print large enough for you to read easily. If childproof caps are difficult for you to use, and if you do not have grandchildren or other youngsters in the house, ask for caps that are easier for you to handle.

It is particularly important to discuss over-the-counter

medications with your pharmacist. Often, he or she will be more readily available to you than your doctor is—for example, on a night when you feel you must have a medication to treat a sudden but not serious condition like diarrhea or a stuffy nose. Talk with your pharmacist before you buy anything, and then call your doctor to be certain that the medicine is right for you.

In my experience, most pharmacists are knowledgeable and often extremely helpful, trustworthy professionals with substantial education and training. Never hesitate to ask your pharmacist about your medications and their proper use.

MEDICATIONS WITH PARTICULAR PROBLEMS FOR THE ELDERLY

Sleeping and Antianxiety Medications

If you use sleeping medicines, don't take them every night. If used too often, they tend to lose their effectiveness and can build up to dangerously high levels in your body. With continuous use, the chance of their doing any good is small, while the opportunity for their doing harm is large. If you take a sleeping pill periodically, make sure that its effects are short-lived, and don't take one of the older, long-acting types (see Table 4). If you use medications for anxiety, remember that, chemically, these are the same medications as those used to

TABLE 4

BETTER AND WORSE SLEEPING AND ANXIETY PILLS

Better	*Worse*
triazolam (Halcion)	diazepam (Valium)
alpraxolam (Xanax)	chlordiazepoxide (Librium)
temazepam (Restoril)	flurazepam (Dalmane)
lorazepam (Ativan)	diphenhydramine (Benadryl)
oxazepam (Serax)	
chloral hydrate	

treat insomnia and thus have the same side effects. All these medications can cause confusion, instability in walking, and sedation.

Although insomnia is inconvenient, if you get tired enough, you will fall asleep. Insomnia will not make you sick, but sleeping pills can lead to illness and injury.

Medications to Treat Colds and Allergies

Stay away from cold remedies. They rarely do much for your cold and have potentially serious side effects. Most cold remedies contain antihistamines, and most antihistamines cause anticholinergic side effects like constipation, difficulty in urinating, confusion, dry mouth, and blurred vision. Antihistamines can make people who have dementia considerably worse, and if you have glaucoma, they will worsen it.

Since it is the antihistamine component in cold remedies that causes these problems, if you must have one, ask your doctor or pharmacist to recommend a medication that alleviates cold symptoms but doesn't contain an antihistamine. If you have allergies, for which antihistamines can have a powerful effect, ask your doctor about antihistamines that do not have anticholinergic side effects. There are now several such drugs, but they can be purchased only with a prescription.

Antidepressants

Some antidepressants have strong anticholinergic side effects and can cause all of the problems described above. The most problematic of these medications is amitriptyline (Elavil). At one time, this was the only antidepressant available, but there are now much safer medications to treat depression in the elderly. Discuss the alternative medications with your doctor.

Medicines for Stomach Cramps

Doctors often prescribe medications called gastrointestinal ("GI") antispasmodics to treat stomach and intestinal cramps. These drugs often combine several medications and are sold under names such as Librax, Bentyl, and belladonna. These medications have strong anticholinergic side effects; in fact, they are used specifically to block the action of the cholinergic nervous system, which stimulates the GI tract (your stomach, small intestines, and colon). Younger people may appropriately use these medications for short periods of time, generally for a viral intestinal infection, but they are not very effective treatment for chronic cramps, gas, or other stomach problems and are dangerous for you to use. Often, aromatic oils (such as peppermint oil, available in pharmacies as spirit of peppermint and in health-food stores as peppermint tea, or in licorice-containing aperitifs such as Pernod) work as well or better and are much safer. However, before using any of these on a regular basis, ask your doctor if it is safe for you. Even too much licorice can affect your health, causing you to retain water and causing your blood pressure to increase.

Medicines for Muscle Spasms

Doctors sometimes prescribe another kind of antispasmodic medicine to treat cramped muscles and lower-back pain. These drugs have such names as cyclobenzaprine (Flexeril), carisoprodol (Soma), and methocarbamol (Robaxin). Because these medications do not work very well in persons of any age, I do not prescribe them. If the dose is raised, they work better but will cause intolerable side effects in an older person. Even in low doses they can cause serious side effects. Avoid them.

Pain Medications (Analgesics)

Always use pain medication cautiously. Tylenol (acetaminophen) and aspirin often provide good relief with minimal risk. In fact, for most kinds of pain, two or three Tylenol every four to six hours is the best choice. Aspirin may irritate your stomach, but when taken with food or an antacid, it is safe for most people. Propoxyphene (Darvon and Wygesic) is no more effective than Tylenol or aspirin but carries much more risk. It is a narcotic and can therefore cause constipation, sleepiness, and urinary retention, and can be habit-forming. I rarely prescribe it. Other narcotics, such as codeine (Tylenol #3) or oxycodone (Percocet, Percodan), are much stronger narcotics and are sometimes needed, but they will assuredly make you constipated and may cause confusion and urinary problems. If you are taking a narcotic pain medication, it is usually necessary to take a stimulant laxative such as cascara, Dulcolax, phenolphthalein (Ex-Lax), or senna as well.

Diabetes Medications

There are many medications available to treat diabetes. (Diabetes and the medications used to treat it are discussed in detail in chapter 12.) To lower blood sugar levels, some people need to inject themselves with insulin, while others can take medications by mouth, known as oral hypoglycemic agents. One of these, chlorpropamide (Diabenese), has been available for a long time, and doctors are very familiar with it. Although this medication is an acceptable choice for younger adults, it is not good for you. It lasts too long in your body. If you get sick, or for some other reason can't eat, the medicine can cause your blood sugar to fall dangerously low and stay low for too long. Moreover, the drug can affect your kidneys' ability to excrete water and therefore can disturb the salt and fluid balance in your body. There are good alternatives to Diabenese; discuss with your doctor which one is appropriate for you.

Antipsychotic Medications

Medications are sometimes prescribed for demented people whose behaviors (wandering, outbursts of anger, and agitation) their families and institutions find troublesome. The use of antipsychotic medications is fraught with problems. Haldol (haloperidol), Mellaril (thioridazine), Navane (thiothixene), and Thorazine (chlorpromazine) are among the more widely used of these medications. Although antipsychotics have a role in treating people who are hallucinating or who have paranoia, *no* reliable evidence demonstrates that they do anything more than sedate most patients who are merely demented.

The side effects of these medications can be severe. They all have anticholinergic properties and thus anticholinergic side effects and can also cause other side effects, such as uncontrollable facial movements, a compulsion to move about, and Parkinson-like stiffness and tremor.

Although there are rare occasions when these medications must be used in patients who are demented—for example, in the presence of genuine psychosis and psychotic symptoms, hallucinations, and paranoia, they are rarely the drugs of choice to control behavior problems. They are best used only if other medications and environmental manipulations have not worked. If they are used, they must be used in small doses and with careful monitoring for side effects.

If someone you care for is taking any antipsychotic medication, discuss the matter with the doctor. Ask:

■ For what specific medical problem the medication has been prescribed and whether the medication has alleviated that problem. If the medication has not solved the problem, why is it being continued?
■ Is there a less toxic medication that might work?
■ Have there been any side effects from the medication, and if so, what should be done about them?
■ Are there alternative approaches to solving the problem other than using a medication?
■ Is it reasonable to discontinue the medication for a time to see if the original problem worsens?

AVOIDING MEDICATION PROBLEMS

What then is the solution? It is not to throw away your medicines but to be careful when taking them.

■ Always weigh the potential benefit of a medication against its potential risk. If your doctor offers a medication, ask how likely it is to help and to harm.

- Do not seek out medication by pressuring your doctor to prescribe for every complaint. If your doctor recommends a nondrug treatment, try it before insisting on a pill. On the other hand, do not be fearful of taking medication; if you have a problem that requires it, discuss its use with your doctor, talk about how the medicine will interact with other medicines you are already taking and other medical conditions you have, and use the new medicine as directed.
- Ask whether the dose is the smallest possible that is likely to help you.
- Do not refill prescriptions without consulting your doctor.
- Be sure that your primary-care doctor, who knows you well, is coordinating all your medication use, and never take or discontinue a medication without first discussing it with that doctor.
- Be certain to get your necessary vaccinations. You need the pneumonia vaccine only once; you need a flu shot every year, in the autumn.
- Be sure that you are taking your medications properly by reviewing them periodically with your primary-care doctor and asking your pharmacist to explain all instructions.

Medications have led to wonderful gains for older persons. High blood pressure, diabetes, glaucoma, heart problems, depression, Parkinson's disease, infections, and hundreds of other acute and chronic diseases can now be treated with medicines. Some medications will help you prevent diseases. Used properly, medicines can lengthen and improve the quality of your life; used improperly, they can cause serious—sometimes catastrophic—problems. You may not be able to choose your enemies, the kinds of diseases that afflict you, but you can choose your weapons against them, and, by working with your doctor and pharmacist, wield those medications for maximum benefit and health.

3

HEART

Beat after beat, day after day, your heart pumps blood to every part of your body. During your waking hours and while you sleep, your heart accomplishes its business of keeping you alive. When your heart works properly, you don't give it a moment's thought. But if it falters, even for a few seconds, you may experience frightening and often terrible consequences.

Doctors know more about your heart than about any other organ in your body. The most advanced technology can measure its every function: powerful medications can alter its speed, force, and electrical system; doctors can open or replace its clogged arteries and repair its valves. Despite all our knowledge and medical technology, however, more older Americans die of heart disease than from any other illness. That fact makes it important for you to understand what your heart does, what can go wrong with it, and what you can do to avoid heart problems.

The four most common heart ailments affecting elders are: coronary artery disease, including angina and heart attacks; arrhythmias; congestive heart failure; and problems with heart valves. After first describing the functions and anatomy of your heart, I will spend the remainder of this chapter discussing these four common heart problems.

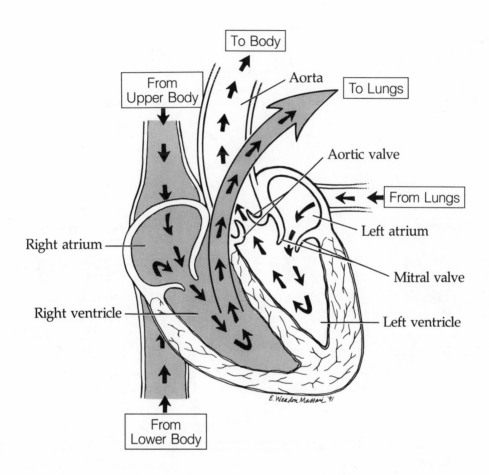

FIGURE 1
The Heart—View Showing Chambers of the Heart

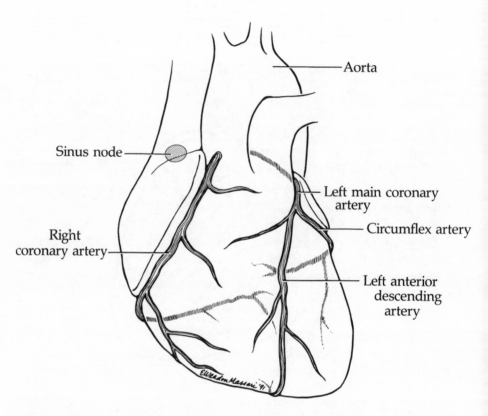

FIGURE 2
The Heart—View Showing Surface of the Heart

THE FUNCTIONS AND ANATOMY OF THE HEART

Your heart is a muscle that pumps blood by contracting rhythmically. Refer to Figures 1 and 2, which show a heart.

Your heart has both a right and a left side, each with its own *ventricle,* or main chamber. The right side takes in blood from your veins and pumps it into your lungs. In your lungs, the blood becomes saturated with oxygen. The oxygenated blood then returns to the left side of your heart, where each contraction pumps it through your arteries to every part of your body.

Each side of the heart has a second chamber, called an *atrium*. When the atrium contracts, it forces blood into the ventricle, allowing the ventricle to fill more quickly and efficiently than passive filling would allow. Normally, the atrium contracts a fraction of a second before the ventricle, assuring that the ventricle fills completely with blood.

Just like a mechanical pump, your heart has valves to control the direction in which the blood flows. Without valves, some blood would course backward through the veins when the heart contracted, and some blood would flow back into the ventricle when the heart relaxed.

Your heart also has complex systems for adjusting both the speed at which it beats and the force of each contraction. On the surface of your heart, a small area called the *sinus node* creates an electrical impulse that stimulates your heart to contract. The speed at which the node fires is controlled by nerves that run to the heart and by chemicals in the bloodstream. These nerves and chemicals also control the strength with which the muscular walls of your heart contract. In addition, your heart can sense when its pumping action is lagging behind the body's need for oxygenated blood and can adjust the force of its contractions to pump more vigorously. These mechanisms of adjustment constitute a remarkable system that allows your body to conserve energy at rest but to increase blood flow quickly when you are active or need to be more alert. Everyone has experienced just how quickly the heart can shift into high gear. A sudden, loud noise makes your heart beat fast and strong almost instantly, a response that occurs as your heart reacts to the sudden release of a chemical called adrenaline—your body's way of putting all its systems on highest alert.

Like any pump, your heart requires a source of energy, and like every other tissue in your body, your heart gets its energy from the oxygen and nutrients carried in your blood. Ironically, your heart cannot directly use the blood that passes through its chambers. Rather, your heart relies on a steady supply of blood from the *coronary arteries* (coronary means "heart"). These arteries, which begin at the largest artery of all, the *aorta,* branch out to supply every part of your heart. A continuous supply of blood through the coronary arteries is critical. If the supply to any part of your heart is less than sufficient, even for a few seconds, your heart will begin to malfunction. A serious interruption in blood supply is what triggers a heart attack.

NORMAL AGE-RELATED CHANGES IN THE HEART

Although scientists know a great deal about how the heart ages, it is often difficult to distinguish the changes due solely to aging from those related to diet, environment, and matters of lifestyle, such as lack of exercise.

Heart Rate and the Sinus Node

Important age-related changes in the heart occur in the *sinus node,* where the cells that stimulate the electrical system of the heart and regulate its contractions are located. As you get older, the absolute number of cells in the sinus node decreases, and the remaining cells become less sensitive to the chemicals that increase heart rate. Thus, the sinus node is less able to increase your heart rate rapidly.

Usually, it doesn't matter that your heart takes a bit longer to speed up, but the extra time can make a difference. For example, when you stand up quickly from lying down or from sitting, gravity makes the blood suddenly pool in the veins of your feet and legs. In order to maintain your blood pressure, your heart needs to rapidly increase the amount of blood it pumps. Since your heart cannot speed up as quickly as it once could, it may not be able to maintain your blood pressure at the necessary level when you stand up, causing you to feel light-headed from lack of blood to the brain. If your blood pressure momentarily falls too far, the wooziness can progress to fainting. Doctors call brief fainting spells *syncope* (rhymes with "recipe"). The syncope itself is not harmful, but the resulting fall can be.

You may experience a quick drop in blood pressure for similar reasons if you strain during a bowel movement or while urinating. This situation poses particular dangers because a fall in the bathroom almost always means that you will hit a hard surface. Thus, try not to strain excessively when going to the bathroom, and get up slowly from the toilet. If you feel light-headed as you stand up, sit back down quickly and stay there until the feeling passes.

The Heart's Output

Along with a decrease in your heart's ability to speed up its contractions, with age comes also a decrease in its ability to contract most forcefully, and therefore to pump blood. At rest and at low levels of exercise, a normal 40-year-old and a normal 75-year-old heart are nearly identical in their ability to pump blood. However, when taxed maximally, your heart cannot match its performance in your younger days. Don't misunderstand: if your heart is healthy and you are otherwise fit, your heart can pump enough blood for you to run a marathon. It's just that this age-related change may limit your speed and endurance, and it will therefore take you longer to complete the course. It doesn't mean that you can't or shouldn't run the race.

The wall of your heart becomes stiffer with age, and a stiffer muscle takes a little longer to relax between contractions. Your ventricles must fill with blood during relaxation, and so your heart needs a little more time to fill with blood than it used to. Under normal conditions, this slower filling will cause you no problem. However, if your heart beats too quickly, it may not be able to fill properly, and therefore it will pump blood less efficiently.

HEART DISEASE

Besides the normal changes that most of us will experience, some of us will also develop abnormal conditions of the heart or vascular system. The four most common and serious of these conditions are coronary artery disease, arrhythmias, congestive heart failure, and problems with heart valves.

CORONARY ARTERY DISEASE

What Is Coronary Artery Disease (CAD)?

We saw earlier that the heart, like all other muscles of your body, requires a constant supply of blood, supplied by the *coronary arteries,* which begin at the aorta and branch off to supply blood to every part of your heart. The *right coronary artery* supplies blood to the right side of the heart. The *left main coronary artery* branches into the *left anterior descending artery* and the *circumflex artery.* (Look back at Figure 2 and find each of these coronary arteries.) CAD occurs most often in the three left-sided coronary arteries.

If you have CAD, fatty deposits, called *plaque,* form in the part of an artery through which the blood flows, called the *lumen;* this condition is called *atherosclerosis.* Plaque also causes the normally smooth surface of the lumen to become irregular (see Figure 3). The narrowing of the lumen, like a blockage in a pipe, means that less blood passes through the artery; the irregular surface of the lumen causes platelets, the sticky blood cells that your body uses to help stop bleeding, to stick there more readily.

If plaque narrows an artery enough, even a small accumulation of platelets can reduce blood flow to a trickle. In severe situations, an artery can become completely clogged, stopping the flow of blood through that artery. If the passage of

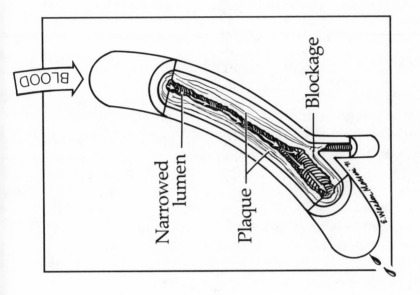

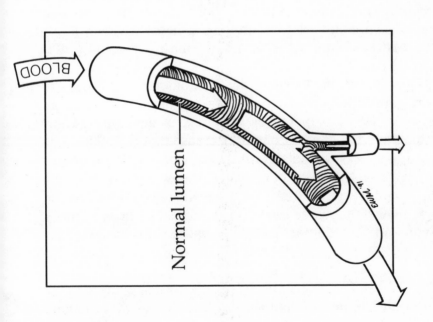

FIGURE 3
A Healthy Coronary Artery (left) and One with Coronary Artery Disease (right)

blood dwindles or stops, a part of the heart will lose its blood supply. One of two serious consequences then occurs.

If there is some blood flow, heart tissue will become starved for oxygen and build up toxins, a condition called *ischemia.* If ischemia persists, or if the blood supply is completely stopped, the affected part of the heart will die, a condition called *infarction* or *myocardial infarction (MI),* commonly called a heart attack or an MI. Ischemia and MIs cause chest pain, *angina pectoris* (angina means "pain" and pectoris means "chest") or, more commonly, just *angina.*

Ischemia is worrisome not so much because it causes pain but because it causes the muscle of the heart to malfunction. Ischemic heart tissue does not contract normally, and if the area of ischemia is large enough, your heart may not be able to pump sufficient blood to maintain your blood pressure at the required levels. Ischemia often produces arrhythmias (discussed later in this chapter) that can cause death.

Myocardial infarction or heart attack is even more worrisome. Your body cannot replace the heart muscle that is killed during a heart attack with normally functioning muscle. The best it can do is to replace it with scar tissue, and scar tissue does not contract. Therefore, a heart attack permanently reduces the pumping action of your heart and may also cause arrhythmias.

CAD is the leading cause of death in older Americans, and you are rightfully concerned with preventing and treating it. We now know what increases your risk of developing CAD and some of what can be done to decrease that risk. Although preventing CAD is better than suffering from it, if your doctor does diagnose CAD, recognize that today there are superb medical and surgical treatments. A diagnosis of CAD no longer means that your days are numbered. There is much that you and your doctors can do to battle CAD and win.

Risk Factors for CAD

Research has determined the several factors that increase your risk of developing CAD. Some of these factors are beyond your control. Others are in your hands, providing you with an opportunity to reduce your risk. The principal risk factors include:

- Genetics: heredity and sex
- Certain diseases, especially diabetes and high blood pressure
- Lack of exercise
- Obesity
- Smoking
- Cholesterol

If you could have chosen your parents and your sex, you could have done a very great deal to reduce your risk of developing CAD: *genetics* plays an important role in this disease. In some families, CAD is common, and in others, it is unknown. Unfortunately, there is nothing you can do to alter the genetic characteristics passed on to you by your parents. Similarly, you can't choose your sex, although you would probably have asked to be born female if CAD had been your main concern. CAD occurs much more commonly in men than in women, a result of nature and of behavior. Estrogen, a hormone found in much higher levels in women, protects the body from atherosclerosis, while testosterone, which occurs in much higher levels in men, promotes it. That much is determined for us. But men's habits compound the discrepancy. More men smoke cigarettes than do women, and smoking increases your chances of developing CAD as much as anything else under your control. Sadly, as the number of women who smoke has increased, the percentage of women with CAD has climbed as well.

If you have hypertension (high blood pressure) or diabetes, you are at a much greater risk of developing CAD. If you also smoke, your chances of developing CAD skyrocket. Controlling your high blood pressure and keeping your blood sugar close to normal greatly reduce the chances that these diseases will lead to CAD. If you also have the good sense to stop smoking, your risk tumbles even more.

Daily exercise powerfully reduces the risk of developing CAD. People who exercise just fifteen minutes daily suffer heart attacks fifteen times less often than do those who do no exercise. Think about that: by doing fifteen minutes of aerobic exercise every day—the kind of exercise that keeps you moving, gets you breathing, and raises your pulse—you reduce your chance of getting CAD by over 90 percent. There is nothing you can do that is more beneficial in reducing CAD risk than this. There's simply no excuse for not starting and sticking with a program of daily exercise at any age! No matter what your other physical ailments may be, you and your doctor can almost always devise an exercise program to meet your abilities.

The statistics are very clear: if you are overweight—that is, if you are *obese*—you are more likely to develop CAD. Losing weight decreases your risk. Of course, if you lose weight not only by controlling your diet but by starting a regular program of aerobic exercise, you will diminish your risk even more and enjoy the enormous psychological and physiological benefits of leading a healthier life.

If you smoke, stop. It's that simple. If you have any other risk factor for CAD, you compound that risk by smoking. There is now good evidence that by quitting, no matter how many years you've smoked or your current age, you will score clear benefits. Your risk of developing CAD will drop immediately, and your lungs will begin to heal themselves as soon as you stop.

Despite these many other factors, most people think only of *cholesterol* as a risk factor for CAD. Indeed, high levels of cholesterol unquestionably pose a risk, but the true extent of that risk for older people has not yet been established.

Cholesterol damages the coronary arteries over years, not immediately. Thus, younger people are well advised to strive for low cholesterol levels so that they reach old age with plaque-free coronary arteries. But for those lucky enough to have reached 80 and beyond, there is no good evidence that lowering cholesterol once they have reached this age substantially reduces the risk of developing CAD. It is true that the higher the amount of cholesterol in your blood (called *serum cholesterol*), the greater your risk of developing CAD. What has not yet been demonstrated is whether reducing serum cholesterol late in old age lowers the risk.

My patients always ask, "What is a normal cholesterol level?" The answer inevitably frustrates them: abnormal cholesterol is a relative thing. Cholesterol levels below 200 appear to indicate the lowest risk; between 200 and 260 presents only a modest increased risk for older people. In younger adults, who can expect to live another forty or fifty years, levels in the mid- or high 200s are of more concern. Cholesterol levels above 260 pose an even greater risk.

Accomplishing a decrease in serum cholesterol levels is not always easy. You can change your diet, reducing the amount of fat you eat, or you can start medication therapy. Both of these alternatives carry a cost. Altering your diet may require a substantial change in your lifestyle, and all the medications used to lower serum cholesterol have side effects. If you and your doctor are convinced that there is a clear-cut benefit for you, either choice may be reasonable. But for many elders, the benefits cannot be demonstrated, and you may decide that it is not worth abandoning favorite foods late in life or taking on the additional complications of a new medication.

If you and your doctor decide to treat your elevated cholesterol with medication, there are several choices. One is niacin, which is among the least toxic medications for lowering cholesterol. An uncomfortable side effect of niacin, however, is flushing. Another medication is cholestyramine (Questran), which binds with cholesterol in your gastrointestinal system, causing side effects of constipation and bloating. The latest medication for treating elevated cholesterol is mevaclor (Lopid). Mevaclor is extremely effective but can cause serious liver and blood complications. While taking it, you will need frequent blood tests. The laboratory charges and the high cost of the medicine make this an expensive form of therapy. Because it can be toxic, use mevaclor only if you have a substantial elevation of cholesterol—generally above 300—and if your risk of developing CAD outweighs the risk of using the medication.

Before we leave this topic, I want to reemphasize that many of the major risk factors other than cholesterol fall directly within your control. There is good evidence that exercising daily, stopping smoking, and losing weight if you are overweight, all reduce your risk of developing CAD more substantially than a small reduction in your cholesterol level. Of course, be sensible about reducing fat in your diet, especially if your cholesterol is high. But even better, stop smoking, lose your extra weight, and most important, exercise daily!

EVALUATION OF CAD

Diagnosing CAD is not difficult, and often no tests are needed. They may be necessary if your doctor is uncertain about your diagnosis or needs to evaluate the extent of your CAD to determine whether you are a candidate for angioplasty or coronary bypass surgery. (Both are explained later in this chapter.) There are two tests that are often used: a stress test and an angiogram, sometimes called an "arteriogram."

One of the most commonly used tests to evaluate your heart for CAD is called a *stress test* or *exercise tolerance test*. It is performed by monitoring your electrocardiogram (often called an EKG or ECG) while you walk or jog on a treadmill.

An EKG produces a written measurement of the electrical activity of your heart. If the blood supply to any part of your heart is insufficient, your EKG is likely to show it. By monitoring the EKG continuously during the stress test, your doctor will be able to determine whether you develop ischemia—whether atherosclerosis in a coronary artery is causing a part of your heart to receive less blood than it needs. If you develop ischemia soon after beginning the test, when the demands on your heart are only slightly increased, there is more to be concerned about than if ischemia develops after you have exercised vigorously for several minutes. Your doctor will therefore note when you develop changes in your EKG and what those changes are.

The stress test performed today often includes the use of *thallium,* a radioactive chemical. After thallium is injected into your veins, it can be detected in your heart with a special scanning device, which can pinpoint the portions of your heart that become ischemic. This information reveals how large or small the area is that is not receiving adequate blood flow. The thallium poses virtually no risk; its radioactivity is very low, and both it and its radioactivity leave your body rapidly.

The most accurate test for determining the extent of CAD is an *angiogram* or *arteriogram*. However, most people with CAD will never need this test. You should have an angiogram only if you and your doctor are considering an angioplasty or coronary bypass surgery. If you know that you are unwilling to undergo either of these procedures, you should not agree to have an angiogram.

An angiogram is a complicated procedure carried out in a specially equipped room of the hospital and performed only by a cardiologist with expertise in the technique. (A *cardiologist* is a doctor who specializes in heart problems. Cardiologists are not surgeons, but some cardiologists perform invasive procedures such as angioplasties; a surgeon who operates on the heart is called a *cardiovascular surgeon*.) In many ways, an angiogram resembles an operation, requiring sterile instruments and highly technical equipment, except that you are awake rather than under general anesthesia during the procedure. Usually, you can expect to stay in the hospital for one day after the angiogram.

Your doctor begins an angiogram by numbing an area in your groin or arm with an injection of a local anesthetic. The anesthetic allows your doctor to insert a needle into one of your arteries without causing you pain. Your doctor then threads a wire through the needle and moves it toward your heart. While watching on an x-ray machine, your doctor guides the wire into the coronary arteries. Your doctor then threads a tiny catheter over the wire and, through the catheter, injects a dye that is visible on x-rays. By injecting dye into each coronary artery, your doctor can determine exactly where blockages occur and to what extent. It requires quite some time to place the catheter into each artery and to take all the necessary x-rays. From beginning to end, an angiogram can last several hours.

To prevent bleeding immediately after the procedure, a heavy weight or tight bandage will be placed over the spot in your groin or arm where the doctor inserted the needle for several hours. You will also be given fluid by vein (intravenously) to help flush all the dye out of your system.

When performed by a skilled and experienced cardiologist, the risk of suffering serious consequences from an angiogram is reasonably low. However, complications can develop. The most common problem is some bleeding where the needle was inserted, but this is rarely serious. Very rarely, the catheter can block a coronary artery, thereby triggering a heart attack or causing your heartbeat to change from its regular rhythm. Some of the equipment in the angiogram suite is there to treat just such a problem.

Treatment of CAD

The first goal in treating CAD is to relieve ischemia and thereby relieve angina. The best kind of treatment for you depends on many factors: whether you have had a previous heart attack; whether your symptoms can be controlled with medication; the number of coronary arteries affected and the extent of the blockage in them; how much physical activity you want to do; whether you are willing to undergo surgery; and your other medical problems. Often, treatment can be accomplished with medication alone. If medication fails, you may need to consider undergoing angioplasty or bypass surgery.

Medications to Treat CAD

If your CAD is very severe—if the blockage is in the biggest of the coronary arteries—it may be necessary for you to have an angioplasty or coronary bypass surgery without first trying medication. More likely, however, your doctor will begin treating, and successfully control, your CAD with medication. The most commonly prescribed medications include nitroglycerin, calcium channel blockers, and beta blockers. Aspirin also plays a role in treating CAD.

The first medication used to treat CAD was *nitroglycerin,* and it remains a mainstay of therapy today. Of course, this kind of nitroglycerin has been stabilized and is not explosive. It dilates, or opens up, the small arteries of your body, thereby reducing the work that the heart must do to pump blood.

When your heart needs to work less, it requires less blood and oxygen.

One form of nitroglycerin, called *sublingual* (sub means "under," and lingual means "tongue"), is taken when you are experiencing angina; by placing the medication under your tongue, your body absorbs it into the bloodstream almost immediately, and you will notice an effect in seconds. When using sublingual nitroglycerin, you must be especially careful of one of its side effects: it can make you light-headed. Always sit or lie down while taking it.

Sublingual nitroglycerin is used to alleviate angina; other forms of nitroglycerin are used to prevent it. These longer-acting preparations are available either in tablet form, such as Isordil, or in an ointment or patch that allows the drug to be absorbed through your skin. Nitroglycerin ointment is spread on a small area of skin every six to eight hours, while a nitroglycerin patch usually lasts an entire day. Although the patch form is more convenient, the ointment is believed to be more effective.

Many people who start on nitroglycerin develop headaches, which usually go away after the first week of use. If you do get headaches, try to bear the pain for a week or two, using acetaminophen (Tylenol) to help you through it. If the headache is intolerable or doesn't go away after two weeks, discuss alternative medications with your doctor.

Another group of medications that helps prevent ischemia are collectively called *calcium channel blockers* and have such names as diltiazem (Cardiazem), verapamil (Calan), and nifedipine (Procardia). These medications help maintain a good flow of blood through the coronary arteries and open up other arteries, thereby reducing the heart's work. Calcium channel blockers are now among the most commonly used medications for angina, and they work very well. Their side effects are usually minimal; some cause a little swelling in the ankles and feet, some slow the pulse, and some reduce blood pressure more than others. The choice of which calcium channel blocker to use depends on an assessment of your CAD, your other medical problems, and the other medications you are taking.

Beta blockers are the third type of medication used to control CAD. Beta blockers—for example, propranolol (Inderal), atenolol (Tenormin), and metoprolol (Lopressor)—work directly on your heart to reduce both its rate and force of contraction, thereby decreasing the work that your heart performs. Beta blockers have been shown to be particularly beneficial to people who have already had one heart attack and may be helpful to people who have CAD and a rapid pulse. However, beta blockers can cause several side effects.

First, by reducing the force of contractions, beta blockers can reduce the functioning of the heart, leading to congestive heart failure (discussed later in this chapter). Beta blockers can also aggravate a relatively common condition called claudication, which causes painful cramping in the legs when walking. If you have breathing problems, such as emphysema or asthma, beta blockers may exacerbate them. Some beta blockers can make you sleepy, and others, especially propranolol (Inderal), can cause depression. Finally, there is evidence that beta blockers are less effective in treating CAD in older people than in younger adults.

You may need to use more than one medication to control your ischemia. For example, your doctor may recommend that you use a calcium channel blocker and a nitroglycerin patch. You may even use several forms of nitroglycerin—tablets during the day, ointment at night, and the sublingual form whenever you experience chest pain. The goal is to find the most effective combination of medications with the least risk of unwanted side effects.

One way to help prevent ischemia and heart attacks is to stop platelets from blocking the narrowed coronary arteries. Aspirin, besides blocking pain, affects platelets, making them less sticky. If you take aspirin, your platelets cannot stick as well to one another and are less likely to block a coronary artery.

The use of aspirin has been widely studied, and research demonstrates that daily use of aspirin can reduce the risk of heart attack in some people. Aspirin therapy benefits men the most, especially men who have already suffered a heart attack. If you use aspirin to treat CAD, you should take one-

half or one aspirin daily. Remember, however, that this treatment is likely to have the side effect of making you bleed more
if you cut yourself.

Angioplasty and Bypass Surgery

If medication fails to control your ischemia, or if your CAD
is very serious when first discovered, you will need to consider undergoing a procedure to improve the blood supply to
your heart. Angioplasty and bypass surgery are the two ways
of repairing blocked coronary arteries. Before either procedure, you will undergo the angiogram, described previously,
to determine whether an angioplasty can be attempted or
whether more radical bypass surgery is necessary.

Angioplasty is performed exactly like an angiogram except
that instead of using an ordinary catheter, your cardiologist
uses one with a tiny balloon on its surface. Your cardiologist
threads the catheter to the spot where the coronary artery is
most blocked. Once the catheter is positioned, the balloon is
inflated to compress the blockage and open the artery. Figure
4 shows how this is done.

If the angioplasty works, you may avoid bypass surgery
altogether. Unfortunately, angioplasty is not always appropriate or successful. If you have many blockages, or if the
blockage is somewhere the catheter cannot reach or cannot
treat safely, angioplasty is not an option. Also, in more than
one in three people, the blockage recurs after angioplasty—
the procedure provides only temporary relief. Rarely, during
the angioplasty a coronary artery suffers damage, requiring
that surgery be performed immediately. That is why you
should have your angioplasty performed in a hospital that also
has excellent cardiovascular surgeons.

The use of a balloon on the catheter is not the only method
of opening up blocked coronary arteries. Researchers are
experimenting with catheters equipped with tiny lasers that
burn away plaque and cleaning heads that clear blockages the
way a Roto-Rooter cleans clogged pipes. However, these techniques are not yet commonly used and have yet to prove
themselves.

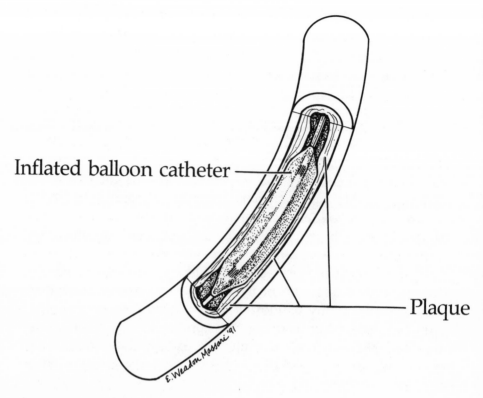

Inflated balloon catheter

Plaque

FIGURE 4
How an Angioplasty Works

The most invasive procedure for treating CAD, and one that involves major surgery, is *coronary artery bypass surgery.* You may hear doctors or nurses refer to it by the abbreviation *CABG* (coronary artery bypass graft), pronounced "cabbage." Your friends may call it simply "a bypass." Although this operation has become commonplace, it is very taxing on the body and should not be performed unless necessary to keep you active or to prevent a heart attack.

Age alone presents no barrier to having bypass surgery, which can and has been performed successfully and safely on persons of all ages. However, other diseases, commonly occuring in older people, especially certain lung diseases and severe atherosclerotic disease affecting blood supply to the brain, may make such extensive surgery particularly risky.

Bypass surgery got its name because the surgeon actually bypasses the blockage in your coronary arteries by grafting on a new blood vessel. At the beginning of the operation your surgeon may remove a vein from your leg to use as the new blood vessel, or he or she may use an artificial vein. Your surgeon attaches the new blood vessel in such a way that it carries blood around the blockage.

Open-heart surgery is complicated. Your surgeon must cut through the protective cage of your breast bone and ribs to reach your heart. The surgical team takes over the normal action of your heart by using a special blood-pumping machine, so that your surgeon can handle your heart. Your surgeon must sew the bypass graft exactly where it is needed and then close and repair the surgical openings in your chest. Yet, despite its complexity, every year many thousands of successful bypass operations are performed.

After the operation, it will be at least several weeks and often several months before you recover completely and are fully active again. For the first days after the surgery, you will stay in an intensive care unit (often called an ICU) so that your doctors and nurses can closely monitor your heart's function. Then, you will slowly begin a program of rehabilitation to help you regain your strength. Even after you have returned home, you will have to limit your activities at first, gradually increasing what you can do. You can expect that your chest will be sore for several weeks and that you will need help with most chores for at least a month.

ARRHYTHMIAS

Your heart's internal electrical system keeps it beating regularly. If the electrical system malfunctions, your heart will beat in an abnormal rhythm. Abnormal rhythms in heartbeat are called *arrhythmias*. Some arrhythmias are harmless, but others are life-threatening because they prevent your heart from contracting and pumping blood properly.

Bradycardia and Pacemakers

When your heart beats too slowly, the condition is called *bradycardia* (brady means "slow," and cardia refers to the heart). If your heart rate falls below 40 beats per minute, or if your heart pauses between beats for more than a second or two, your blood pressure will fall, your brain will not get blood, and you will become light-headed or even faint. Several medications used to treat various medical conditions, such as beta blockers—for example, propranolol (Inderal), verapamil (Calan), digoxin (Lanoxin), timolol eye drops (Timoptic), and methyldopa (Aldomet)—can cause bradycardia as a side effect. Most often, however, bradycardia is caused by a problem in the heart's electrical system. Fortunately, bradycardia can be controlled by a *pacemaker.*

A pacemaker is a small electronic device that stimulates the heart when its own electrical system functions too slowly. In a minor surgical procedure, the pacemaker is placed just under the skin of the chest; a tiny wire runs from it to the wall of the heart. The wire is threaded to your heart through a vein while the doctor determines the position of the wire with x-rays.

Recent studies indicate that in America more pacemakers are implanted than medically necessary. If your cardiologist recommends that you have a pacemaker, be certain that you really need it. Before you agree to the procedure, confirm that your bradycardia has or is very likely to cause medical difficulties. Do not have a pacemaker implanted unless two cardiologists agree that it is necessary and is likely to be beneficial.

Atrial Fibrillation

Normally, your heart beats at a regular pace, each beat initiated by an electrical stimulation from a special area on the heart known as the sinus node (see Figure 2). That stimulation causes the *atrium* to contract first and the *ventricle* to follow immediately thereafter. Atrial fibrillation occurs when the normal electrical stimulation is replaced by an irregular and rapid one that fails to cause the atrium to contract normally.

You may experience atrial fibrillation from time to time over months or years without complication. However, atrial fibrillation sometimes causes the ventricle to contract very rapidly as well, leading to an emergency requiring immediate medical care.

When atrial fibrillation is most serious, you may faint, become short of breath, feel palpitations, or experience chest pain. Your doctor will be able to determine that you have atrial fibrillation by feeling your pulse, listening to your heart, and taking an electrocardiogram.

If you do have atrial fibrillation, your doctor will be most concerned about how fast your heart is beating and whether it is pumping properly. If your heart is beating too quickly, you will probably be given digoxin, a medication that slows it down. If your heart rate is so fast that your heart cannot pump properly, it may be necessary to give it a gentle electrical shock to force it back into a slower and regular rhythm. Fortunately, an electrical shock is rarely needed; medication usually controls the situation.

The first time you experience atrial fibrillation, your doctor will try to discover why it started. He or she will want to determine if you have suffered a heart attack, have had a blood clot that damaged your lungs, have an overactive thyroid (the cause of atrial fibrillation in President Bush), have a faulty heart valve, or whether you are taking a medication that overstimulated your heart.

Your doctor also will want to determine whether your atrial fibrillation occurs continuously or only intermittently by recording the beating of your heart over a longer period than an electrocardiogram provides. You will be provided with a *Holter Monitor,* a portable device that you will wear for an entire day as it records your electrocardiogram on magnetic tape. This extended record will demonstrate whether you experienced atrial fibrillation during that day and, if so, how often. Although the Holter Monitor is used most frequently to measure atrial fibrillation, it is also employed to monitor all the arrhythmias discussed in this chapter.

If atrial fibrillation continues, small blood clots can form in your heart and eventually break off, causing a stroke. Although this is not a common complication of atrial fibrillation, it can be serious, so to prevent it, your doctor may prescribe an anticlotting medication called Coumadin. This drug, however, also prevents clotting throughout your body and may lead to dangerous bleeding. Thus, you and your doctor must weigh carefully the benefits and risks of using Coumadin. For example, if you have a tendency to fall, have cancer, have had bleeding in your gastrointestinal tract, or drink alcohol heavily, it may not be safe for you to use Coumadin. If you do take Coumadin, your blood must be tested, every few days at first, and then every few weeks or months, to be sure that you are taking the proper amount. When you start on Coumadin, be certain that you understand the risks and your doctor's schedule for monitoring your blood tests.

Ventricular Arrhythmias

Ventricular arrhythmias occur when your heart's electrical system becomes irritated. An abnormal electrical discharge overrides the heart's normal electrical pathways, akin to a short-circuiting. The result is a *premature ventricular contraction (PVC)*. A single PVC rarely causes any problem; however, the heart does not pump well during a PVC, and if several occur in succession, you can experience light-headedness or fainting. However, PVCs can also produce dangerous arrhythmias, leading to a medical emergency. For example, on occasion PVCs can override the heart's normal rhythm entirely, leading to *ventricular tachycardia* (tachy means "fast" and cardia refers to the heart) or *ventricular fibrillation*. These life-threatening arrhythmias most commonly occur during or shortly after a heart attack. Both ventricular tachycardia and ventricular fibrillation interfere with your heart's ability to pump blood, and can lead to death from *cardiac arrest,* when your heart stops beating entirely.

If your doctor is concerned that you are at risk of developing ventricular tachycardia or ventricular fibrillation, he or she may perform highly technical tests or decide to treat you with medications and measure the effectiveness of the drug therapy. Medications, called *antiarrhythmics,* such as quinidine, procaine, lidocaine, mexilitine, and amiodarone, help prevent ventricular arrhythmias. They are potent medications with serious side effects and should be used only when necessary.

CONGESTIVE HEART FAILURE

What Is Congestive Heart Failure?

The heart, like every pump, has two functions. In one direction, it pumps blood forward, through the arteries, to every part of your body, just as a fire engine pumps water onto a fire. In the other direction, the heart removes blood from the veins, just as sump pumps clear water out of a flooded basement. If your heart cannot remove enough blood from the veins, blood backs up, overfilling your vascular system, a condition known as *congestive heart failure*. Your body retains too much fluid, a condition sometimes called overhydration.

Congestive heart failure has two immediate consequences. First, when your heart can't remove sufficient blood from the veins that serve your lungs, a backup in these veins causes congestion in your lungs. As a result, your lungs fill with fluid, a condition called *pulmonary edema*. Pulmonary edema makes it difficult to breathe, often most notably when you lie down, a symptom called *orthopnea*.

Second, because your heart can't completely drain the blood from other veins of your body, you may develop swelling called *edema*. Edema generally gathers in your feet and lower legs because of the pull of gravity, but it can form in any part of your body below your heart. While you sleep, edema may settle in the lower part of your back, and after you have gotten up it may move to your feet. Edema can also occur in several organs, causing swelling in your liver and malfunction of your kidneys.

Evaluating Congestive Heart Failure

If you have congestive heart failure, your doctor will want to determine its cause. Your medical history, especially if you have had one or more heart attacks, may explain the origin, and a physical examination may provide all the necessary information. Sometimes, however, a test is needed to determine the cause or to choose the best treatment for you. One commonly used test is an *echocardiogram,* which uses sound waves to show how your heart is functioning. The test is painless and essentially without risk. The echocardiogram will tell your doctor whether your heart is squeezing uniformly, whether one particular area is malfunctioning, whether your heart's valves are working properly, and the overall size of your heart and the thickness of its walls. With this information your doctor can determine whether surgery is needed to repair a faulty valve or, more usually, whether a medication is warranted, and if so, which type.

Treating Congestive Heart Failure

Diuretics, such as furosemide (Lasix), are the mainstay of treating congestive heart failure. These medications (also known as "water pills") force your kidneys to produce more urine, pulling more water from your blood and thereby reducing the volume of blood that your heart must pump. Diuretics are reasonably safe, but your dose must be adjusted to your particular need; too much can cause you to become dehydrated. If you start to become dehydratd, which can easily happen on hot days or if you cannot drink or eat due to a flu or stomach-ache, stop or reduce your diuretic and call your doctor immediately for advice. Most diuretics also cause your body to lose potassium, and most people using diuretics for congestive heart failure must take supplemental potassium.

The medicine digoxin (Lanoxin) helps some people with congestive heart failure because it stimulates the heart to pump more vigorously. In the past, digoxin was the preferred treatment, but recently doctors have learned that this drug is not nearly as effective as we once thought. Many people with congestive heart failure need not use digoxin. If you take digoxin for congestive heart failure, ask your doctor if it is really helping you or if you can discontinue it.

If you have severe congestive heart failure, medications such as captopril (Capoten), enalapril (Vasotec), and hydralazine may help. They reduce the strain on the heart by opening up your arteries. When it is required to move the same volume of blood but through wider channels, the heart's pumping action improves. If diuretics alone cannot control your congestive heart failure, your doctor may recommend that you also take one of these medications.

HEART VALVES

Your heart has four valves that control the filling of each of its chambers and ensure that blood flows in the correct direction. If a valve becomes leaky, called *regurgitation,* blood will flow backward. If a valve becomes narrowed, called *stenosis,* the flow of blood will be blocked.

The *aortic valve* and the *mitral valve* (refer to Figure 1) most commonly develop these two problems. If your valve problem is mild, you may not experience any symptoms, but over time the faulty functioning of the valves may harm your heart. Eventually you may develop shortness of breath, palpitations, arrhythmias, angina, and fainting.

Evaluating Valve Function

If one or more of your heart valves functions improperly, your doctor will be able to hear through the stethoscope a *murmur,* a soft noise created by blood flowing through the narrowed valve or flowing backward. Some people have murmurs even though their valves are functioning normally; usually your doctor can distinguish an innocent murmur from one that indicates a malfunctioning valve. If you have a murmur that indicates you might have a faulty valve, your doctor will recommend an echocardiogram. This is the test, described earlier, that uses sound waves to measure the heart and its function.

Repairing Faulty Valves

Often a valve problem is so mild that no special treatment is necessary. In that case, your doctor will check you every six months or so to be sure that the situation is not worsening. If the valve's function deteriorates, or if your heart becomes strained by the faulty valve, you may need to have the valve repaired.

If the valve is narrowed, restricting blood flow through it, it can sometimes be fixed with a procedure called a *valvuloplasty*. A valvuloplasty is performed by a cardiologist in a procedure similar to an angioplasty. The cardiologist positions a catheter at the narrowed valve and, using a balloon, is able to open it. However, valvuloplasty is not always possible, is often not permanent, and can't be used to treat a leaky valve. In those cases, the only alternative is surgery. Open-heart surgery to repair or replace a heart valve is as major an operation as bypass surgery but may be the only way to save your heart.

The heart is an amazing and complex organ. It pumps blood to every part of your body, regulates the frequency of its beat with a remarkable electrical system, and adjusts the forcefulness with which it pumps depending on how active you become.

Like any other part of the body, the heart can experience disease, and its complex systems can develop problems. Coronary artery disease is common in late life, the product of smoking, lack of exercise, high blood pressure, and high cholesterol. Fortunately, your doctors have many medications to control coronary artery disease and two procedures, angioplasty and coronary artery bypass surgery, to help those for whom medications alone cannot provide adequate treatment. Many other problems such as arrhythmias, congestive heart failure, and valve problems can also be treated successfully.

Although the diagnosis of coronary artery disease or any other heart problem is bound to alarm you, many of the most remarkable advances in modern medicine have occurred in this field. There is a great deal that you and your doctors can do to treat successfully the more commonly occurring cardiological problems of late life.

BLOOD

Of all the organ systems in our bodies, blood seems to us the most vital, closely bound up in the way we feel about ourselves and others, something evident in our everyday language. Tired blood is what we have when we are fatigued, but when we are well, it is strong blood we boast of. We call anything or anyone essential to our well-being our lifeblood. Blue blood flows through the veins of noblemen, but common blood flows through the rest of us. And, between us and people we don't like, there is bad blood. Truly an amazing substance, blood has, in our bodies, even more varied functions and uses than in our speech.

As blood circulates through the arteries and veins, it brings oxygen to every tissue in the body and takes away carbon dioxide and other waste products. Blood also performs many other tasks, helping your body fight infections, acting as a reservoir for water, and even controlling the loss of itself if injury causes you to bleed.

Blood is made up of liquid and cells. The liquid consists of water and protein while the cells are of three kinds: red blood cells (RBCs), white blood cells (WBCs), and platelets. Bone marrow produces the cells of your blood, which (with other organs) make the proteins. Water in our blood comes from the liquid we ingest and is stored in the tissues surrounding the blood vessels.

RED BLOOD CELLS

Red blood cells (RBCs) are fantastic works of body engineering. They are filled with a chemical called hemoglobin, which, with the help of iron, combines with and holds on to oxygen. When RBCs pass through the thin blood vessels of our lungs, they become saturated with oxygen. As they course through the arteries, the RBCs deliver oxygen to the tissues of the body and carry carbon dioxide away.

The health of every tissue of your body depends on an adequate supply of the oxygen that your RBCs deliver. If blood flow is inadequate, tissues will be starved of oxygen, become damaged, or die. In other chapters you will learn that inadequate delivery of oxygen causes angina and heart attacks, strokes, and bed sores.

When RBCs become saturated with oxygen in the lungs, they become bright red; when they give up their oxygen, they darken. You can see this in your skin, which takes on a healthy red flush when it receives oxygen-rich blood, most noticeably when you blush. If your blood lacks adequate oxygen, however, your skin develops a frightening gray or blue color, a condition called *cyanosis.*

RBCs live for about 120 days, after which your body recognizes old and tired RBCs, filters them out, and destroys them. However, your body saves the iron of the old RBCs and recycles it in new ones. As long as RBCs are not lost due to bleeding, the iron levels in your body remain normal.

Age does not affect the life span of RBCs or reduce the amount of hemoglobin in them. Although the total number of RBCs in your body falls slightly with age, this decrease occurs because the total volume of your blood decreases. The only age-related change of medical importance is that your bone marrow produces RBCs more slowly. Under normal conditions, this change presents no problem. Difficulties arise only if you develop some other condition that requires large amounts of new RBCs more quickly than the marrow can manage.

Anemia

Anemia, the most common blood problem, is a decrease in the number of RBCs in the blood to the point where you have too few to deliver adequate oxygen to all the tissues of your body. You may appear pale because your skin lacks oxygen-rich blood and you may feel tired or listless because your brain and heart receive less oxygen. You may also be physically weak because your muscles lack the oxygen they need to perform best. If you also have atherosclerosis, a narrowing of the arteries from fatty buildup that decreases blood flow, anemia further impairs the delivery of oxygen to your heart, brain, or legs. Anemia and atherosclerosis together can result in chest pain, shortness of breath, strokes, or pain in the legs called claudication.

To check your blood for anemia, your doctor usually performs one of two tests. The first measures the proportion of RBCs to liquid in your blood, a proportion known as the *hematocrit*. An hematocrit of 40 means that 40 percent of your blood is made up of red blood cells. The other test measures the amount of hemoglobin in your blood.

Although common, anemia is not normal. If you are anemic, you and your doctor will want to know why. Anemia is usually caused by a loss of blood, by having your RBCs destroyed more quickly than they are replaced, or by a reduction in the rate or number of RBCs your bone marrow produces.

Iron-deficiency anemia, one form of the condition, occurs if your body is low in iron. Your body normally recycles its iron when it destroys old RBCs to make new ones. Therefore, if your iron is low, you are probably losing RBCs through bleeding. This situation commonly occurs after surgery or a traumatic injury. If it happens at other times, you may be leaking blood into your stool, a warning sign of colon cancer or a bleeding ulcer. If you have iron-deficiency anemia, your doctor will want to determine whether it results from a gastrointestinal problem and, if so, if the problem is an indication of cancer or a bleeding ulcer.

Another kind of anemia is due simply to the effects of chronic disease on your bone marrow's ability to produce RBCs. Your doctor determines whether your bone marrow is functioning properly by measuring the number of newly formed red blood cells, called *reticulocytes*. If your reticulocyte count is low and you do not have iron-deficiency anemia, your anemia is likely caused by inadequate production of RBCs, not by their loss.

Any serious illness tends to suppress the production of new RBCs, and this effect is particularly apparent as you age. Doctors call this the *anemia of chronic disease*. Despite its name, the anemia of chronic disease occurs not only in the presence of chronic (long-term) illnesses but with short-term, serious illnesses.

The anemia of chronic disease rarely calls for direct treatment itself; usually, treating the underlying illness will cure the anemia. However, if you have anemia of chronic disease, your bone marrow will be slow to produce new RBCs after blood loss from surgery or trauma, and you may remain anemic longer than otherwise would be expected.

Most other causes of anemia are from disease in the bone marrow that seriously impairs the production of RBCs. Sometimes cancer, especially breast or prostate cancer, spreads to the marrow, destroying the cells that produce RBCs. There are also two cancers, *leukemia* and *multiple myeloma,* that actually start in the bone marrow, causing anemia. Toxic substances, including some medications, and exposure to large doses of radiation can also damage the ability of bone marrow to produce RBCs.

The bone marrow will also fail to function normally if it lacks certain necessary nutrients. For example, if you become deficient in folate or B_{12} (two important vitamins), you will develop anemia. Or, if the amount of iron in your blood falls low enough, through excessive blood loss or a diet lacking in iron, your bone marrow will malfunction, producing an insufficient number of RBCs. A normal diet usually contains adequate amounts of these nutrients for most people. If you need supplements, your doctor can tell you which ones you need and how to get them.

If your bone marrow seriously malfunctions, your doctor may suggest a *bone marrow biopsy* to diagnose the problem. This test is generally performed by a *hematologist,* a doctor specializing in blood problems. The hematologist will anesthetize a spot on your hip, insert a special needle into your hip bone, and withdraw a small sample of the bone marrow. During the biopsy you will feel pressure, but the anesthetic agent usually prevents any severe pain. When the anesthetic wears off, however, you can expect to be a little sore for several days.

The least common cause of anemia in older people is the overly rapid destruction of RBCs within the body. Your body normally destroys RBCs only when they are old, but sometimes it destroys RBCs unnecessarily, a condition called *hemolytic anemia.* Some medications and autoimmune conditions can cause hemolytic anemia. If your doctor suspects this situation, he or she will draw blood samples to test for it.

If your hematocrit—the ratio of RBCs to total blood volume—falls too low or too rapidly, a blood transfusion may be needed to raise it quickly. A transfusion is simply the mechanical transfer of blood into your body. There is no absolute number on the hematocrit scale that determines when you need a transfusion; every situation is different. If an injury, surgery, or a problem in your gastrointestinal system causes you to lose blood rapidly, or if you have anemia and develop a warning sign of catastrophic illness—chest pain, shortness of breath, confusion, or fainting—you may need a transfusion immediately. If you have chronic heart disease, have had strokes, or have serious lung disease, your doctor may recommend that you receive a transfusion even in the absence of these signs. However, transfusions should be reserved for serious medical situations. If your doctor suggests a transfusion although you have none of the symptoms above, ask whether it can be delayed safely in order to allow time for other treatments to raise your hematocrit.

Although transfusions usually cause little problem, they

pose at least three risks: you can develop a tranfusion reaction, catch a viral illness, and become overloaded with fluid.

Before any transfusion, the blood bank compares the donated blood with your blood to be certain that the two are compatible. Despite these tests, sometimes the transfused blood triggers a reaction against it in your body. These transfusion reactions are usually mild—chills and fever—and pass quickly. Occasionally, however, transfusion reactions are severe, causing kidney damage, breathing problems, and cardiac arrest.

The blood bank also takes precautions to exclude diseased blood. Unfortunately, tests for this purpose are not perfect, and some extraordinarily small fraction of donated blood is thus infected with hepatitis or the AIDS virus. The chances of getting either of these diseases from a transfusion is now extremely low, but it is not zero. Some doctors may recommend that a relative with a similar blood type donate blood for you to reduce this risk. Although you may have every confidence in your family, there is no assurance that a relative doesn't carry a communicable disease. Many people are unaware that they carry hepatitis or the AIDS virus. If you know in advance that you may need a transfusion—for example, if you are planning on surgery—discuss with your doctor the possibility of putting aside ("banking") some of your own blood.

WHITE BLOOD CELLS

White blood cells (WBCs) are the body's army. WBCs recognize foreign substances that enter the body and destroy them. They will attack viruses and bacteria that invade your bloodstream, splinters of wood, glass, or metal that lodge in your skin, and even cancer cells. And, unless we trick them, WBCs recognize and destroy transplanted organs because they are not your own.

Of course, WBCs are not always successful. When they fail, we suffer infections or other diseases. Yet, much more often than you realize, your WBCs prevent such problems long before they become severe enough to require treatment.

The bone marrow produces several different types of WBCs, each of which has a different task to perform. Some recognize foreign substances and release a chemical alarm to alert the rest of your body. When the cells of recognition sound the warning, your body releases other kinds of WBCs from their armories and rapidly begins producing replacements. That is why your WBC count goes up when you have an infection. Some WBCs produce proteins that help destroy foreign cells, and others attack foreign objects directly, like little "Pac-Mans," chewing up the foreign substances and digesting them with enzymes. Still other WBCs shut down the alarm system once the foreign object is destroyed so that the killer WBCs don't destroy anything that they shouldn't.

As we get older, the proportion of some of the different kinds of WBCs changes, and their activity decreases. Because of these normal changes, you are more susceptible to some infections. For example, you are more likely to develop pneumococcal pneumonia and to become more seriously ill from it. Skin infections tend to spread more quickly, and viruses, like herpes zoster (discussed in chapter 6) are harder to control.

Problems with WBCs

For WBCs to fight infections and work effectively as part of your immune system, they must be present in adequate numbers and function properly. Some circumstances can decrease the number of WBCs available, and others can affect how they function. For example, some medications poison the bone marrow, causing a dramatic fall in the number of WBCs. Although this side effect is rare, it occurs occasionally with antibiotics and commonly with drugs used to treat cancer. Other medications, particularly steroids (prednisone, for example), affect the function of WBCs, leaving your body less able to fight infections. If you develop any sign of an infection—fever, cough, skin sores, pustules, or redness—while you are taking steroids, contact your doctor promptly.

Leukemia is a cancer of the bone marrow that can dramatically affect the number and function of your WBCs. There are several different kinds of leukemia, two of which, *chronic lymphocytic* and *acute myelogenous,* occur more commonly in the elderly. Chronic lymphocytic leukemia (CLL), is by far the most common in older people. As its name implies, it affects lymphocytes, a kind of WBC. It is called chronic because it progresses slowly, over years. Most people with CLL have it for many years, often requiring very little treatment and experiencing few symptoms. Sometimes, however, the disease progresses rapidly, requiring treatment with potent medications.

Acute myelogenous leukemia (AML) occurs in people of all ages and is much more serious than CLL. It affects the myelocytes, the WBCs that fight infection. Those who have AML generally succumb to fevers, infections, bleeding problems, and anemia soon after the disease develops. Chemotherapy (drug therapy) can sometimes cure AML, but is often not successful. Since the therapy is intensive and toxic, it is not appropriate for everyone. As with any kind of cancer, if your doctor recommends treatment, you should understand fully, before you begin treatment, your chances of recovery and the side effects that you are likely to experience.

PLATELETS

Blood is meant to remain in your blood vessels; it is not supposed to leak internally or spill from the body through cuts. To control the loss of blood, your body has a complex system to control bleeding. One part of that system is the platelet.

Platelets (pronounced pláte-lets) are smaller than other blood cells and are sticky, adhering one to another and to the cells around them to patch the place where blood is escaping. At the site of bleeding they move into action, becoming even more sticky, piling up, and releasing chemicals that stimulate the rest of the body's clotting system. Remember the last time you skinned your knee? At first, blood flowed briskly through the many small abrasions. Within minutes, the bleeding slowed, and minutes later it was little more than a slight ooze.

Soon, a scab formed, allowing the skin underneath to heal. All this was accomplished by the blood's platelets and its clotting proteins.

There are no measurable changes in platelets as you get older. Their number remains constant, and they are as active as they always were. Nevertheless, many older patients comment that their skin bleeds more easily now. This bleeding tendency occurs because your skin has thinned and thus tears more easily, not because of a change in your blood or its components. Unless you suffer an abnormal condition or take a medication that affects platelets or the clotting proteins, your body's mechanisms to stop bleeding work as well now as ever.

Several medications, notably aspirin, affect platelet function. Even at very low doses, aspirin makes platelets less sticky. If you take aspirin, you will bleed more and longer. Moreover, aspirin irritates the stomach, which can itself lead to bleeding. Drugs called nonsteroidal antiinflammatories (NSAIDs), such as ibuprofin (Advil), are similar to aspirin in this way. Acetaminophen (Tylenol) does not affect the function of platelets and is, accordingly, generally a safer pain-relieving medicine than aspirin.

Aspirin's effect on platelets is not always bad. Blockages in small arteries contribute to heart attack and stroke. Because aspirin makes the platelets less sticky, it has the effect of "thinning" your blood so that platelets don't stick together to block arteries narrowed by atherosclerosis. There is evidence that some people, especially men who have already suffered a heart attack or stroke, can reduce the chance of suffering another heart attack or stroke by taking half an aspirin daily. This evidence, which has received much attention in the media, has led some doctors to recommend a daily aspirin as preventive medication. However, it is not clear that everyone benefits from daily aspirin. Before you begin taking aspirin for this purpose, discuss it with your doctor.

BLOOD PROTEINS

There are many different proteins in the blood. Some proteins merely pass through the blood on their way from where they were produced to where they have their effect. For example, insulin is made in the pancreas but is carried in the blood on its way to the body's muscles and fat, where it works. Here, I will discuss only those proteins that assist blood in its assigned tasks, namely the clotting proteins, which help control bleeding, and antibodies, which help WBCs fight infections.

More than a dozen different *clotting proteins* work with the platelets to control bleeding. The body's system for controlling bleeding is so complex because blood must begin to clot quickly, stop clotting as soon as the leak is fixed, and never clot unnecessarily. If a clot forms where it shouldn't, it can clog a vital artery or vein, causing medical emergencies such as heart attack, stroke, deep vein thrombosis (called a DVT), or pulmonary embolism (a blood clot in the lung). Fortunately, the clotting system tries to prevent the formation of unnecessary clots, and happily, the system works just as well in old age as it did in youth.

Many of the clotting proteins are made in the liver. In order to produce adequate amounts of them, your liver must function properly and your diet must include vitamin K, found in green, leafy vegetables. Anyone who has serious liver disease or is seriously malnourished may not be able to make these proteins.

For specific medical reasons, you may be given medications, called *anticoagulants,* that block vitamin K so that the liver cannot make these clotting proteins. One such medication is Coumadin. Your doctor might give you this anticoagulant if you develop a blood clot in your leg, if you have a valve in your heart replaced, or if you suffer a stroke. Coumadin is a very effective medication and may be essential in preventing further illness. Older people are more sensitive to its effects, however, so your doctor must monitor your dose of the medication carefully with frequent blood tests. If you take Coumadin, or any other anticoagulant, follow your doctor's instructions precisely, have your blood tested frequently, and take care of any bleeding immediately by applying pressure to the bleeding site and keeping pressure on it for at least ten minutes. Don't use aspirin if you take Coumadin because together they can cause serious bleeding. If you use anti-coagulants, never hesitate to call your doctor if you have an injury, even a minor one. If you fall or otherwise hit your head or develop any large black and blue area, contact your doctor immediately to find out if you need medical attention for possible internal bleeding.

Antibodies, which help WBCs fight infection, comprise the other important type of blood protein. In your blood, you have many thousands of different antibodies, each one of which recognizes and helps destroy one specific foreign substance, called an *antigen.* The first time your body encounters a particular antigen—a bacterium, virus, or cancerous cell—there is a delay before your body knows that the antigen is harmful and attempts to destroy it. However, once your body has met an antigen, your body remembers it forever. That memory is carried in specialized white blood cells that quickly produce the correct antibody if ever they encounter the same antigen again.

The antibody system can recognize and destroy many kinds of antigens, but it is particularly good at fighting viruses. That is why we get most viral infections, like measles and mumps, only once in our lives. One of the great advances in medicine was the discovery that through vaccinations, we can teach the body to recognize foreign antigens and become immune to them before we are infected with the disease and it has done major damage. Vaccines do this by exposing your body to a virus particle that has either been killed or otherwise altered so that it can't cause an infection but can stimulate your body into producing antibodies that protect you from the real virus.

For the most part, vaccines work as well for you now as when you were young. Moreover, you may benefit from your many years of exposure to viruses, which have given your body time to produce a great variety of antibodies to over-come them. Although many viruses change little, if at all, some viruses change in subtle ways with time. These changes mean that an antibody that your body developed to combat the virus once will lose a battle with the changed form of the same virus. For example, the influenza (flu) virus alters its shape constantly, which is why you need a flu shot every year. Flu vaccine is prepared to protect you against the current, most prevalent type of flu.

Antibodies also fight infections other than viruses. They can often kill bacteria, although they are not quite so adept at it. If a bacterial infection is minor, your antibodies may be able to destroy the infection, but a large bacterial infection may be able to reproduce quickly enough to overwhelm the protective system. Although they are not as effective as vaccinations against viruses, scientists have developed vaccines against some bacteria. The vaccination against pneumococcal pneumonia is one good example, and I generally recommend it for all my patients. It is usually needed only once in a lifetime and will help you avoid or fight this serious illness.

Working with WBCs, antibodies can even destroy some cancer cells. Cancer cells have unusual properties that sometimes allow antibodies to recognize them as being abnormal. More often than we realize, cancer cells are destroyed by our own antibodies and WBCs before a tumor grows large enough to overcome our immune system. There are suggestions, however, that as you get older your antibodies and WBCs lose some of their ability to recognize and destroy cancer cells, explaining, in part, why the elderly suffer from cancers more commonly than do younger people.

WATER AND BLOOD VOLUME

More than half of blood is water, and, surprisingly, it is as salty as the sea. All the cells and proteins I have discussed so far in this chapter are suspended in your blood thanks to this water.

When you drink water, it is absorbed in the gastrointestinal system and enters the bloodstream. The water in the blood moves in and out of the tissues surrounding blood vessels as needed, keeping the tissues well hydrated. When there is too much water in the system, the kidneys process it into urine, which you excrete. When there is too little water, the kidneys try to conserve water and, by making you feel thirsty, your body prompts you to drink.

Overhydration and Dehydration

Our bodies take great care to keep the volume, that is, the amount, of our blood just right. Yet, because of age-related changes, disease, and medications, you may suffer from too much water in your system (overhydration) or from too little (dehydration). Both conditions can result in serious medical difficulties.

Overhydration may be caused by kidney or liver disease but most often occurs because of heart problems, and therefore it is discussed in chapter 3, which discusses the heart. However, *dehydration* generally occurs for other reasons, which I will discuss here.

It is never normal to become dehydrated. As soon as your body senses that it is becoming dehydrated, your kidneys begin to conserve water by producing concentrated urine that carries away waste products with as little water as possible. As you age, your kidneys are less efficient at concentrating urine. Thus, you will continue to lose water through your urine even when you are dehydrated.

While your kidneys are at work conserving water, your brain triggers your thirst, prompting you to drink and thereby increasing the amount of water in your body. For reasons we don't fully understand, with age you do not become thirsty as quickly or as intensely. Therefore, the impetus for you to drink weakens, making serious dehydration even more likely. Light-headedness, fever, sleepiness, and confusion are signs of de-hydration, which also aggravate the situation by making it even harder for you to realize that you must take in water!

If you cannot easily get to water or if the weather is hot, the risk of dehydration increases. If you are bedridden or not mobile, be certain that a good supply of water, juice, or other liquid is at hand. In hot weather, be certain that you drink enough—at least two quarts (eight cups) of fluid a day—even if you aren't thirsty. It may be necessary to set a timer or an alarm clock to remind yourself to drink.

You must be particularly cautious if you take diuretics ("water pills"), one of the most commonly used medications. Generally, diuretics are prescribed to prevent you from retaining too much water. One type of diuretic, thiazide, is very good treatment for high blood pressure. More powerful diuretics, such as furosemide (Lasix), are used to treat congestive heart failure. If you become dehydrated and are taking one of these medications, you may need to reduce your dosage. If you are ill and having trouble taking in food or water, if you are vomiting for any reason, or if the weather gets hot and you perspire heavily, contact your doctor to discuss how to balance your need for the medication with the necessity to avoid dehydration.

In addition to controlling the amount of fluid in the bloodstream, your body also closely controls the salt content of the blood. If the salt content gets too high, you will become thirsty. Since eating salty food causes you to drink and retain more water, it can raise blood pressure and cause sweling. However, if you are dehydrated, a little extra salt will help you rehydrate.

ABNORMAL BLOOD PROTEINS

Although there are several conditions that can affect the proteins in the blood, there are two that are special to late life. One of these, *multiple myeloma,* is a cancer of the blood cells that produce proteins. The other, *macroglobulinemia,* is similar in many ways but is not cancerous.

In multiple myeloma, a cell called a *plasmacyte* becomes cancerous and, like other cancerous cells, begins reproducing without control. These cells produce abnormal proteins that have harmful effects on the kidneys and decrease the body's ability to fight infection. People with multiple myeloma also develop anemia. If your doctor suspects that you have multiple myeloma, blood and urine samples and, probably, a bone marrow biopsy will be necessary to make a certian diagnosis.

Without treatment, multiple myeloma is usually fatal within a year. Fortunately, this cancer responds well to treatment, usually without severe side effects. Treatment includes the use of two drugs: prednisone, a steroid, and melphalan (Alkeran). When treated with these medications, most people with multiple myeloma will be free of problems from the disease for several years or longer.

In macroglobulinemia, the body produces abnormal proteins, but no cell is cancerous. Fortunately, their effects are much less harmful than those of multiple myeloma. In fact, the abnormal proteins often cause no medical symptoms or harm at all and are discovered only as part of laboratory investigations for other health problems. The only real concern is the possibility that macroglobulinemia will develop into multiple myeloma, a conversion that occurs in about one in ten patients within five years. Therefore, if you have macroglobulinemia, have your doctor check twice each year for signs of multiple myeloma.

Blood is a complex fluid made up of several kinds of cells, many kinds of proteins, water, and salt. It performs a myriad of vital functions. The normal changes occurring in your blood as you get older generally do not cause symptoms or noticeable changes in the way you feel, but they do make it more likely that you will experience additional medical problems if you develop a disease. Happily, the few blood diseases that occur with some frequency in later life are not common, and most can be treated effectively.

BONES

Your bones do much more than merely support you. They contribute actively to the maintenance of your good health. As you get older, your skeletal system experiences changes that often lead to medical conditions such as arthritis and fractures, and in women, osteoporosis. In this chapter, I first want to familiarize you with what your bones are and what they do. Knowing that, it will be easier for you to understand both the normal age-related changes of bones and the abnormal conditions that affect bones and cause disease in them.

THE COMPOSITION AND STRUCTURE OF BONES

Bones are made up of three principal parts. The outer surface is called the *periosteum* (peri- means "around" and -osteum refers to bone). Blood vessels enter the bone through the periosteum, carrying oxygen and other nutrients to the *cortex*. The cortex is the hard, white part, which you usually think of as bone. Within the cortex is the *marrow,* a soft, pulpy material responsible for manufacturing blood cells.

The cortex is constructed of a combination of minerals,

primarily calcium, in what scientists call a *polysaccharide matrix*. Polysaccharides are complex chemical substances made up of sugarlike building blocks. The minerals provide strength; the polysaccharides give flexibility, permitting bones to withstand minor stress without breaking.

Throughout your life, special bone cells, called *osteoblasts* and *osteoclasts,* form and reform your bones in a process referred to as bone remodeling. Thanks to these specialized cells, your bones can grow, repair damage, and remain physically healthy.

Your body has three types of bones: *long* or *cortical bones; flat or compact bones;* and *trabecular bones.*

Long bones, also known as *cortical bones*, like your leg and arm bones, owe their strength to their shape. They are formed into stiff, hollow rods, so that they are light yet capable of supporting great weight. Think of how much weight even a thin piece of paper can hold up when it is rolled into a tube. That is the principle behind the shape of your long bones. Of course, they would be even stronger if they were solid, but think how heavy your limbs would be if your long bones were solid bone.

Flat bones, also known as *compact bones,* like your skull and hip, gain strength by stacking together large amounts of dense bone material. Flat bones also occur in conjunction with long bones where extra strength is needed. For example, the part of the thigh bone that fits into the hip joint is made up of flat or compact bone.

The third kind of bone, *trabecular bone,* makes up the vertebrae of the spine. Think of trabecular bone as a compromise between long and flat bone. It is honeycombed, combining some of the strength of flat bones with the lighter weight of long bones.

The differences between the various types of bone rarely make a difference in how you feel. They do, however, explain why people with osteoporosis tend to fracture flat or trabecular bone rather than long bones. I will discuss that fact in detail later, in the section on osteoporosis.

The Functions of Bone

As structural support, your bones do much more than hold up your weight: they give rigidity to your limbs and transform the action of muscles into movement. Your bones also have nonstructural functions, including the storage of calcium and production of blood.

Movement

Most of your muscles attach, at least at one end, to a bone. When the muscle contracts, it pulls the bone, moving it. Where a muscle attaches to another muscle, the contraction results in a change of shape rather than in the movement of a limb. A few muscles work in this latter way—for example, the muscles that change the expression of your face; your stronger muscles, however, lift, propel, and push you by attaching to your bones.

Nonstructural Functions

Your *bone marrow* manufactures red blood cells, white blood cells, and platelets. These blood cells play a vital role in maintaining your health and are discussed in detail in chapter 4. For example, white blood cells fight infection, and platelets help stop bleeding. That is why your bones form an integral part of your immune system and of your system for clotting blood. Although there is marrow in all of your bones, some bones, most notably the breast bone (the sternum), hip bone (the ileum) and spinal column bones (the vertebrae), are more active than others in producing blood cells.

Your bones not only are made up of calcium, but they also serve as a reservoir of this important mineral. When you take in an abundant supply of calcium, your body deposits it in your bones and withdraws the mineral in times of need. Only rarely does this storage system malfunction. Certain diseases, such as kidney failure and some cancers, can cause your bones to release too much calcium, sending the calcium level in your blood dangerously high but driving the level in your bones perilously low. More commonly, the mechanism operates unnoticed and without problem.

AGE-RELATED CHANGES IN BONES

Changes in the Composition of Your Bones

From cradle to grave, your bones undergo a continuous, but unevenly paced, transformation from extremely pliant to brittle. An infant's bones are very flexible, which meets the baby's needs and allows for the rapid changes that accompany early growth. But soft, pliable bones are unsuitable for the rigors and stresses of adult life. During adolescence the bones achieve a near perfect balance of strength and flexibility, allowing us to perform all sorts of physical feats without a high risk of bone damage.

After adolescence you experience two important changes. First, during young adulthood, the mineral content increases, strengthening your bones further but causing a loss in flexibility. Later, at the end of middle age, your bones begin to lose density, mostly from a loss of mineral content but also from a loss of the polysaccharide matrix in which the minerals are held. When these losses occur, your bones do not regain their youthful flexibility but rather lose strength while remaining brittle. If your bones lose enough density and become so weak and brittle that they break from minor trauma, the condition is called *osteoporosis,* described in detail later in this chapter.

Changes in the Shape and Activity of Bones

Bones also alter their shape throughout life. During childhood, your bones grew rapidly in length, under the stimulation of growth hormone. After puberty, this growth stopped but another, subtler change occurred. Your bones, particularly your long bones, continued to grow thicker.

When you were young, your bones were biologically very active, remodeling at a rapid pace. A broken bone healed quickly, often with little more medical attention than a plaster cast. After adolescence, for reasons we still don't understand, this activity decreases. The speed at which bone remodels and repairs slows; bones grow slowly and, if fractured, take much longer to heal.

With time, the amount of marrow in your bones also decreases. You have about 15 percent less marrow now than when you were a young adult. Under normal circumstances, that amount is still sufficient to produce the blood cells you need. However, if you must quickly generate large numbers of cells—for example, after blood loss from an operation or accident—you may not be able to meet the demand and may require a blood transfusion to tide you over until the emergency passes. The decreased amount of marrow explains why you recover more slowly from anemia. (See chapter 4 for a full discussion of anemia.)

OSTEOPOROSIS

What Is Osteoporosis?

The normal age-related changes in your bones result in your reaching late life with bones that are thicker, less flexible, and weaker. If the loss of bone density—the loss of minerals and polysaccharide matrix—continues, you will develop *osteoporosis*. Osteoporosis occurs when your bones cannot meet the demands of your usual activity. If you suffer from osteoporosis, your bones become so frail that they break or collapse even without severe stress.

Everyone loses bony mass at approximately half a percent per year after age 40, but this rate nearly doubles in women during the decade following menopause. This rapid loss occurs in women because with menopause, the level of a hormone necessary to build calcium into bones in women, called *estrogen,* declines. Ten years after menopause, a woman will have lost approximately 10 percent of her total bone mass. With time, bone loss continues: by age 75, a woman can have lost nearly one-fourth of the bone mass she had in middle age.

Since it is not age alone but the lowered levels of estrogen that lead to more rapid bone loss, osteoporosis can occur at a young age in women who have had their ovaries removed surgically.

Risk Factors

Some people are at higher risk of developing osteoporosis because of genetics, disease, lifestyle, or the medications they take. Certain of these factors cannot be controlled; we can't, for example, choose our sex or heredity.

Men are at a lower risk of developing osteroporosis because they generally have greater bone mass than women and do not experience the hormonal changes associated with menopause. Osteoporosis occurs much more commonly in women than in men.

Among women, black women suffer osteoporosis less often than white women because they reach menopause with greater average bone mass, not because they lose bone mass more slowly. Among white women, those who are fair-haired and fair-skinned reach menopause with a lower bone mass than do others and, accordingly, are more likely to develop osteoporosis. Diseases can contribute to the development of osteoporosis, too. For example, multiple myeloma (a form of blood cancer), hyperparathyroidism (a disease of calcium metabolism), liver diseases (including alcoholism), Cushing's disease (an abnormality of steroid production), and kidney disease may all cause or accelerate osteoporosis.

Unlike the other risk factors, lifestyle and, to a lesser degree, the use of medications are within your control, so it is important to understand how medication, diet, and exercise affect osteoporosis. Some medications, principally steroids (for example, prednisone), greatly increase the risk of osteoporosis. A little later in this chapter, you will learn how you can actively protect yourself by altering aspects of your lifestyle.

The Evaluation of Osteoporosis

The earlier osteoporosis is diagnosed, the more likely you are to be helped by treatment to slow its progress. If you suspect that you may be developing the disease, see your doctor.

Your doctor will ask you about risk factors for osteoporosis: do you have a family history of the disease; do you use certain medications such as steroids like prednisone; do you suffer any of the diseases that increase calcium loss—hyperparathyroidism or kidney problems; do you drink large amounts of alcohol; are you physically inactive?

Your doctor will then examine you and may order blood tests to measure how your liver and kidneys are functioning or to determine the level of certain hormones. The physical examination will give your doctor little information unless, for example, you have already suffered compression fractures (discussed below) and have developed some curvature of the spine.

Your doctor may also recommend tests to measure the density of your bones. This measurement can be obtained with a specially equipped CAT scanner, but other tests, especially the *dual photon absorption,* are more commonly used. In this test, a technician passes an invisible beam through a bone, usually your wrist bone, to measure its density. Although the test is safe and painless, I seldom recommend it. The test generates interesting information but only rarely alters treatment. If your doctor suggests that you undergo dual photon absorption, ask why the test is needed and how its results will change your therapy.

Fractures from Osteoporosis

Although osteoporosis weakens bones throughout the body, the flat and trabecular bones suffer greater damage than do long bones. Remember, long bones gain strength primarily from their shape; flat and trabecular bones attain strength through their large mass and density. Age and osteoporosis decrease bone mass, placing the flat and trabecular bones at special risk. Thus, older persons in general, and people with osteoporosis in particular, suffer flat and trabecular bone fractures more often. When long bones break, the fractures occur usually at their ends, where they are actually made up of flat bone. For example, you are more likely to suffer hip fractures or wrist fractures than fractures in the middle of your legs or arms.

Compression fractures—that is, the collapse of a bone—are common complications of osteoporosis. Your spine is built of individual vertebrae, stacked like bricks, which carry the weight of your body. The vertebrae are made up of trabecular bone; the spinal cord, the most important nerve in your body, runs from your brain to the bottom of your spine through a hole in the center of the stack of vertebrae. Osteoporosis weakens the vertebrae so that even minor stress can cause them to collapse partially.

When a vertebra collapses, it often compresses more in front than in back, which may lead to stooping, a loss of height, and an increase in the curve of the spine. This condition is known as *scoliosis*. Sometimes the curve can be so pronounced that the spine forms a hump, known as a *gibbous*.

More devastating than the scoliosis is the pain associated with compression fractures. Even slight movement makes the pain worse, and unfortunately it is not possible to put a cast on the back to prevent movement or to relieve weight from the spine. Many patients are most comfortable lying in bed, but compression fractures heal slowly, and it is often impossible to remain immobile long enough to allow complete healing. Worse, long periods of bed rest themselves pose serious risk—bed sores, pneumonia, blood clots, and muscle weakness among them.

The most serious complication of vertebral compression fractures is pressure on the spinal cord. Fortunately, this complication is rare, but if it occurs, it can lead to serious neurological damage.

Currently there is little effective treatment for replacing the bone loss of osteoporosis, but recent information suggests that some medications, discussed below, may help. Although fractures of the hip and wrist can be repaired with casts or surgery, osteoporotic bone heals slowly. If you suffer a compression fracture, your doctor can prescribe medications to ease the pain, but the fracture itself must heal in its own time. In short, osteoporosis is much better prevented than treated.

Preventing and Treating Osteoporosis

Very little is known about preventing osteoporosis in men, and most of the following discussion applies only to women. Women who have had no warning signs of osteoporosis should strive to prevent it, and those who already have some osteoporosis need to slow or stop its progression.

One of the best ways to prevent osteoporosis is to come to menopause with as much bone mass as possible. To do this, younger women should consume adequate amounts of calcium. At this time, however, there are no clear data on whether a diet rich in calcium benefits you later in life. Nevertheless, I—and most other doctors—recommend such a diet. It may help, and there is no evidence that it harms.

One gram of calcium daily is adequate but 1½ to 2 grams is probably even better. Many foods contain calcium, including all dairy products. Alternatively, calcium can be taken in tablet form. Calcium carbonate (Tums) is an inexpensive alternative, but may cause stomach gas. Calcium gluconate and calcium oxalate are equally effective and do not cause gas, but are more expensive; they are available at pharmacies, health food stores, and vitamin shops. Although some people recommend bone-meal tablets, I advise my patients to avoid them because bone meal may contain trace amounts of lead.

To utilize calcium, your body requires vitamin D, which is found in green leafy vegetables and, in America, as an additive in milk. Vitamin D can also be taken in tablet form. For convenience, some calcium preparations are combined with vitamin D, for example, Oscal-D.

To process calcium, your body must first convert ordinary vitamin D to an active form. This conversion occurs when you expose your skin to the sun. Only a small amount of sunlight is needed. Merely exposing your hands, forearms, face, and head for half an hour every few days is enough. In fact, longer exposure doesn't appreciably increase the level of activated vitamin D but does increase your risk of getting skin cancer (see chapter 6). Sitting behind a window is not good enough: the glass filters out the ultraviolet light, which activates the vitamin. If you live in a cold climate, you will need to balance the need for sunshine against the risks of wintry weather. It makes little sense to solve the calcium problem at the cost of a broken wrist from a fall on the ice.

Your protein and alcohol intake present two other dietary concerns. A high-protein diet will cause your bones to give up calcium, weakening them. However, a diet with inadequate protein also poses health risks. For the moment, there is not enough evidence to recommend a low-protein diet as therapy for osteoporosis; still the evidence is good that a diet with very high levels of protein is harmful. As with most issues affecting diet, balance is the key to good health. Ask your doctor to refer you to a dietitian to establish the right diet for you and to teach you about which foods are high in protein.

The effects of alcohol are clearer: consuming large amounts of alcohol increases your risk of developing osteoporosis. If you already have the disease or if you have risk factors for developing it, limit the amount of alcohol you drink.

Another good preventative is regular physical activity. Although experts debate whether exercise actually prevents osteoporosis, we do know that physical activity strengthens your bones. In response to exercise, bones become denser and stronger. Weight-bearing exercise, such as walking, running, dancing, and jumping, is most beneficial. Unless you must limit your exercise, frequent participation in any of these activities may be very helpful in preventing osteoporosis.

If you are a woman, you can prevent bone loss if you replace the estrogen loss brought on by menopause. However, estrogen therapy is of benefit only while it is administered. If you stop, you will lose bone mass just as if estrogen therapy had never been started, and at the same rapid pace that occurs during the first ten years after menopause.

Until recently, estrogen replacement was reserved for especially serious cases of osteoporosis. Doctors feared that the side effects of estrogen therapy, especially the possibility that it increased the risk of uterine and breast cancers, outweighed the benefits. Now, however, we find that low doses of estrogen will slow osteoporosis yet bring little or no increased cancer risk. Accordingly, most experts now recommend estrogen replacement at the time of menopause for women who are likely to develop osteoporosis. However, for women more than ten years past menopause, estrogen therapy holds little promise of benefit because the majority of bone loss related to changes in estrogen levels has already occurred.

You must go to your doctor for estrogen. He or she will discuss the risks and benefits and explain the two ways of taking it. One is to take estrogen for three weeks each month but not in the fourth week. The other is to take estrogen for three weeks and then to take *progesterone* (another hormone whose levels fall substantially after menopause) during the fourth week. Many experts prefer the second method, in which estrogen and progesterone are cycled in monthly courses, but these recommendations are currently being revised. Ask your doctor about the most recent thinking.

Estrogen therapy causes the side effect of monthly uterine bleeding in some women, just as they experienced prior to menopause. If you have uterine bleeding while taking estrogen, see your doctor to determine whether the estrogen or something else is to blame. Often, a change in the dose of the medication will stop the monthly bleeding. If the bleeding persists, you may nevertheless continue the therapy unless you find the situation intolerable.

Treatment After Bone Loss Has Occurred

Once osteoporosis has developed, it is particularly important to slow or stop the loss of bone. Several treatments can be of help.

Follow a diet rich in calcium and vitamin D and be certain to get out in the sun regularly. A tablet that combines calcium and vitamin D, such as Oscal-D, is often the simplest way to ensure that you get what you need. Some doctors also recommend supplemental tablets of fluoride, a mineral that enhances bone formation. There is scanty evidence that fluoride helps but little to suggest that it is harmful. It probably can't hurt you.

Aside from the prescriptives above, you can also take several medications to facilitate bone formation. *Calcitonin* is a naturally occurring hormone that stimulates bone to incorporate more calcium. Calcitonin supplements are expensive, difficult to administer (because the drug must be injected by needle, although a nasal spray is currently being tested), and the dose must be very carefully monitored. Too much calcitonin can decrease the level of calcium in your blood, leading to serious side effects. We don't yet know if calcitonin really builds bones that better withstand the fractures and compressions brought on by osteoporosis. For the moment, consider its use to be experimental, and do not take it unless you are under the care of a doctor who specializes in osteoporosis.

One of the most exciting new treatments for osteoporosis is *editronate*. This medication may not only slow or arrest bone loss but actually reverse it. This medication holds great promise, although its use is not yet routine.

To summarize, most women should take care that their diets are rich in calcium and vitamin D and receive regular exposure to the sun. If you have begun estrogen therapy, continue it under your doctor's guidance, as long as you are comfortable. Both young and older women should participate in some weight-bearing exercise daily. You can always take a short but brisk walk in the sun; it's fun and healthy. Consider all other therapies for the prevention or treatment of osteoporosis to be experimental at this time and use them only under the guidance of a doctor who is a specialist in the disease.

FRACTURES

Causes of Fractures

Bones break for many reasons other than osteoporosis. Injuries from car accidents, falls, and sports are not the sole province of the young. One other, and fortunately rare, cause of fractures in the elderly is cancer. Breast, prostate, and lung cancers all have a particular tendency to spread to the bone. When a cancerous tumor weakens a bone to the breaking point, a *pathological fracture* occurs. Pathological fractures may need to be fixed surgically and beamed with radiation to slow the growth of the cancer and strengthen the bone.

How Bones Heal

Fractured bones heal themselves in two stages. First, your body creates strong connective tissue to bridge the ends of the break and then generates new bone to mend the break permanently.

Usually, a doctor must realign and secure the broken bone under a rigid cast of plaster, plastic, or metal to assure that it heals properly. The cast keeps you from moving the affected area so that the bone can repair itself in the right shape as quickly as possible. Some fractures—of the hands or feet, for example—do not require casting, while others like broken ribs can't be casted. If you suffer a simple fracture, your primary-care doctor may be able to take care of it. If the break is serious, your doctor will probably refer you to an *orthopaedic surgeon,* a specialist in repairing broken bones.

Some fractures, such as hip fractures or those that break bones in several places or shatter the bone, require more than a cast to hold the pieces together while they heal. A surgical procedure known as an ORIF, an acronym for "Open Reduction and Internal Fixation," may be necessary. ORIF uses screws or bolts to align and hold bone fragments together, permitting the break to mend as sturdily as possible. ORIF is particularly useful for treating hip fractures, because it allows healing to occur relatively quickly.

HIP FRACTURES

Falls are especially troublesome because of the risk of hip fractures. "Old age begins with the first fall and ends with the second," the novelist Gabriel García Márquez observed. Happily, advances in medicine have proved the good author wrong. Today, there are excellent treatments for hip fractures and, though serious, a broken hip is no longer the sure harbinger of death and disability it once was.

Some experts believe that sometimes the hip actually breaks before the fall and the ensuing impact with the ground. These doctors suggest that a sudden and violent contraction of a muscle of the leg may cause the hip to break, particularly if the bone is weakened by osteoporosis. If they are right, the fall actually occurs after the fracture, not the other way around. Of course, a hip can also break if you slip from a ladder, get injured in an accident, or otherwise suffer a serious trauma.

ORIF

If you break your hip, you will be less concerned about why it happened than with what you can do to fix it. The good news can be said in one word: ORIF (Open Reduction and Internal Fixation), the surgical procedure in which broken bones are aligned and secured with the use of metal parts.

Before ORIF was developed, a hip fracture inevitably meant months in bed. The broken bones were held in place by traction, with heavy weights suspended from pulleys at the foot of the bed. For many patients, this cure was more catastrophic than the fracture itself. The prolonged bed rest often led to loss of independence, weakness, and the development of pneumonia, bed sores, and blood clots, and many people never healed sufficiently to walk well again. ORIF has speeded recovery, reduced the incidence of complications, and allowed hundreds of thousands of older persons to walk properly and painlessly after fracturing a hip.

Orthopaedic surgeons use several different ORIF procedures to repair hip fractures, depending on the location and extent of the fracture. Figure 5, showing the hip, will help you understand where breaks commonly occur. If neither the head of the femur nor the socket in which it sits is badly damaged (A), the surgeon can sometimes hold the break

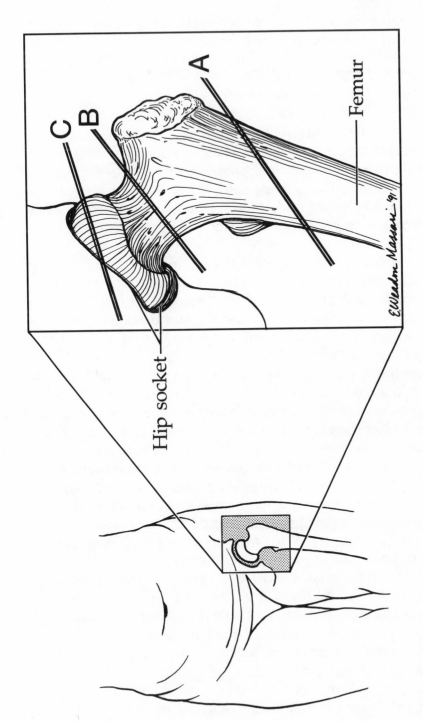

FIGURE 5
The Hip and Types of Hip Fractures

together with steel pins or a special kind of steel clamp. However, if the head of the femur is damaged (B), a metal replacement may need to be attached to the healthy portion of the femur. In the most serious cases, when both the head of the femur and the socket in which it sits are damaged (C), a total hip replacement may be required. In this operation, both parts of the joint are replaced, the head of the femur with a steel replacement, and the socket with a steel-and-plastic cup.

Although this may sound gruesome, it is substantially less risky and promises greater hope for recovery than weeks in traction. Even with a total hip replacement, you can reasonably expect to get out of bed, albeit with assistance, in just a few days.

Complications can occur with any operation, and with hip surgery there are three particular concerns: blood clots in the leg, pain, and confusion. Other complications, like poor placement, slipping of the artificial femur head, and infection, occur very rarely if the operation is performed by an experienced and skillful surgeon.

The trauma to and immobilization of your hip and leg create a risk that you may develop a *blood clot* in a vein in your leg. Blood clots can be dangerous because the solidified blood not only blocks the vein where it occurs, but it can break off and travel to your lungs, where it will cause a *pulmonary embolism,* a serious medical emergency. To help prevent blood clots, your doctor probably will prescribe an anticoagulant medication (a "blood thinner") known as Coumadin. You may need to take Coumadin for as long as six weeks after surgery. During that time the dose of the drug will be adjusted according to the results of periodic blood tests.

After a hip repair, almost everyone will experience some pain, and your doctor will usually prescribe medication to alleviate it. Always be careful when using narcotic pain medicines. (See chapter 2 for more information on this.) They can cause confusion, sedation, severe constipation, and increase the risk of pneumonia. Unless the pain is severe, avoid narcotics and ask that other medications be used. If you must take a narcotic, switch to less risky medicine when the pain diminishes. If you are taking a narcotic, a family member or friend should be alert for the medication's side effects and should also discuss with your doctor how to balance pain relief with the need to avoid the narcotic's side effects.

If you undergo any surgery, and especially if your hip is surgically repaired, you may develop one serious complication, *postoperative confusion*. Confusion is most likely to occur in people who had some dementia prior to the operation, but anyone can experience it. The stress of the operation, the anesthesia and other medications, and the lack of sleep that sometimes occurs in hospitals create a situation in which confusion easily develops. Your anesthesiologist and surgeon can decrease the likelihood of confusion by reducing some of your medications during and after the operation. Be certain to discuss this possible complication with your doctors before your operation.

Your family and friends should be alert for changes in your mental abilities. If you seem confused, they should insist that a geriatrician or internist evaluate you. You will most likely recover from postoperative confusion within several days, but the complication may persist for as long as several weeks. Unfortunately, and for unknown reasons, a small percentage of older people who develop postoperative confusion never fully recover.

Rehabilitation for Hip Fractures

Shortly after the operation is finished and the anesthesia has worn off, rehabilitation begins. At first, this process may involve simply moving and stretching your affected leg to prevent stiffness. Soon, however, you will begin more intensive and more complex physical therapy to improve strength and flexibility. You will work with at least two professionals during the rehabilitation process: a physical therapist and an orthopaedic surgeon. Of the two, you will see and work more closely with your physical therapist.

The most important element of successful rehabilitation is your own active participation. Rehabilitation *is* work, hard work that can sometimes be painful and disheartening. Although optimism may be difficult, there are good reasons to remain confident: your chances of an excellent recovery are very good.

Try to find a physical therapist who has experience with the elderly, especially if you have memory problems or feel you might need an extra push toward optimism. Above all, you must feel comfortable with your therapist. If you don't, find another one. The therapist will understand, both of you will be happier, and your rehabilitation will be more effective if you have confidence in your therapist and get along well with him or her.

Although physical therapy usually begins in the hospital, it doesn't end there. If you are able to work very actively with your therapist, you may gain great benefit from an intermediary stay in a rehabilitation hospital or nursing home with good physical therapy services. There, you can recover fully, regain your strength and self-confidence, and become mobile and independent again. This accomplished, you can return home self-reliant and safe.

If you have other health complications and can't participate so vigorously, therapy can be performed at home, although it will be more limited in what it can accomplish, and your progress will therefore be slower. Usually, you will need help during this recovery period at home. Before you are discharged from the hospital, discuss with the hospital social worker the necessary arrangements for the assistance you may need.

In general, you can expect to make an excellent recovery from a hip fracture or hip replacement, although it might not come as swiftly as you would like. Count on six weeks or thereabouts before you can walk easily, go up and down stairs, or comfortably get in and out of cars. With time, however, you should expect to have the same freedom of movement, and sometimes even more, than you had before your injury.

ARTHRITIS

Arthritis occurs when there is damage to a joint, the place where two or more bones meet. *Arthritis* means an inflammation of a joint, and *arthralgia* means pain in a joint, but these terms are often used interchangeably. Several medical conditions can damage your joints. Two of the most common conditions are *rheumatoid arthritis* and *degenerative arthritis.*

Rheumatoid Arthritis

Rheumatoid arthritis is one of the so-called autoimmune diseases, a disease in which your body reacts against some part of itself, in this case the lining of the joints. Rheumatoid arthritis does not commonly begin in old age; it generally afflicts children or younger adults. Although you can develop rheumatoid arthritis in your later years, if you have the disease, it probably started when you were younger and has survived with you into old age. Accordingly, I will not discuss rheumatoid arthritis here.

Degenerative Arthritis

Degenerative arthritis, also called *osteoarthritis* or *degenerative joint disease* (DJD), is a disease of old age. To understand DJD, you need to understand a little about anatomy.

Where bones meet at joints, their surfaces are covered with a hard, slippery, and glistening material—*hyalin cartilage.* If bone met bone without any intermediary tissue, every motion you made would be accompanied by the friction and eventual damage of hard bone grinding against hard bone. Thanks to the cartilage at these meeting places, bones slide smoothly against one another.

With time, the cartilage in your joints can become damaged, particularly if you have stressed your joints through unusual activities or if your job required you to repeat the same movement over and over again for years. For example, a postal carrier who hauled a mail sack over one shoulder may have damaged the cartilage in his shoulder joint, while a housekeeper who carefully scrubbed floors by hand and polished silver and wood year in and year out may have damaged the cartilage in the small joints of her fingers and hands.

Eventually, damaged cartilage wears away, exposing the

surface of one of the bones in the joint, which in turn quickly damages the cartilage on the surface of the other. The result is a joint in which bone rubs against bone, creating irritation and pain at first, and then inflammation and swelling, which decreases movement in the joint and increases the pain. Over time, the irritation may deform the joint, a development especially noticeable in the hands, where the knuckles may become enlarged. This condition can be very painful if it occurs in the neck, where bone spurs may impinge on nerves.

Typically, in addition to the small joints of the hand, DJD affects the joints that have borne the most weight and done the most work during your lifetime—the knees, hips, and hands. If you have had an unusual profession, you may find that other joints—perhaps your shoulder, wrists, or neck—have also developed DJD.

Although DJD is common in late life, it generally remains mild. If you have DJD, you may experience stiffness or pain, but only rarely will your joints become noticeably swollen or inflamed. Fortunately, DJD usually does not progress so far as to limit your activity. If the disease does cause you substantial pain or interferes with your ability to do your job, talk to your doctor about treatment.

Medications called *nonsteroidal antiinflammatory drugs* (NSAIDs) provide the best treatment for controlling the pain of DJD, although acetaminophen (Tylenol) also works well. These medications are available in prescription and over-the-counter forms. Aspirin is a NSAID, and there are many others, such as naproxyn (Naprosyn, Anaprox), ibuprofen (Motrin, Advil), and indomethacin (Indocin). NSAIDs have two important effects: they block pain and reduce inflammation (which, in turn, reduces pain even further).

As with all medications, NSAIDs must be used with caution. They irritate the stomach and may produce diarrhea, upset stomach, and ulcers. They affect platelets (an element of the blood responsible for clotting) and may make you bleed more if you are injured. They can decrease kidney function and cause you to retain fluid. Despite their many side effects, however, you can reap substantial benefits from NSAIDs if you use them properly, under the guidance of a doctor.

Physical therapy can also help. For example, changing the way you walk by shifting your weight with a cane or walker may reduce the pain of DJD in the hip or joints of the leg. Warm soaks may also reduce pain.

If a joint, particularly your hip, becomes severely damaged by DJD, consider surgery to replace the joint. Discuss surgical options with your doctor if the pain becomes intolerable or if DJD prevents you from doing the things you want to do. Surgery carries risk at any age, and you should not rush into the operating room. On the other hand, age alone is no reason to stop you from having an operation if it will relieve pain and allow you to continue work or participate actively in your hobbies.

Surgery to replace the hip joint is now common and is almost always successful in decreasing pain and improving movement. (Hip replacements are discussed earlier in this chapter, in the section on hip fractures.) Unfortunately, the replacement of other joints is not yet routine, although there has been recent progress in replacing knee and ankle joints. Surgical repair or placement of the joints of the fingers, hands, and shoulders can be performed but cannot yet be recommended for most people.

PAGET'S DISEASE

Paget's disease is characterized by abnormal activity of the bone cells in which the affected bone grows larger than it should and is weaker than the healthy bone around it. Often, the weakened area will then fracture. Usually, in the absence of a fracture, Paget's disease causes no symptoms and is diagnosed fortuitously, by x-rays performed for some other reason. Occasionally, however, Paget's disease can cause serious problems.

If the disease occurs in the bones of the hip, the abnormal growth can cause a deformity that damages the joint, leading to degenerative arthritis. If it occurs in the bones of the skull, it results in enlargement of the head.

The affected bone also can impinge on nerves where they

run through or between the bones. One feared complication is damage to one of nerves that runs through the skull. For instance, Paget's disease may damage the otic nerve (which carries information from the ear to the brain through a narrow passageway in the skull) and lead to hearing loss. Additionally, Paget's disease may affect the tiny bones in the ear (the ossicles) that conduct sound, further decreasing hearing abil-ity.

Generally, Paget's disease is not treated unless the affected bone is damaging a joint or nerve. Your doctor might pre-scribe medications that slow the rapid bone formation of Paget's disease if you have a serious complication. People with Paget's disease must be careful not to spend too much time in bed, since calcium levels increase if an afflicted person does not walk and otherwise exercise regularly.

A Halloween skeleton suggests that your bones are lifeless—an image that is far from true. Your bones are full of life and are essential to your well-being. Unfortunately, medical prob-lems with bones and joints often disable older people. Today's surgical procedures to replace joints, however, have brought great benefits to many, and scientists have begun to learn more about preventing and treating arthritis and osteoporosis. Many more successes in treating the medical problems of bones are on the horizon.

6

SKIN

S kin serves many functions. As a barrier, it repels dirt and water, stops many harmful chemicals from entering your body, prevents injury, and protects you from the harmful rays of the sun. Like a wrapping, it holds your body's soft tissues together. But the skin is also an active system, with sweat glands which cool, sebaceous glands which oil and lubricate, and hair follicles which produce both the hair on your head and the finer hair elsewhere on your body. The skin produces cells that actively fight infection by recognizing and destroying bacteria and viruses, and it even has a role in nutrition, converting inactive vitamin D into its active form so that the body can use it. In addition, the skin communicates with the brain through fine nerve fibers, allowing you to experience sensation, both painful and pleasurable. Despite all these important functions, we usually consider skin only in cosmetic terms, since it is, after all, one of the first things we notice about others and about ourselves. At all ages, we want our skin to look good. At all ages, we should also want our skin to be healthy.

Parts of the Skin

As Figure 6 shows, the skin is made up of several layers, each serving a different purpose. The outermost layer is made of *keratin,* a tough protein whose main function is protection. Areas needing the greatest protection, the hands and feet, have the thickest layers of keratin. Next comes a thin layer of cells called the *epidermis,* which produces keratin and pigmentation, which determines complexion. When the skin is exposed to sunlight, the epidermis produces more pigment. That is why skin darkens when exposed to the sun, resulting in the tan some of us covet. Also in the epidermis are the cells that, when exposed to sunlight, convert vitamin D to its active form so that calcium can be properly absorbed and metabolized. The next layer, the *dermis,* contains the major functioning components of the skin—the blood vessels, nerves, hair follicles, and glands. Cells in the dermis provide the body's first defense against infection. Under the dermis is the *subcutaneous fat,* which gives the skin much of its characteristic texture. At all ages, women tend to have more subcutaneous fat than men.

HOW YOUR SKIN CHANGES AS YOU AGE

Every layer of the skin changes dramatically with age. The pigment-producing cells in the epidermis and those cells in the dermis that fight bacteria and viruses become less active: hair—which, after all, is part of the skin—tends to turn gray, and the skin becomes less efficient in warding off infections. The dermis becomes thinner, and, at the same time, the small blood vessels supply less nutrition to it. With reduced blood supply, even small cuts heal more slowly. The number of glands that secrete moisturizing oils decreases, as does their activity and, thus, your skin tends to be drier. Most important, perhaps, you lose thickness in the layer of subcutaneous fat. While this loss might seem at first like a blessing, in fact it is a misfortune because subcutaneous fat works like padding under a carpet or a tablecloth, protecting both the skin on top and the layers of tissue below. Thinning of the dermis and loss

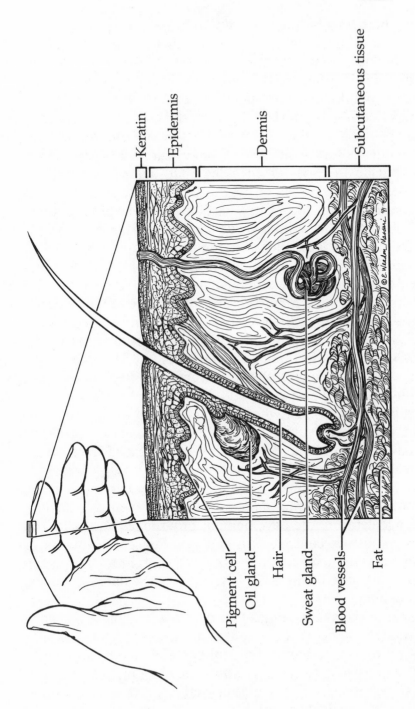

FIGURE 6
The Skin

of subcutaneous fat leave your skin more susceptible to cuts and bruises. Subcutaneous fat also insulates, and because it is thinner, you are more likely to become chilled.

Loss of subcutaneous fat also explains in part why wrinkles develop. Wrinkles occur when the deeper layers of skin provide inadequate support to the epidermis. Without the under-padding—without subcutaneous fat—to smooth the surface, the epidermis forms tiny folds that appear as wrinkles. There is no reason to consider wrinkles unattractive, and in some cultures they are marks of the status of revered old age. The great actress Anna Magnani once admonished a photographer not to remove the wrinkles from her face in his photograph. As she said, "It took a lot of living to put them there!"

Nonetheless, most people dislike wrinkles, and for centuries cosmeticians have helped paint them away. The best ways to prevent and minimize the appearance of wrinkles are to avoid sunshine and to keep your skin moist. Recently, a medication called Retin A has shown some promise in treating wrinkles. Retin A is similar to vitamin A but has several side effects. First, it makes the skin very sensitive to sunlight, causing it to burn easily. Second, Retin A is absorbed through the skin into the body, where it can be toxic to other organs. Third, it is expensive. Since Retin A's effectiveness in treating wrinkles is minimal and because it can cause side effects, I generally do not recommend it.

Many normal changes are accelerated by exposure to the environment. Sunshine is the most potent enemy of healthy skin, accelerating the development of wrinkles and, with too much exposure, causing skin cancers. Sunscreen lotions or creams applied to the skin block the harmful rays of the sun and provide one of the best ways to slow the damage caused by sunshine.

Some of the skin changes that occur with aging are normal age-related changes, while others are caused by exposure to the environment, including sunlight and harsh chemicals. Most are harmless, although they are often distressing. Certain skin growths are unattractive, and dry skin can be uncomfortable. If you develop any kind of skin problem that bothers you, whether a new dark spot or itchy skin, talk to your doctor. Although some skin problems require consultation with a *dermatologist*—a doctor who specializes in diseases of the skin—many common conditions can be diagnosed and treated by your primary-care physician. Speak with him or her before seeing a specialist.

There are several ways to diagnose skin problems. Your doctor will begin by asking you questions: when did you first notice the problem; have you ever had anything like it before; have you put anything on your skin or taken any new medications; have you tried to treat it with anything; and does it itch, burn, or hurt? The doctor will then examine your skin closely, noting where the problem occurs, its color, whether it is raised or flat, and whether it is blistered or scaly. The doctor may recommend treatment with a cream or ointment applied directly to the problem site or may want to take a small piece of the growth or rash, called a *biopsy,* in order to inspect it under the microscope or to determine if a fungus grows from it.

Your primary-care doctor may be able to perform a skin biopsy or may refer you to a dermatologist. Regardless of who does the biopsy, the procedure is generally the same and usually causes very little discomfort. After the affected skin is anesthetized with an injection, a small sample is taken with a tiny round knife. The local anesthetic assures that the biopsy is painless. The sample is then sent to a laboratory for evaluation, which usually takes several days to complete.

COMMON PROBLEMS

Dry Skin—Xerosis

Your skin produces less oil as you get older, which is why you may suffer from overly dry skin. Although it is water in the skin cells that keeps your skin moist, it is the oil in those cells that keeps the water from evaporating. Thus, natural skin oils play a crucial role in keeping skin moist and comfortable. If the skin becomes too dry, it may itch, burn, crack, or scale, a condition called *xerosis.*

To treat dry skin or xerosis, you must prevent the skin from losing its moisture by either minimizing the loss of oil or supplementing the oil that your body produces, or both.

Although daily cleanliness is, as a general rule, a good thing, people with xerosis should bathe or shower only once a day, at most. The temperature of the water does not make much difference in the amount of oil that is lost, but very hot water may itself irritate the skin. If you have dry skin or xerosis, avoid scrubbing with brushes or rough washcloths; instead, use a natural sponge or soft cloth. Use a gentle soap, one with moisturizing oils and free of harsh detergents. Your pharmacist can recommend an appropriate product. Dry yourself with a soft towel, patting the skin rather than rubbing it. If you take baths, consider adding bath oil to the water, but be extremely careful if you do: bath oils can make your tub treacherously slippery. Bath preparations containing oats or chamomile can be especially soothing to dry skin.

After bathing or showering, apply a moisturizer to help the deeper layers of the skin retain water. Many different brands are available, varying widely in their ingredients and price. Generally you should avoid products containing fragrance, as these may irritate sensitive skin. Moisturizers containing urea are particularly helpful in treating very dry skin and xerosis. Again, ask your pharmacist for advice.

Replacing lost oil may not completely cure dry, irritated skin. Serious xerosis sometimes requires the use of medicines, usually creams containing steroids, which decrease inflammation and irritation. But topical steroids should not be used too often or over too large an area because they are absorbed through the skin, affecting other parts of the body. Some steroid creams are available over-the-counter at the pharmacy; stronger ones require a doctor's prescription.

Birthmarks, Skin Tags, Keratoses, and "Liver Spots"

Growths and blemishes you were born with are often called "birthmarks." These have gained particular notoriety since the Soviet leader Mikhail Gorbachev took to going without a hat, exposing the birthmark on his forehead. Other kinds of skin marks can form at any age, and older persons develop them commonly. Generally, these marks are harmless and are best left alone. However, if a very dark growth suddenly appears, no matter how small, or if any sore does not heal within two to three weeks, show it to your doctor. These developments are warning signs of skin cancer (discussed later in this chapter); don't ignore them.

Small tab-like protrusions that look like bits of extra skin and are the same color as the surrounding skin are probably *skin tags* and generally cause no problem. However, if they occur where they become irritated from clothing, they may bleed. In such cases, skin tags can be removed. If skin tags do not cause problems, leave them alone.

Another common skin growth looks like a small mound of flaky, cracked, waxy skin, darker in color than the surrounding skin, but not black. These are called *senile* or *seborrheic keratoses* and can occur anywhere on your body. You don't have to have them removed, but, if you wish, your doctor can freeze them with a touch of liquid nitrogen, a very cold liquid that kills skin cells on contact. The dead keratosis then flakes off over several days' time, leaving normal skin below. This procedure usually does not leave a scar and causes only a pinprick of pain.

Flat patchy areas of darkness, often brown and resembling large freckles, are popularly called *liver spots*. In fact, they have nothing at all to do with the liver. Because they are flat they can't be cut off, and freezing them is generally not advised. They are best left alone or covered with makeup. If you devleop a patch of darker skin that continues to darken, show it to your doctor to be sure that it is not cancerous.

Rashes

Your skin demonstrates its displeasure at something to which your body is allergic or to something irritating by developing a rash. Rashes can occur anywhere on the body; they can develop all over or may appear in one small area, depending on the cause. The most frequent causes of skin rashes are allergies, irritations, and infections.

When your skin touches something to which you are allergic, the resulting rash is called *contact dermatitis.* The best known cause of contact dermatitis is poison ivy, but there are many others. For example, you may be allergic to certain metals or to a specific laundry detergent. After touching these materials you may develop a rash. While a contact dermatitis remains confined to the area of skin that has touched the substance, in a systemic allergic reaction, the skin responds to something *in* your body, such as a medication, to which it is allergic, with a rash that can appear all over.

Irritants are things that cause your skin to develop a rash even though you are not allergic to them. For example, caustic soaps or lye used in housecleaning can cause an irritation rash although you do not have a specific allergy to them. Scratching, as well, can be so irritating that it causes a rash to form. Thus, while you may get minor contact dermatitis after touching something to which you are allergic, scratching the rash may worsen it because of the further irritation of the skin.

If you develop a rash and think it is caused by allergy or irritation, first determine the source of the problem and eliminate it. If the rash continues or is bothersome, apply an over-the-counter steroid cream (for example, hydrocortisone) to the affected area. If the problem persists, contact your doctor; you may need a stronger steroid preparation, available only by prescription. However, you must be cautious in using a steriod on rashes because the medicine can aggravate the situation if the rash is caused by a bacteria or fungus instead of an allergy or irritant.

Bacterial, fungal, and *viral rashes* differ from everyday irritation or allergic skin reactions. Although bacterial infections are the least common of the three, they are serious, sometimes posing potentially catastrophic danger. A bacterial infection that spreads into the deeper layers of the skin is called *cellulitis.* Don't confuse cellulitis with the harmless condition of fat accumulations popularly called cellulite. Cellulitis often begins with a cut, scrape, or small infection—a mosquito bite that becomes inflamed or a skinned knee suffered in a fall, for instance. It generally appears as a red rash, warm to the touch. When it occurs on a limb, it may cause lines of redness to streak up a leg or an arm. You may experience painful swelling and develop a fever. If your rash matches this description, call your doctor or go to a hospital emergency room. Cellulitis is dangerous and requires treatment with antibiotics. If it is not caught quickly, you may have to be hospitalized for intravenous administration of antibiotics. In extreme situations, cellulitis can be life-threatening.

Fungal infections, such as athlete's foot, are common and generally occur in the folds of skin that trap moisture—in the groin, between the toes, or under the breasts, for example. Fungal infections may become bright red and often itch or burn. Because fungus requires moisture to grow, your first line of defense is to keep the affected area dry and covered with talc. Medicated powders, containing talc and an antifungal agent, available over-the-counter at the pharmacy, may be particularly helpful. Antifungal agents are also available without a prescription in cream form, but the best preparations require a doctor's prescription.

Many different viruses can cause a rash. *Herpes zoster,* for example, is particularly common and troublesome in older people. Herpes zoster is the same virus as that which causes chicken pox. Although they are both in the same virus family, herpes zoster differs from herpes simplex, the virus that causes cold sores.

If you have ever had chicken pox, you are at risk of developing herpes zoster. During the initial infection with chicken pox (which you may have had as a child), the virus caused the blisters that are the hallmark of herpes zoster. After the blisters disappeared, the illness appeared to have ended, but in fact the virus did not vanish. It continued to live in a quiet state in the nerves of the skin, causing no symptoms. Your body's immune system keeps the virus dormant, and in most people the virus never causes problems again. However, in some people and particularly in old age, it can reawaken to cause a herpes zoster infection. Doctors don't know why the virus reactivates but believe it has something to do with a failure in the immune system, although this explanation does not mean that your immune system is abnormal or that you will develop other immunological problems.

When the herpes zoster virus reawakens, it comes to the

surface of the skin and produces a rash with tiny blisters (often called *shingles*); the rash can be very painful and takes weeks to heal. As long as the blisters are present, you can infect other people with the virus. Therefore, you should be sure to keep the area covered and to wash your hands before touching anyone else. Once the blisters disappear, the affected area may remain darker in color than the surrounding skin and may continue to be painful. This enduring pain, called *postherpetic neuralgia,* can last for months or even years after the rash disappears. If you develop a rash that may be herpes zoster, see your doctor. If it is herpes zoster, a prescription steroid medication, called prednisone, taken by mouth, may help prevent postherpetic neuralgia.

Skin Cancers

Although skin cancers are the most common kind of cancer, they are rarely fatal. If discovered and treated early, they generally do not cause serious health problems. When untreated, however, as with other kinds of cancer, they can enlarge and spread into surrounding organs. If skin cancers metastasize (that is, spread to other places in the body) or grow into surrounding tissues, serious medical complications and even death can follow. The three common kinds of skin cancer are squamous cell, basal cell, and melanoma.

Squamous cell skin cancers are related more to sun exposure than to aging; many years of exposure to the sun cause them, generally on the face, head, shoulders, and arms. Not surprisingly, people who live in sunny regions such as Florida and southern California are at highest risk. Squamous cell skin cancers may first appear to be small sores that do not heal. Slowly, over weeks or months, the sores enlarge. Occasionally, squamous cell cancer metastasizes, spreading to faraway parts of the body. Any sore on a part of your skin that has been exposed to the sun that does not heal in a few weeks is suspicious, and your doctor should examine it.

If caught at a very early stage, a prescription medication called 5-fluorouracil (5FU) can sometimes remove squamous cell cancers without surgery. 5FU is applied directly to the skin. You should put it only on the area your doctor tells you to and leave it on only for as long as directed. If you can't safely apply and remove 5FU yourself, arrange to have a family member, friend, or visiting nurse help you.

If the cancer is more advanced, you must have it removed surgically, a simple procedure when the cancer is small. In the doctor's office, the dermatologist will numb the area around the cancer with an injection of a local anesthetic and then cut out the cancer. The tissue will then be sent to the laboratory for microscopic analysis to determine if the borders of the sample are free of cancer. If they are—that is, if the analysis demonstrates that all of the cancer was removed—nothing more needs to be done. If not, a second procedure may be necessary to remove the remaining cancer. Generally, the most uncomfortable part of the whole procedure is the initial injection of anesthetic. Of course, if the cancer is large, you will feel some pain after the procedure, while your skin heals.

When the cancer is large or occurs on the face, especially near the eye or lips, it may be removed by a dermatologist trained in the special, microscopic surgical technique called *Mohs*. Mohs (rhymes with "hose") allows the dermatologist to remove the cancer while looking at it under a microscope. In this way, the dermatologist can remove tiny fragments of the cancer, being certain to get it all without damaging adjoining healthy tissue. As with the removal of small squamous cell cancers described above, the Mohs procedure is painful only for the moment that the anesthetic is injected.

Basal cell cancers are the most common kind of skin cancer, and they too are related to sun exposure, occurring most often on exposed skin. Basal cell cancers start as small depressions, often as small as one of the *o*'s on this page, with pearly white borders; they enlarge very slowly, taking weeks to become easily noticed. These cancers are even less likely to spread than are squamous cell cancers. They can, however, grow to a large size if left untreated. As they grow, they destroy healthy skin. They are generally removed surgically, with the same procedures used to excise squamous cell cancers.

Melanomas are the least common but most dangerous of

the three skin cancers. Because melanomas are cancers of the pigment-producing cells of the epidermis, they are usually (but not always) darkly pigmented. They generally appear as dark blue or black growths and may be flush with the skin or raised. In black-skinned people, melanomas are particularly difficult to see, because they may be only slightly darker than the normal skin color.

Have your doctor look at any new dark spot or growth on your skin. Melanomas, if found early, can be removed in their entirety by the dermatologist. If they're not detected early, they grow down into the deeper layers of the skin and then metastasize to other parts of the body. Metastatic melanoma is rarely curable and is usually fatal.

The best way to reduce your chances of developing all types of skin cancers is to avoid exposure to the sun. If you like to spend time outdoors, protect your skin with clothing, a hat, and, for areas that are not covered, a sunscreen. Sunscreens are rated with a number; the higher the number, the more protection the cream or lotion affords. Ratings of 15 to 30 provide the best protection.

BED SORES

Pressure can kill skin because it prevents blood from flowing, and without blood, skin dies. When skin dies, an ulcer will form, called a *pressure ulcer,* a *decubitus ulcer,* or, commonly, a *bed sore*. Unless treated carefully, a skin ulcer can become infected. The infection sometimes spreads into the adjacent bone or even throughout the body. Accordingly, promptly show all ulcers, even shallow ones, to your nurse or doctor.

Normally, even when sitting or sleeping, you move frequently, shifting your weight so that no one area experiences pressure for very long. If pressure persists in one place for more than approximately two hours, the underlying skin will die. Usually, discomfort causes us to shift position much more frequently than every two hours. However, some diseases— diabetes, spinal-cord injuries, and dementia among them— affect the ability to sense discomfort. Other conditions or illnesses, such as weakness, arthritis, and those that require restraints, also make it difficult to move. This is when the danger of developing pressure ulcers is greatest.

When a person is confined to bed or a wheelchair, pressure is usually most intense on bony spots like the bottom of the spine (the sacrum), the hip, and the heel of the foot, but ulcers can form anywhere on the body that suffers prolonged pressure.

Older people are particularly at risk of developing pressure sores since their skin has become thinner and lost some of its blood supply with age. Thus, it is more susceptible to injury and will repair more slowly than younger skin. Poor nutrition, especially lack of protein, also weakens the skin and allows pressure ulcers to form more easily.

Pressure ulcers can—and should—be prevented. Persons who cannot move themselves should be moved by someone else at least every two hours. It takes great effort to shift someone's weight that often, but less frequent movement is not acceptable: it will not prevent ulcers. Generally it is best to turn bedridden persons from side to side, using pillows for support. A hospital bed may make this job easier: it takes less strength to move someone if the bed is at the right height. Persons confined to chairs are best shifted by using pillows. Protect the most vulnerable spots of the body (the base of the spine, the heel, and elbows, for example) with soft cotton or fluffed wool. Protective mattresses and special cushions filled with water or air also help to distribute weight and prevent ulcers. A good hospital-supply store should be able to recommend what is best for your particular situation.

Hospitals and nursing homes sometimes use foam pads or mattresses, often called egg crates because they look like the boxes that eggs come in. Although these mattresses are generally more comfortable, they do little to prevent pressure sores from forming. A person placed on an egg crate must be turned just as frequently as a person on an ordinary pad or mattress! Air-filled mattresses (rarely used at home) are a little better but are really beneficial only if they are part of a mechanical system that regularly changes the pressure to different areas of the mattress every few minutes. If you are at risk of developing pressure sores, be certain that your caregivers do not rely on mattresses or other devices alone. The only sure way to prevent ulcerations is frequent changes in the position of your body and of the cushions that support you.

Keep your skin as healthy as possible. For example, powder the areas of your skin that tend to become damp, such as your buttocks and thighs, with talc; change bedclothes and sheets whenever they become wet from perspiration or incontinence; and moisturize patches of dry skin. Be certain that you eat a balanced diet—one rich in protein and supplemented with vitamin C and zinc is particularly helpful. Your body needs protein to rebuild damaged skin, and both vitamin C and zinc promote healing of skin wounds.

If an ulcer forms, continue the same measures generally used for prevention and contact your doctor or, in a nursing home or hospital, alert the nursing staff and attending doctor. Prompt medical attention is crucial.

Dead skin can prevent healing in the layers below it and can trap infection. Therefore, dead skin, called an *eschar,* often needs to be removed from the ulcer. The procedure of removing an eschar is called *debriding.* Debriding should be done only by a doctor. Generally it is not a painful procedure because only dead tissue is removed, and dead tissue does not feel pain. If live tissue must also be removed, the doctor will use a local anesthetic to minimize the discomfort.

Special dressings and skin treatments may be helpful in getting pressure sores to heal more quickly. For shallow ulcers, protective dressings, made of gauze and sometimes coated with Teflon so that they will not stick to the skin, may be all that you need. Other dressings, sold under the name of Duoderm or Opsite, put directly over the ulcer and left in place for several days, allow the skin to heal and may even encourage growth of new skin. "Wet to dry" dressings are useful if there is some drainage of fluid from the ulcer. In this case, a gauze dressing is moistened with a salty solution and applied to the ulcer; the dressing is not removed until it has dried. The drainage from the wound adheres to the dressing and is pulled off along with the dressing. Once the drainage has stopped, "wet to dry" dressings should no longer be used, since they may slow the growth of fragile new skin. If an ulcer has any sign of infection, the doctor may order a dressing or washing with Betadine, a liquid containing iodine, to help clean out the infection. Once an infection has been cleared up, Betadine dressings should be discontinued so as not to inhibit the growth of new skin. Infected ulcers may also require additional treatment with antibiotics taken by mouth, injection, or intravenously, depending on the circumstances.

Sometimes pressure ulcers occur on several body surfaces at the same time, making it impossible to position a person so that pressure is removed from all the affected areas at once. When this happens, it may be necessary to get specialized nursing care that includes the use of a special mattress. The water or air mattresses discussed above may be helpful, but occasionally an air-blown sand mattress is needed. These mattresses, generally used only in hospitals, are extremely heavy and require reinforced floors, and care-givers need special training to use them safely.

It is better to prevent bed sores than to have to treat them. If you do get them, however, you need prompt and aggressive treatment to avoid serious complications. Part of your treatment should include analyzing why the sores formed. The answer to that question will help you prevent others from forming.

Most of the changes that age brings to the skin generally cause few, if any, health problems, and manifest themselves only cosmetically. By using common sense—avoiding direct sunlight, especially without the use of sunscreens, applying moisturizers to dry skin, bringing new growths or sudden changes in the health of your skin to the attention of your doctor—you can avoid many of the few serious skin problems of aging. For the two most serious health risks—skin cancers and bed sores—early detection and treatment can lead to a cure. If you are confined to bed or a wheelchair, insist that you receive proper preventive care. If you develop a pressure sore, have your nurses and doctor treat it immediately. An occasional bed sore may develop if you are confined; if they occur regularly, you probably are not receiving adequate care. Talk to your doctor and, if necessary, get yourself into more attentive professional hands.

7

MOUTH AND TEETH

The mouth and its various parts are remarkable for the many functions they perform. As part of the gastrointestinal system, your teeth begin the digestive process by mechanically softening and breaking food apart, while saliva moistens food (to allow for easy swallowing) and begins to break it down chemically with enzymes. The surface of your tongue is covered with taste buds, which allow you to enjoy the flavor of food. Independent of its role in digestion, your mouth also shapes sounds so that you can form words, helps you change the tone of your speech, and alters the expression of your face.

In subtle ways the mouth changes with age. These changes alone usually do not cause difficulties. However, several medical problems can develop as a result of disease, medications, or the use of dentures. By being alert to those problems and by maintaining good oral hygiene, you will preserve your oral health and continue to enjoy the pleasures of eating, speaking clearly, and smiling.

TASTE

With age, the number of taste buds on your tongue decreases, and your nose becomes less sensitive to some scents. Since taste and smell work together to allow you to appreciate the flavor and aroma of foods, these changes may lessen your enjoyment of eating.

You require nearly twice as much sugar or salt than do younger people to sense these familiar tastes, which is why you may find that many foods seem bland. In contrast, your ability to sense bitter tastes does not decrease. Thus, the bitter element in some foods may overwhelm its other flavors, leaving you with an unpleasant or metallic taste in your mouth. Finding food bland and bitter may spur you to add large quantities of salt or sugar to make your food more palatable.

For most people, more salt and sugar present no medical problem. However, if you have high blood pressure (hypertension), certain heart troubles—such as congestive heart failure—or diabetes, you may need to restrict your salt or sugar intake. If so, you will discover that some alternatives work equally well in enhancing the flavor of food. Experiment with herbs such as oregano, rosemary, thyme, cinnamon, nutmeg, garlic, various kinds of pepper, and onion. You are likely to find that choices such as these make your food more interesting and flavorful than handfuls of salt or sugar.

DRY MOUTH AND XEROSTOMIA

Many older people experience dry mouth as a minor annoyance. Dry mouth usually occurs not because the glands of your mouth produce less saliva now, but because the supporting tissues of your mouth become thinner with age and hold less moisture. As a result, your mouth dries out more quickly. This normal change can be aggravated by medications, dehydration, and other causes.

Your saliva glands have become very sensitive to medications that have anticholinergic side effects (see chapter 2). By

blocking the actions of acetylcholine, these medications reduce the amount of saliva your glands produce. Antihistamines used to treat colds or allergies, some
antidepressants, and medications used for motion sickness
are the most common offenders in causing your mouth to feel
dry. If you already experience chronic discomfort from dry
mouth, taking anticholinergic medications will aggravate the
situation.

Dehydration, whether it occurs due to medications, to
warm weather, or to drinking inadequate amounts of water,
also reduces saliva production and dries the membranes of
the mouth. Diuretics ("water pills"), medications that force
your body to lose water, may make your mouth feel dry and
can lead to dehydration. In hot weather your body loses extra
water because you perspire more, and if you do not drink
enough liquids you will also become dehydrated. Any one of
these causes of dehydration will aggravate dry mouth. So can
other situations.

Ill-fitting dentures may cause you to leak saliva onto your
lips or to push them into place frequently with your tongue or
lips. Both of these occurrences lead to the loss of moisture.
Less commonly, infections in the mouth can irritate fragile
membranes, leading to pain and dryness.

Xerostomia

When dry mouth is more than a mild annoyance, the condition is called *xerostomia* (*xero* means "dry" and *stomia*
means "mouth"). Xerostomia is uncomfortable and can affect
chewing, swallowing, and digestion. If you suffer from xerostomia, talk to your doctor or dentist. It may be a symptom
of some other illness, but even if it isn't, your doctor or dentist
will likely be able to help you.

Xerostomia, if caused by a medication, is best treated by
stopping or changing the medication; if it is caused by ill-
fitting dentures, refitting your dentures may help. Even if the
exact cause cannot be identified, there are ways to treat xerostomia. Often, frequent sips of water or sucking on a
lozenge or hard candy, especially a sour one, will control the

problem. Alternatively, your doctor or dentist may recommend that you use prescription lozenges or drops to stimulate your saliva glands to produce more fluid and help your mouth's membranes remain moist.

TEETH

Healthy teeth allow you to chew your food, assist you in shaping your words, and maintain the shape of your face. Without sound teeth, you may chew your food incompletely, making the food difficult to swallow, more likely to get stuck in your throat, and harder to digest. Lost teeth make it more difficult to speak clearly, interfering with your ability to make yourself understood. And, as anyone who wears dentures knows so well, without teeth, your cheeks and lips collapse inward, distorting the shape of your face.

Age is no reason to take less good care of your teeth than when you were younger. Brush your teeth carefully at least twice, and floss them at least once, every day. Visit your dentist regularly—every six months is a good rule of thumb— to have your teeth cleaned and your mouth examined. If you develop a sore tooth or other problem with your teeth or mouth, do not wait for your regular checkup: call your dentist and ask for advice.

As we all know, by the time people reach old age, many of them have lost their natural teeth. Happily, Americans today take better care of their teeth, and the percentage of our older population wearing dentures has fallen dramatically in the past thirty years. Although well-fitting dentures are often a tolerable substitute for natural teeth, unfortunately they are less functional and often uncomfortable. If you wear dentures, take good care of them. Clean them regularly so that you can look your best and avoid unpleasant breath. If you lose or gain weight or have not worn your dentures for several weeks, they may need adjustment. If your dentures feel uncomfortable, consult your dentist.

Badly fitting dentures make it difficult to chew well, may cause pain, and can lead to the development of sores. Sores under your dentures can be painful, and chronic irritation can lead to *leukoplakia,* damaged tissue that looks white and can develop into mouth cancer. Even if your dentures feel comfortable, look in the mirror periodically to examine your mouth when you are not wearing your dentures. Be sure that there are no signs of leukoplakia or sores. If you notice anything suspicious, bring it to your doctor's or dentist's attention promptly. As part of your regular checkups, your doctor and dentist also should look carefully under your dentures and throughout your mouth and throat for hidden problems.

If your dentures do not fit well, your dentist will likely be able to adjust them to make them more comfortable. However, if your dentures persistently bother you, stop you from eating foods you enjoy, or embarrass you, ask your dentist about newer kinds of artificial teeth. Developments in dentistry have led to alternatives that may not have been available when your dentures were made.

MOUTH AND THROAT CANCER

Cancer of the mouth or throat, *oral cancer,* is not common but is very serious. Smokers and people who chew tobacco develop it more often. By the time oral cancer is discovered, it is often incurable.

Oral cancer begins in the thin tissue lining the mouth or throat, often appearing as an erosion that does not heal or a white area that persists. If it occurs in the front part of the mouth, you may notice it when it is still in an early stage, but if it occurs in the back of the mouth, it may go unnoticed for some time. Unfortunately, these cancers quickly grow down into the rich network of veins, arteries, and lymph glands around the mouth and throat, making them difficult to remove.

If an oral cancer is discovered at an early stage, a surgeon (either an oral or an ear-nose-and-throat surgeon) may be able to remove it entirely with a simple operation. However, if the cancer has grown large, deeper tissues will have to be removed for the operation to be successful. Operations on large mouth or throat cancers are complex and often have serious complications. If your doctor recommends an operation for oral cancer, first understand fully what is involved and what the doctor expects to achieve. Ask whether the operation is likely to remove all of the cancer, so that you can expect a cure, or whether the operation will remove only part of the cancer. Ask whether the operation will leave you disfigured and whether it will affect your ability to speak or to swallow. Only after you have this information will you be able to decide whether you wish to undergo surgery.

Sometimes, a cancer specialist (an *oncologist*) will recommend radiation therapy to treat oral cancer. Radiation therapy may shrink the cancer or slow its growth and may be recommended before, after, or in place of surgery. Although oral cancer responds to radiation therapy, this treatment rarely cures it. The oncologist may also recommend chemotherapy—that is, therapy with medications. Unfortunately, however, chemotherapy is not very successful at treating oral cancers.

Both radiation therapy and chemotherapy have potential side effects that can make you quite uncomfortable. Therefore, be certain to discuss carefully exactly what your doctors hope to accomplish by starting you on either kind of therapy, and be certain that you fully understand the effects of the therapy on the rest of your body. Armed with that knowledge, you can make a sensible choice as to whether the therapy is worth its burdens.

Sadly, modern medicine does not yet have good treatment for oral cancer unless it is discovered early. Examine your mouth and throat regularly for signs of trouble: sores that recur or do not heal, a buildup of whitish plaque under your dentures, or persistent irritations. If you notice any of these, bring them to your doctor's attention at once. Have your dentist and your doctor examine your mouth and throat carefully when you go for regular checkups. Early detection remains the best way to survive oral cancer. Never ignore any of its warning signs.

Age alone should not affect your ability to eat, smile, and speak clearly. Nevertheless, with age, your mouth does become susceptible to problems, most of which are minor. Medications or illness may cause your mouth to become dry, cavities and gum disease may affect your teeth, and oral cancer, although not common, can occur. You must care for your mouth as vigorously as ever to prevent difficulties and to discover illness early, when it can be treated most successfully. Fastidious care of your mouth and teeth and an awareness of the few trouble signs should permit you to keep this important part of your body healthy and trouble-free.

8

VISION AND EYES

No one—at any age—needs to be reminded of the importance of preserving good eyesight. While many ailments are difficult to bear, impaired vision often poses the greatest challenge. The English poet John Milton, who grew blind in his old age, wrote, "O loss of sight, of thee I most complain!" That same complaint is justifiably voiced today by anyone who suffers vision loss. Even minor impairment may lead more readily to falls and fractures, errors in taking medication, and new fears. If your vision is reduced, you may develop a reluctance to leave the house and to interact socially. In the seventeenth century, there was little help for John Milton. Today, there is a great deal that medicine can do to help you keep your vision healthy and to improve your sight if you do suffer vision loss.

Figures 7 and 8 show two views of the eye. Figure 7 depicts the eye as though you were looking at your face in a mirror (frontal view); figure 8, as you would see the eye if you could look through the side of your head (cross-sectional view). The eye is complex, but understanding its basic structures will help you appreciate what your specific problem may be and what can and should be done about it.

Look at the illustrations and try to imagine a beam of light

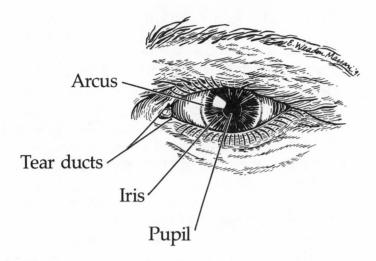

FIGURE 7
The Eye—Frontal View

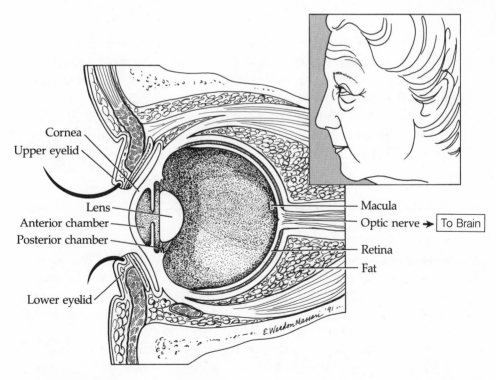

FIGURE 8
The Eye—Cross-Sectional View

entering the eye. The light enters the eye by passing first through the *cornea,* a clear, domed structure on the surface of the ball of your eye. It then passes through the *pupil,* a remarkable apparatus that regulates the amount of light entering more deeply into your eye. The pupil opens (dilates) or closes (constricts) like the aperture of a camera lens, adjusting all the time to different lighting situations. In dim light, the pupil dilates to let in as much light as is necessary to see; in bright light, it constricts, to protect your eye from being overwhelmed by an abundance of light. The *lens* focuses the light before it is projected onto the *retina,* where specialized nerve cells sense the light and transform it into electrical impulses. Those impulses speed along the *optic nerve* to your brain, where they are decoded, permitting you to experience sight.

COMMON AGE-RELATED CHANGES

Many normal physical changes occur to the eye as you get older, affecting how you see the world. For example, you have probably already noticed how difficult it is to focus on anything less than three feet away or how difficult it is to see anything when first entering a dark room. Here, I will discuss three such changes—presbyopia, arcus senilis, and adaptation to light—and two common problems, dry eyes and ptosis.

Presbyopia

Most older people find it difficult to focus on close objects. This change, called *presbyopia* (*presby* means "aging," *opia* refers to the eye), usually becomes noticeable by age 50 and, for the most part, develops regardless of whether you used glasses earlier in life, whether your vision has been excellent or poor, or whether you have been an avid reader.

Presbyopia occurs because the lens of your eye becomes less elastic with age. When an object is close to your eye, muscles within your eye pull on the lens, causing it to become thinner so that the image projected onto the retina is in clear focus. This process is called *accommodation*. Your lens, which has been accommodating for many years, loses some of its ability to thin itself, causing close objects to be less well focused. If you hold the object a little farther away, you require less accommodation to see the object clearly. This common discovery—that moving the object away lets you see it better—has led to the quip that if only our arms were longer, we wouldn't need reading glasses!

Arcus

Another common and normal change is the development of a grayish ring around the outside of the *iris,* the colored portion of the eye. This ring is called *arcus senilis* (Latin for "ring of old age") or simply *arcus,* for short. If arcus occurs in younger people, it can signal disease, but in you its occurrence is almost always harmless.

Adaptation to Light

It is also normal for you to find that you adapt to dim light more slowly than you used to. That is, if you move from the lawn on a sunny day into a house with the curtains pulled, it will take you longer to see well when you step inside than it once did. You may also have noticed that the amount of light you require to see, known as the *visual threshold,* has become higher. Even after allowing adequate time to adapt to dim light—for example, if you walk into a darkened restaurant at lunchtime—you may still not be able to see as well as you would like or as well as your children can.

Dry Eyes

Many older people suffer from dry and itchy eyes. Often, this dryness is caused by a normal change in the tear glands, which produce fewer tears, as you get older. Thus, you may find that your eyes itch, burn, and turn red even when the weather is not hot, dry, or smoggy. If dry eyes bother you, use eye drops (one brand is Artificial Tears) to supplement your natural tears. These drops can be bought without a prescription at the pharmacy. However, since dry eyes can be a symptom of certain diseases, you should tell your doctor what you are experiencing and that you want to try using drops. He or she may want to have an eye doctor (an *ophthalmologist*) examine your eyes to rule out the possibility of some more serious cause.

Ptosis

With age, the ball of the eye tends to sit more deeply in the eye socket, because the pad of fat located behind the eye becomes thinner. This normal change can cause your eyelids to align badly or to sag, a problem called *ptosis*. Ptosis in turn causes tears to spread less evenly over the eye and to evaporate more quickly. If ptosis is severe, tears will actually spill onto your cheeks, a condition known as *epiphora*. When ptosis is mild, using artificial tears may be enough to alleviate your discomfort and prevent chronic dryness from damaging the cornea. When ptosis is advanced, discomfort and redness of the eyes and eyelids can become more of a problem than eyedrops can handle. Fortunately, relatively simple surgery can usually correct the situation. The procedure is performed by an ophthalmologist or by a plastic surgeon trained in correcting these problems.

ABNORMAL VISION LOSS

Vision loss and blindness are all too common in older people even though these conditions are not the result of the normal changes of aging. Half of all blindness occurs in persons over age 65, and 3 percent of persons over age 85 are blind. Sadly, these statistics, which measure "legal blindness," understate the severity of the situation. Many older persons suffer from visual problems serious enough to affect the quality of their lives although they don't qualify as "legally blind."

The diseases that most commonly lead to visual loss in the elderly are cataracts, glaucoma, diabetes, and macular degeneration. I will discuss each of these diseases in some detail. For the moment, it is important to recognize that these diseases do not inevitably lead to impaired vision. Cataracts can usually be surgically removed and vision restored. Glaucoma can generally be controlled if diagnosed early, preventing loss of vision. Good control of diabetes can help allay the complications that lead to blindness; avoiding blindness is one of the most important reasons why diabetes must be diagnosed early and treated properly. Unfortunately, macular degeneration can't be prevented and is only rarely treatable.

CATARACTS

What Are Cataracts?

The lens of the eye often develops an opaque or cloudy area called a *cataract*. A cataract can form throughout the lens or in just one portion of it. In either case, if the cataract becomes dense or large enough, it prevents light from passing properly through the lens to the retina, so your vision becomes hazy and blurred.

Under unusual circumstances cataracts can occur in younger people, but they occur most commonly in the elderly, causing 15 percent of people over age 50 and more than 50 percent of people over age 75 to suffer some vision loss. Cataracts can occur in anyone but appear more frequently in people with diabetes, people who have used steroid medications such as prednisone, and people who have had an eye injury. Cataracts are particularly common in people whose eyes have had years of unprotected exposure to bright sunshine, because the ultraviolet in sunshine damages the lens.

Because cataracts are not painful, and because they usually affect vision slowly, over years, you probably won't become aware that you have a cataract in its early stages. Nevertheless, as the cataract progresses, symptoms occur. Your vision gradually becomes dull and fuzzy. In bright light, you may experience uncomfortable glare because the cataract scatters the light before it reaches your retina. When the cataract becomes "mature," that is, fully developed, you may find it impossible to read clearly or to tolerate bright sunshine.

It does not require a specialist to diagnose a cataract. Your primary-care doctor will be able to see the cataract when examining your eye with an ophthalmoscope. The ophthalmoscope, a flashlight-like instrument with a lens, lets your doctor look into your eye. To your doctor, the cataract will look like a dark gray, opaque area that obscures his or her view of the back of your eye. If your doctor finds that you have a cataract, you will need to see an ophthalmologist for a more precise evaluation. The ophthalmologist will use eye drops to dilate your pupils in order to inspect the cataract fully, and to determine its size and density, and will also look for other problems that might be affecting your vision. This examination is virtually without risk or pain, although it will take several hours before your pupils return to normal.

Treating Cataracts

Although no treatment can stop a cataract from growing larger or denser, it is generally a good idea to protect your eyes from strong sunlight. Almost any pair of glasses can be treated so that they filter out the harmful ultraviolet (UV) rays of the sun. If you live in a sunny climate or spend much time outdoors, be certain that your glasses filter UV light. Further, because certain medications such as steroids (e.g., prednisone) can cause cataracts, if you have an early cataract and are using prednisone or a comparable medication, ask your doctor if you can stop the medication or use some other drug.

If your cataract is not yet mature, there are practical steps you can take to lessen its effects on your sight. The principal concern is to reduce glare, both inside and outdoors. Bright, glaring light causes your pupil to constrict. When your pupil is constricted, the light entering your eye is more likely to pass through the cataract and be affected by it. Less bright and indirect light causes the pupil to dilate, allowing more light to enter the eye through the clearer parts of the lens. Therefore, try to arrange the lighting inside your house so that it is neither too bright nor direct. Indirect light—for example, light that is reflected off walls and ceilings—is preferable to light pointed directly at you, a book, or other objects. Outdoors, wear sunglasses. Unfortunately, these practical steps provide only partial and temporary relief. A mature cataract can be treated satisfactorily only by surgical removal. But how do you know when it is time to have surgery?

The best way to determine if it is time for an operation is to ask yourself this question: Does the cataract so affect your sight that you cannot comfortably do what you need or want to do? For example, if you enjoy collecting stamps or doing needlepoint, you will need very good vision or else have to give up your hobby. Such a situation might argue for early surgery. If you do not do fine, close work but rather watch television or movies, it may not be important to remove a cataract until it interferes more substantially with your vision. In short, it is time to have the cataract removed when the cataract makes it difficult for you to see clearly the things you want or need to see. Until then, it is too early to have surgery, even if your doctor says that the cataract is large and dense. There is no advantage in delaying surgery for a cataract, but neither is it wise to have any operation before it is needed.

Before you decide to have surgery, it is important to know if you have other eye conditions that might affect the success of the operation. For example, glaucoma (discussed on p. 141) must be controlled prior to having cataract surgery. Some diseases, such as macular degeneration or diabetic retinopathy (both are discussed later in this chapter) may affect vision more than a cataract. If you have either of these diseases, removing the cataract may not improve your vision. In that case, the decision to have an operation must be especially carefully considered.

Today, cataract surgery is generally performed as an outpatient procedure—that is, without admission to the hospital. If you have cataracts in both eyes, each will be treated in a separate procedure, usually several weeks apart. General anesthesia is rarely used. In all likelihood, you will be awake during the surgery. You won't, however, feel any pain because drops containing a local anesthesia will be put in your eye before the operation. In addition, your doctor can give you medications to keep you calm and relaxed. Although it may give you "the willies" to be awake for the operation, general anesthesia dramatically increases the risk of surgery. Be thankful if you can have the procedure without it.

Today there are several different methods for removing a cataract. The *intracapsular extraction method* involves removal of the entire lens and much of the capsule—a sac of tissue that helps secure the lens in place—that supports it. The *extracapsular extraction method* removes the whole lens but only part of the supporting capsule. Most experts believe the second method is safer and better. Sometimes, doctors dissolve the lens with sound waves that shatter the cataract in a process known as *phacoemulsification*. These sound waves are special frequencies that can't be heard and do not cause pain or damage to other structures of the eye.

When cataract surgery is performed by a skillful ophthalmologist, the procedure is generally safe and can be very successful in restoring vision. However, no operation is without risk; the two principal complications of cataract operations are hemorrhage and infection. The most common is hemorrhage, or bleeding into the eye. Hemorrhage rarely occurs, but when it does, it can lead to blindness in the affected eye. You can also get an infection, a serious situation. Ask your ophthalmologist how best to care for your eyes after surgery and what are the signs of hemorrhage and infection that you should look for. If an eye becomes red, more painful, or begins leaking fluid, if your vision changes, or if you develop a fever in the weeks after surgery, contact your ophthalmologist immediately.

The fact that the operation is an outpatient procedure shouldn't lead you to expect that you will be back to full function right away. Your eye will probably be uncomfortable for a few days or even weeks. To reduce pressure on your eye, you will need to avoid bending over, lifting heavy packages, and other kinds of strain. You will need to put drops in your eye for at least several days, and will also have to wear a patch over the eye, which makes it difficult to judge distances. In short, you will need to recuperate, and between the eye patch and other restrictions, you will face new challenges in cooking, eating, and using the bathroom. Given all this, talk to your ophthalmologist and to your primary-care doctor well before the procedure so that you will understand how the operation will affect your activities. Determine what extra help you may need after surgery, and be certain to arrange for that help well in advance.

During a cataract operation, the ophthalmologist removes all or part of the lens of your eye. The resulting changes in vision caused by the procedure are called *aphakia*. Aphakia causes the eye to magnify what it sees by nearly one-third, decreases peripheral vision, and alters, but does not eliminate, your eye's ability to focus light. In the past, the only option for people with aphakia was to wear thick glasses. Now, a contact lens can correct the magnification. However, it may be difficult for you to insert and remove, clean, and disinfect contact lenses. If so, you may prefer or need to wear glasses to correct your vision. Another solution to aphakia is to have a new lens placed in the eye where the old one used to be. This procedure is called a *lens implant*. Lens implants are done when your old lens is removed, during the operation. Before surgery, discuss with your ophthalmologist whether a lens implant is right for you. This step in the operation adds a little extra risk but will eliminate the need to wear corrective lenses after surgery.

GLAUCOMA

What Is Glaucoma?

Glaucoma, the leading cause of blindness in the United States, affects more than 2 million people. Although glaucoma is not preventable, the blindness that results from glaucoma *is*. Glaucoma occurs when the pressure of the liquid in the eye (the *intraocular pressure*) becomes too high. (By the way, the liquid that fills the eye is not the same as tears, and glaucoma and the production of tears are not related.)

Your eye is essentially a pliant ball that maintains its shape because it is filled with liquid. If the pressure of that liquid becomes too high, you will develop problems. The increase in pressure brought about by glaucoma usually begins slowly, and at first there are no symptoms—you will experience neither pain nor changes in vision. Nevertheless, over time, the increased pressure works its damage. At first, it destroys the nerve fibers in the retina that are farthest from the optic nerve, leading to a loss of peripheral vision. This causes your field of vision to narrow; eventually, you will begin to see the world as though you were looking through a tunnel. Later, the increased pressure affects nerve fibers closer to the optic nerve, affecting your central vision and leading eventually to blindness.

Most glaucoma is of the type called *open-angle glaucoma.* We don't know the exact reason why it occurs, but the problem seems to involve a decrease in the amount of fluid that flows from one part of the eye to the other. If the fluid cannot pass freely, the pressure builds. A rarer type of glaucoma, *angle-closure glaucoma,* can occur suddenly. Unlike open-angle glaucoma, angle-closure glaucoma can cause severe pain and sudden changes in vision. Angle-closure glaucoma is a medical emergency that requires immediate attention.

Screening for Glaucoma

Because glaucoma usually does not cause symptoms when it starts, you should see an ophthalmologist yearly to be tested for the disease. There are three parts to the examination. First, using the ophthalmoscope, the doctor will examine your retina and look at the optic nerve. If you have glaucoma, your optic nerve may have a changed appearance. Second, the ophthalmologist will test your peripheral vision, the earliest visual change caused by glaucoma. Peripheral vision may be tested with a wall chart and a moving object on the end of a pointer, or it may be tested with a machine that uses a large dome and a moving light. Third, the ophthalmologist will measure the pressure in your eye. This procedure is painless, takes only a few moments, and can be done with several different types of instruments. The doctor first numbs your eye with a drop of local anesthetic and then measures the intraocular pressure with a tiny instrument, often mounted on a much larger piece of equipment, that touches the cornea. If any of these tests suggests glaucoma, further tests may be needed to make a certain diagnosis.

Treating Glaucoma

Reducing intraocular pressure will prevent damage to the nerves of the retina and prevent loss of vision. Intraocular pressure is reduced either with medications or by a surgical procedure.

Most often, your doctor will prescribe eye drops to be used several times a day. Although the drops are generally safe, the medication in them gets absorbed into the bloodstream and can cause side effects elsewhere in your body. Prescription eye drops, after all, are potent medicines.

One kind of glaucoma medication, pilocarpine (Pilocar), causes the pupil to constrict and thus the area around it to open, allowing more of the fluid in the front chamber of the eye to escape, thus lowering the intraocular pressure. When the pupil is constricted, however, it is more difficult to see well in dimly lit places. Thus, if you use pilocarpine, it is important that you have adequate lighting when reading or doing detailed work. Further, if you also have cataracts, this medication may worsen your vision because of its effect on the pupil.

It makes sense that if constriction of the pupil is beneficial in glaucoma, dilation, which can lead to increased pressure, is not recommended. Medications with anticholinergic properties (discussed in chapter 2) will cause the pupil to dilate. Thus, if you have glaucoma you should not use these medications. Although a doctor generally won't prescribe medications with anticholinergic properties if you have glaucoma, your doctor may forget or simply not know that you have the disease. Moreover, many over-the-counter medications, such as most cold medications and sleeping pills, are anticholinergic. If you have glaucoma, never take *any* medication before asking your doctor or pharmacist whether you can use it safely.

The second kind of eye drops commonly used to treat

glaucoma, like timolol (Timoptic) or betaxolol (Betoptic), are known as *beta-blockers*. These medications decrease the amount of fluid that your eye makes. They are generally safe drugs but they can reduce blood pressure and slow the heart. Be certain to tell your eye doctor if you have any heart or blood pressure problems and, of course, discuss the use of these drugs with your primary-care doctor before taking them.

The third kind of eye drops contains epinephrine (Epitrate) or dipivefrin (Propine); they also decrease the amount of fluid that the eye makes but do not slow the heart or reduce blood pressure.

If these medications do not lower your intraocular pressure or if side effects make it impossible to use them, there are other medications you can try. Some of them, such as Diamox, are taken as pills rather than used as drops. In short, a tolerable medication can generally be found to control intraocular pressure.

For angle-closure glaucoma, surgery is the best treatment; for open-angle glaucoma, surgery is appropriate if medication is not effective, if medication side effects are not acceptable, or if other health problems render you unable to use the medications properly. The surgery is a short procedure generally performed with a laser in the ophthalmologist's office. *Laser iridectomy,* as the treatment is called, creates small holes in the meshwork through which the fluid in the eye drains. When performed by an experienced ophthalmologist, the procedure is relatively safe and painless. After surgery, you generally will not need to continue to use medications to treat intraocular pressure, but you should continue to visit your ophthalmologist periodically to have the pressure checked.

DIABETIC RETINOPATHY

One of the serious complications of diabetes is vision loss. Although diabetes causes 7 percent of all blindness in the United States, this complication is not inevitable and many diabetic persons never develop significant visual loss. But the complication is common, especially in those who have had the disease for more than ten years. Good control of blood sugar is the best way to prevent diabetes from affecting the eye. If you have diabetes, you must see an ophthalmologist yearly so that, if needed, treatment can be started early. (Diabetes is discussed in detail in chapter 12.)

Elevated blood sugar harms the small blood vessels that bring nutrients and oxygen to the retina. Weaknesses, called *microaneurysms,* can develop in these blood vessels. When the microaneurysms break, they cause small hemorrhages, or leakages of blood, into the retina. These hemorrhages damage the retina, and if a hemorrhage occurs in the most sensitive part of the retina, the *macula,* vision loss can occur quickly. If left untreated, diabetes causes a second problem, called *proliferative retinopathy,* the growth of abnormal blood vessels, which further impairs vision.

Ophthalmologists can detect microaneurysms, hemorrhages, and the growth of new blood vessels by using an ophthalmoscope. However, the best way to examine diabetic retinopathy is with a medical procedure called *fluorescein angiography,* the purpose of which is to photograph the blood vessels and any leakage from them. In this examination, a special dye—fluorescein—is injected into a vein of your arm. The dye travels through your bloodstream to your eye, where it can be detected by photographing the retina with a special camera. If microaneurysms exist, if any of the blood vessels are leaking, or if abnormal blood vessels are growing into the retina, they will appear on the photographs. Although the examination itself is not painful, you may have some discomfort when the pictures are taken because of the bright light that is used, but this is a small price to pay when this information is needed. In addition, for a few hours after the test, your urine may have an odd color as your kidneys excrete the dye from your body.

Treatment of Diabetic Retinopathy

Excellent studies have shown that treatment with laser therapy benefits diabetic persons who have retinal changes.

Although the most minimal changes of diabetes on the eye, called *background retinopathy,* generally do not require treatment, do not wait until you suffer noticeable deterioration in vision to seek evaluation. After all, the whole purpose of treating diabetic retinopathy is to prevent vision loss. Ophthalmologists who are expert in the care of diabetics can tell you when it is time to start treatment.

The treatment involves focusing a laser on the small blood vessels, burning them in a procedure called *photocoagulation.* Photocoagulation reduces hemorrhaging and stops the growth of new blood vessels without unduly damaging the fragile retina. Happily, the retina does not sense the burning, and you should not experience pain from the procedure.

So, you see how important it is to exercise tight control of your blood sugar to help prevent complications from diabetes. You could save your sight! If you are undergoing treatment with an ophthalmologist for visual changes associated with diabetes, you also should be under the care of an internist, geriatrician, or endocrinologist who is experienced in caring for diabetics.

MACULAR DEGENERATION

What Is Macular Degeneration?

The *macula* is the central portion of your retina; it contains the highest concentration of light-sensitive nerves. If the macula degenerates—that is, if you suffer *macular degeneration*—your vision will become blurred, and it will become difficult to see smaller objects, such as the print on this page. Macular degeneration affects your central, rather than your peripheral, vision. There are two types of macular degeneration: the more common one is called *nonexudative* or *dry macular degeneration;* the less common type, called *exudative* or *wet macular degeneration,* can lead to the greatest loss of vision.

The reasons why the macula deteriorates are not fully understood. But once started, the situation tends to progress so that more and more light-sensitive cells in the macula are lost. The first signs of the disease may be changes you notice when looking at fine print, which may appear blurred, or at parallel lines that may appear wavy rather than straight. Or you may find that your glasses just can't bring things into focus.

The macula is difficult to examine. If you or your doctor suspects that you have macular degeneration, an ophthalmologist must evaluate the situation. If your ophthalmologist confirms that you have macular degeneration, ask to be referred to an ophthalmologist who specializes in the disease.

Unfortunately, little can be done to treat dry macular degeneration other than using proper glasses, good lighting, magnifying lenses, and other aids for the visually impaired. For those with the less common form of the disease, wet macular degeneration, there is some evidence that laser treatments may be helpful. However, laser treatments will not benefit everyone who has wet macular degeneration; the results are not nearly as good as when lasers are used for persons with diabetic eye changes. Because the treatment for this disease is somewhat controversial, obtain a second opinion before agreeing to it.

OTHER CAUSES OF VISION LOSS

Many other diseases, injuries, and infections can cause loss of vision. Certain inherited diseases, such as retinitis pigmentosa, lead to blindness, but vision loss from this disease usually becomes evident before old age. Also, strokes can damage the part of the brain that senses vision (see chapter 13). Even a brain tumor can affect vision, but this cause of visual change is rare. If a blood vessel bursts in the eye, the hemorrhage can cause a loss of vision. This condition is not the same as a burst blood vessel on the surface of the eye, which usually has little or no effect on vision but may instead be only a cosmetic problem. *Temporal arteritis* is a disease that causes blood vessels to become inflamed and, if left untreated, can block the blood supply to the eyes, causing sudden blindness. *Retinal detachment* occurs when an area of the retina lifts or is pulled from its underlying surface, with a subsequent loss of vision in one or more parts of the normal visual field. This problem can usually be repaired with a laser, which effectively welds the retina back in place.

Many older people are bothered by "floaters," tiny dark spots that seem to float through your vision periodically. These are caused by darkened spots in the fluid that fills the eye. Floaters are not usually a sign of anything serious, and there is rarely anything that can be done to eliminate them.

As a rule, most of the illnesses that affect the eye should be treated early to obtain the maximum benefit from treatment. That is why you must consider any sudden change in your vision or pain in your eyes as an emergency, requiring immediate medical evaluation. Changes that occur over weeks or months also require prompt medical attention. If you notice even a slow or gradual change, don't delay having a proper evaluation just because it's "hardly anything."

AIDS FOR THE VISUALLY IMPAIRED

Even when medication and surgery can't correct visual loss, the use of visual aids can often make your life more enjoyable and easier. For example, high-quality magnifying lenses can be very helpful, especially when mounted on stands for reading, worn as glasses for watching television or movies, or held by hand for many other tasks. Proper lighting is important, and your particular condition will determine whether you should use direct or reflected lighting and whether a stronger intensity is best for you. Night-lights in the bedroom, bathroom, and hall are generally a good idea because they reduce the need for the eye to adapt to darkness. Your ophthalmologist and your optometrist (the person who fits and advises about glasses) can help you decide if tinting, ultraviolet filters, or other special products should be incorporated into your glasses.

Large-print books and newspapers may enable you to continue to read even if you have advanced vision loss. Many libraries carry large-print books, and several major newspapers print special editions for the partially sighted. You can also get a phone with large keys, which many persons with reduced vision find easier to use.

Several excellent organizations assist persons who have loss of sight, including the American Association for the Blind and the Society for the Partially Sighted. Branches of these organizations exist in most major American cities and can be located in your phone book.

Your sight is so precious that you must make every effort to preserve it. See an ophthalmologist each year so that potential problems can be diagnosed early, often the key to minimizing loss of vision. If you notice anything unusual with your eyes or in how you see, consult your doctor. When it is your sight that is at issue, you have nothing to gain from delay, and much potential benefit from prompt medical care. If you do suffer vision loss, recognize that you still have a great deal of living to be done, much of which can be made easier with visual aids. Recall that John Milton, mentioned at the start of this chapter, wrote his masterworks, *Paradise Lost* and *Paradise Regained,* after he was completely blind.

9

HEARING AND EARS

I f you do not hear well, the impact on the quality of your life can be enormous. If it is difficult to follow conversations, you are likely to avoid social situations. If you shout in response to questions or force your friends to shout at you, you may be shunned. If you give a bizarre answer to a question simply because you didn't hear it clearly, others may wrongly think that you are confused. Worse, if you can't hear warning sounds—fire alarms, smoke detectors, car horns, or the sounds of people approaching—you can endanger yourself and others. Too often, people wrongly ignore the early signs of hearing loss and attribute the change to "just getting old." Sadly, this reaction causes many people with treatable hearing loss to suffer unnecessarily.

Mild hearing loss is so common that it is often difficult to determine whether age or many years of exposure to noise is the real culprit. Regardless, 25 percent of people over age 65 and over half of all persons in nursing homes suffer some hearing loss. What is certain is that the normal changes in hearing, attributable to age alone, do not lead to severe hearing impairment. Getting old does not inevitably mean "going deaf."

When many people think of hearing loss they think of deafness, but deafness is only an extreme condition in which people can hear little or nothing even with the assistance of a hearing aid. Fortunately, most hearing loss is not so extreme, and although the problem is generally not treatable with medication or surgery, most people can be helped substantially with hearing aids.

HEARING VS. UNDERSTANDING

The softest volume that you can hear is called your *auditory threshold*. Your ability to distinguish different sounds is called *discrimination*. Thus, your auditory threshold determines what you can hear, and your ability to discriminate determines what sounds you can understand. If you can't hear certain sounds or sounds of a certain pitch, your ability to discriminate may be impaired. That is why many people with mild hearing loss complain not that they can't hear but that they can't understand. They hear the conversation but can't make out the words, or they hear the music but can't distinguish the instruments. Hearing loss may make sounds seem indistinct, just as poor eyesight makes objects appear blurred.

When many sounds occur at the same time, you may have even more difficulty understanding. Thus, although in quiet settings you may be able to understand every word of a conversation, when it is noisy—when several conversations are going on at the same time at a party, or when there is constant background noise—you may have real difficulty understanding. This situation can be particularly distressing if, for example, you have a large family. Holidays, which should be joyful times, may become an enormous challenge because it's so tough to get what your grandson is telling you so earnestly amid the din of many people gathered in one room, all talking at the same time. If your hearing is good, you can separate sounds and concentrate only on the ones you want. If it is not, focusing on any one sound is difficult because you hear them together as an indistinguishable noise. If you cannot discriminate adequately, you may become disoriented, appear confused, or seem depressed and unwilling to participate in social activities.

THE EAR

Each part of your ear contributes to good hearing (see Figure 9). The ear lobe (the *pinna*) captures sounds; the *auditory canal* brings sound from the outside to the *eardrum;* the eardrum begins the transfer of sound to the brain; the *ossicles,* a set of bones, transmit and magnify the vibrations of the drum; the *cochlea* holds both the hair cells that sense sound and the cells that sense position and movement; and the *otic nerve* carries information to the brain. Although with age the eardrum becomes thinner and more translucent and the ossicles become stiffer, these changes usually have little effect on your ability to hear. Other age-related changes, however, do affect how you hear.

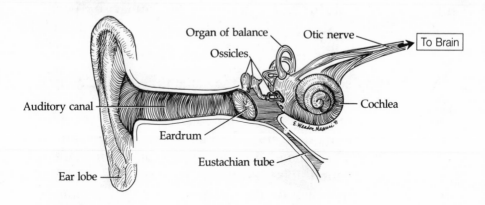

FIGURE 9
The Ear—Cross-Sectional View

PRESBYCUSIS

Age-related changes in the hair cells, which sense sound, can lead to *presbycusis* (presby means "aged," and cusis means "hearing"), the most common hearing problem for elderly persons. With presbycusis, you lose the ability to hear high-pitched sounds, but can still hear midrange and lower-pitched sounds. Presbycusis usually affects both ears.

Presbycusis is often so mild that it frequently goes unnoticed or is discovered by accident through routine hearing tests performed by a doctor or a nurse at a seniors' center. Although presbycusis generally advances, albeit slowly, it does not usually lead to deafness. You may notice, however, that certain music, like the sound of a violin or flute, doesn't sound as brilliant as it used to. Certain high-pitched voices—of small children and some women—may become more difficult to understand. Electronic devices that emit high-pitched tones, such as electronic timers, alarms, or beepers—also become difficult to hear. Most important, loss of high-frequency hearing may affect your ability to discriminate, so that conversations blur and spoken words become difficult to understand. This is often most noticeable at parties or gatherings when there is background noise.

Since presbycusis affects only the ability to hear high-pitched sounds, it is easy for an *audiologist,* a hearing expert, to recognize the condition. It is also the kind of hearing loss that responds best to hearing aids, which can be adjusted to amplify the high-pitched sounds more than low-pitched sounds, correcting the problem without making every sound uncomfortably loud.

NOISE-INDUCED HEARING LOSS

Another very common cause of hearing loss has nothing to do with aging but rather with long exposure to loud noises, a condition called *noise-induced hearing loss.* Loud noise can damage the fragile cells that sense hearing, the eardrum, and the ossicles. This kind of damage doesn't occur from brief exposure to loud noise but to years of abuse. People who have worked in factories, used certain kinds of machinery, or spent substantial time where blaring noises were common are most likely to develop this kind of loss. Noise-induced hearing loss generally can be helped substantially with hearing aids.

Today, more care is taken to shield workers from loud noises, but even the younger generation may not escape noise-induced hearing loss. There is considerable fear that youngsters who listen to pounding music at discotheques and through headphones at high volume will suffer more noise-induced hearing loss than did your generation. Although an occasional loud rock concert is unlikely to hurt your grand-daughter's ears, many hours of such exposure may do her hearing considerable damage.

SENSORINEURONAL HEARING LOSS

Even without exposure to loud noise, the fragile cells and bones that sense and transmit sound can be damaged, leading to *sensorineuronal hearing loss.* There are many causes of this condition, and it is therefore difficult to pinpoint an exact reason why it occurs.

Certain drugs—like the antibiotics gentamicin, tobramicin, and vancomycin—can damage these cells; so can aspirin, if taken in high doses. If you use aspirin several times a day, one of the warning signs that you are taking too much is a buzzing or ringing sound in your ears, called *tinnitus.* If this reaction occurs, call your doctor and reduce your dose of aspirin.

Diseases too may damage the nerves and structures of the ear. For example, a tumor, *acoustic neuroma,* can cause such damage. *Paget's disease,* discussed in chapter 5, can cause surrounding bones to impinge on the nerve that carries information from ear to brain (the otic nerve). Infections that get into the brain (meningitis) may destroy the structures of the ear that sense or transmit sound.

Obviously, the treatment of sensorineuronal hearing loss depends on its cause. If it is caused by a medication or a disease, stopping the medication or treating the underlying disease may be the best available treatment. Sometimes surgery is needed. For example, if your problem is caused by a malfunction of the ossicles, an *otolaryngologist* (an ear-nose-and-throat specialist) may perform an operation that allows these small bones to function better, but such treatment is rarely needed or beneficial in the elderly. If these treatments don't help, a hearing aid may be beneficial.

SUDDEN HEARING LOSS

A sudden loss of hearing is never normal. If you experience it, get prompt medical attention. The cause may be easily remedied—for example, an accumulation of ear wax can be the culprit—or the cause may be something serious.

No one is sure why we have ear wax; one thought is that it repels insects and stops them from entering the ear. Whatever its purpose, when wax accumulates, it can block the ear canal and stop sound from reaching the eardrum. Never attempt to remove ear wax with cotton swabs. This home treatment often compacts the wax, worsening the situation. Cotton swabs can also damage the lining of the ear canal or the eardrum and can lead to painful and dangerous infections.

If wax is the problem, your doctor or your doctor's nurse will "irrigate" the ear, trying to remove the wax with water. If the wax is too hard to remove, for several days you may have to use drops that soften the wax and then return to the doctor's office for another irrigation. If wax accumulates regularly in your ears, you may want to use these drops every few weeks to help dissolve the wax before a clog forms. The drops, sold under such names as Debrox and Ceruminex, can be purchased from your pharmacy without a prescription. Letting warm water from the bath or shower flow into the ear canal also helps prevent wax buildup.

Ear infections can trouble elders just as severely as they trouble toddlers, causing pain, dizziness, and hearing loss. *Otitis externa* (inflammation of the external ear), infections in the ear canal, are painful and often occur after swimming in a pool or lake. For this reason, it is sometimes called "swimmer's ear." This condition occurs because water containing bacteria and fungus gets trapped in the ear canal. Since the infection involves only the outer ear, it is generally treated with drops that contain antibiotics and antifungal agents. Swimmer's ear can usually be prevented by putting a few drops of a mixture made of equal amounts of alcohol and vinegar into the ear immediately after swimming. These solutions are available at your drugstore, but I generally tell people to prepare their own—at one-tenth the price.

Otitis media (infections of the middle ear) occur in the chamber of the ear behind the drum. They can be painful, cause fever, affect hearing and balance, and should be treated by your doctor without delay. Treatment usually consists of antibiotics taken by mouth.

EVALUATING HEARING LOSS

Since you may not recognize mild hearing loss, your primary-care physician should check your hearing during your regular visits. That screening may include simple questions about hearing but should also involve limited testing.

Some doctors have an *audiometer* or *audioscope,* machines for testing hearing, and use it routinely. Others, myself included, will test your hearing by asking you to repeat words whispered several feet from your ear; if there is no suspicion of any problem, this simple and less-expensive test is a reasonable alternative to using the audiometer.

Your doctor should also examine your ear canal and drum with an *otoscope,* a type of flashlight with a narrow beam of light and a cone-shaped end that allows him or her to point the beam into your ear. The ear canal has a natural bend, but by pulling gently on your ear lobe, your doctor can straighten the entire length of the canal and view your eardrum. By doing this, your doctor can be sure that there is no infection of the canal, accumulation of wax, or change in the drum indicating infection in the middle ear.

If there is any suspicion of hearing loss, your doctor will refer you to an *audiologist,* a highly trained professional who specializes in testing hearing and advising about the use of hearing aids, and perhaps request specific tests or an overall hearing evaluation. In an overall evaluation, the audiologist will generally perform at least two tests. The first, *pure-tone audiometry,* measures your hearing; the second test determines your ability to discriminate sounds—that is, to understand words. For both tests, the audiologist will ask you to wear earphones.

In the first test, the audiologist will play frequencies of sound through the earphones to test the full range that your ear should be able to hear and to determine your auditory threshold—i.e., the minimal intensity necessary for you to hear the tones. The audiologist may repeat the first test in a slightly different way to determine if you hear sound more easily when it is conducted through the bones surrounding your ears rather than through the air in your ear canal. Thus, the audiologist may be able to identify whether your hearing problem is in the drum and ossicles which transmit sound or in the nerves and structures which sense sound. The audiologist will produce a graph from this information, showing how severe your hearing problem is and whether your ability to hear in the lower, middle, or upper frequency range is most affected. In the second test, for auditory discrimination, the audiologist plays words, rather than tones, at different volumes.

These tests will give you and your physician important information: the kind of hearing loss you have; whether you are suffering from presbycusis or some other hearing problem; how severe your hearing loss is; and whether one or both ears are affected. With this information your audiologist and doctor will be able to recommend the best treatment.

HEARING AIDS—AMPLIFICATION

When hearing loss occurs suddenly, it is most often due to an accumulation of wax or an ear infection, both of which are easily treated. When hearing loss is chronic, medical or surgical treatment is rarely helpful. Less than 1 percent of people with a hearing loss can be helped with treatment other than that provided by hearing aids.

A hearing aid amplifies sound to compensate for your loss of hearing. Your hearing aid is adjusted for your particular losses, by amplifying those frequencies that you hear least well. Technological advances have made it possible to produce very small hearing aids that offer excellent clarity. Unfortunately, many of my patients tell me that they are embarrassed to wear a hearing aid. This is difficult to understand, particularly when a patient looks at me through his or her glasses! Just as glasses correct problems with vision, hearing aids correct problems with hearing. Neither of these aids should cause embarrassment: most of us will need to use one or both at some time in our lives. In so visible a role as president, Ronald Reagan wore a hearing aid without any embarrassment and set a good example for all of us.

Of course, like glasses, hearing aids take some getting used to. At first the earpiece may be uncomfortable, and learning to adjust the hearing aid takes time also. But a hearing aid will allow you to enjoy the sounds of life, to participate fully in social settings, and will put an end to that scolding: "Why don't you listen to me? And stop shouting—you should get your hearing checked!" Once you get used to it, a hearing aid will greatly increase the joy you take in life.

Regardless of size, all hearing aids have similar parts. A microphone picks up sound, a battery-powered amplifier makes the sound louder, a volume control (sometimes called the "gain") regulates the amount of amplification, a small speaker plays the sound, and an earpiece, fitted into the ear canal, transmits the amplified sound to your eardrum. Tiny hearing aids, barely visible once in place, can fit in the ear canal. Because of their size, however, they are difficult for some people to put into and to remove from the ear, and the volume dial may be too small to use easily.

Slightly larger hearing aids, worn behind the ear, are connected by a small tube to an earpiece inserted into the ear canal. This type of hearing aid is easier to operate and maintain. If your hearing loss is very severe, there are larger and more powerful hearing aids that are worn elsewhere—for example, from a chain around your neck.

Hearing aids mounted on your glasses can be particularly helpful if you have severe hearing loss on one side. If your hearing is so bad in one ear that a hearing aid won't improve hearing in that ear, the glasses-mounted hearing aid can help by taking sound from the bad side, amplifying it, and delivering it to the better ear. Even with such amplification, however, people with severe hearing loss on only one side often experience an additional difficulty: with all sound coming through one ear, it is difficult to locate sounds. You may hear a shout or car horn but be unable to tell whether it comes from the left or the right, back or front. Hearing aids mounted on glasses may also be useful if you have dementia or if you just have a tendency to lose things.

Most people who wear hearing aids usually use one in the weaker ear, but you may want to have an aid in each ear if your hearing is poor on both sides. Your audiologist will advise you about this alternative and will also work with you to make the earpiece as comfortable as possible. The audiologist fits your earpiece by making a mold of the outer part of your ear canal. Often, adjustments must be made after the initial fitting. You will find that it takes a few weeks to adjust to the feel of wearing a hearing aid; you may prefer to begin wearing it for only several hours a day, gradually increasing the wearing time. But once you get used to it, it is generally best to wear the hearing aid whenever you are awake.

The audiologist is also responsible for teaching you how to care for and adjust your hearing aid. Hearing aids are expensive, and when you purchase one you are also paying for instruction. You should learn how to clean your hearing aid, change its batteries, and adjust the volume, which is best set at a level high enough that you can hear what you need to but not so high that louder noises are amplified to uncomfortable levels or that electronic "feedback"—a squealing sound—occurs. Some people turn up the gain until the aid squeals and then turn it back a bit, but it is better to adjust it more precisely. In particular, learn how to turn the volume down in case you suddenly come into a very noisy place. If your aid has an adjustment for tone, also learn how to set it properly. Finally, ask your audiologist whether your hearing aid has a telephone setting. Hearing aids with this feature may make using a telephone much easier, if you have the correct kind of telephone.

Sudden loss of hearing requires a doctor's prompt attention, but this doesn't mean that you should ignore hearing loss that occurs more slowly, attributing the situation to "getting older." Although chronic hearing loss usually is not curable, hearing aids enable millions of older persons to hear well and to continue to enjoy the music of life. By working with your doctor and your audiologist, your particular hearing problem can be identified and the correct kind of hearing aid obtained. Recognize the hearing aid for what it is: a tremendous boon to your life.

10

CONSTIPATION AND THE GASTROINTESTINAL SYSTEM

The gastrointestinal (GI) system has two primary functions: it digests food and eliminates waste. When your GI system works properly, you hardly notice it. But if something goes wrong, you can feel miserable. Although the GI system can malfunction at any age, older people commonly suffer from GI problems, most often from constipation. Accordingly, most of this chapter will discuss constipation and how to treat and prevent it. The end of the chapter discusses several other GI problems. Figure 10 depicts the principal components of the GI system, described in some detail in the first part of this chapter.

WHAT IS THE GI SYSTEM?

The GI system is an active pipeline, constantly working to process food into energy. Attached to this long tube are organs, such as the liver and the pancreas, which participate in the digestion of food. Food enters the GI system when you eat, and it emerges as waste when you have a bowel move-

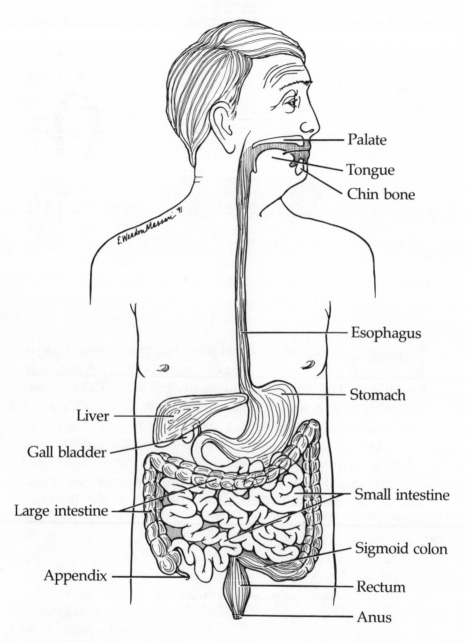

FIGURE 10
The Gastrointestinal System

ment. Along the way, food is ground up and converted into liquid, its nutrients are absorbed into the body, and certain waste products of the body are deposited into the waste food. Finally, the liquid waste is changed back into a semisolid form and eliminated from the body. At any point along this long journey something can go wrong, affecting your health.

Digestion starts in the mouth. There, you chew food and moisten it with saliva, which contains enzymes, chemicals that begin to break down and thus digest what you eat. During the process of swallowing, the coordinated actions of the tongue, the roof of the mouth (the palate), and the cheeks push food into the *esophagus*. Muscles in the wall of the esophagus contract in waves, propelling chewed food into the stomach. The rhythmic movement of the muscles within the esophagus (and throughout the entire GI system) is called *peristalsis*. As I will point out later in this chapter, many GI problems are directly related to interruptions or changes in the speed of the body's peristaltic action.

The *stomach* is a sac with glands in its muscular walls; the muscles grind food, and the glands produce digestive acids and enzymes. The stomach liquifies food, dissolving nutrients and permitting them to be absorbed into the body. The stomach also stores food, passing it on in measured quantities into the next part of the GI system, the small and large intestines.

The names *small* and *large intestines* are somewhat misleading: the small intestine, at more than thirty feet in length, is much longer than the large intestine. However, the diameter of the small intestine is substantially narrower than the diameter of the large intestine, and it is to that measurement that the terms *small* and *large* refer. The functions of the small and large intestines are so complementary that they are often referred to together simply as the intestines. The large intestine is also commonly called the *colon*. Helpful bacteria grow throughout the intestines, aiding in the digestive process. That is one reason why you may experience GI problems when you take antibiotics: the medicine often kills the good bacteria in your intestines as well as the bad ones that are causing sickness elsewhere in your body.

As peristaltic action moves food through the small intestine, the food's acidity is neutralized with bicarbonate and most of its nutrients are absorbed into the body. In the large intestine, water is removed from the mostly digested food, turning the waste into semisolid *feces* or *stool,* and waste products from elsewhere in the body are deposited into the feces.

The last two sections of the large intestine, the *sigmoid colon* and *rectum,* absorb even more water from the stool and store the waste until enough has accumulated to stimulate a bowel movement.

During a bowel movement, several things happen in a coordinated process. As the muscles of the abdominal wall tighten, and thus increase pressure on the colon, peristaltic action forces the feces toward the anus. At just the right moment, a ring of muscles called the *anal sphincter* relaxes, allowing the stool to pass.

Other organs assist in the digestion and absorption of food and are considered part of the GI system. The *liver* produces *bile,* which makes digestible certain components of food, such as fats; the *gallbladder* stores bile until it is needed. The liver also serves other functions: metabolizing drugs, inactivating toxins in the blood, and producing chemicals that are part of the body's blood-clotting system. The *pancreas* produces several digestive enzymes, for example, the insulin needed to digest sugar and bicarbonate for neutralizing stomach acids.

The *parasympathetic nervous system* governs all this activity. It is the system that sets the rate at which food and waste pass through the GI tract and controls the production of the enzymes, acid, and bicarbonate made by the liver, gallbladder, and pancreas. By adjusting the speed of passage (called *transit time*), it also controls the absorption of nutrients, the frequency of bowel movements, and the amount of water passed out with the stool.

NORMAL AGE-RELATED CHANGES IN THE GI SYSTEM

For the most part, the normal age-related changes occurring in the GI system do not themselves cause GI problems.

They do, however, predispose you to such problems when factors like diet, lifestyle, inactivity, medication, or illness come into play. In particular, the parasympathetic nervous system is much more readily slowed down in the elderly, for example, by certain medications. The section on constipation will explain why this is important.

Taste and *smell* work together, allowing you to appreciate the flavor and aroma of foods. Both senses become duller as you grow older. For reasons that are not understood, as you age, you experience a decreased capacity to smell and your tongue loses some of its taste buds. You may notice that some foods you once found flavorful now seem bland. That is because you require nearly twice as much sugar or salt as you did when young to reach the threshold at which your body can sense these tastes. You also may be surprised to discover that some foods taste bitter. Bitter taste predominates over other tastes, such as sweet and sour, as you grow older. These changes in taste and smell do not necessarily lead to health problems. They can, however, influence how you cook and what you eat, and that in turn can affect your health.

The stomach's capacity to produce acid decreases with age. While this decrease does not result—as one might hope—in less frequent development of ulcers or of "sour stomach," it does occasionally lead to incomplete digestion of some foods and alterations in the population of the helpful bacteria that normally live in the small intestine. The net result is that your body may absorb less of some nutrients.

The weight of the *liver* and the blood flow through it decrease by nearly half between ages 25 and 80. Although an octogenarian's liver is sufficient to perform necessary functions under normal conditions, if challenged by something unusual (a poisonous substance, for example), it may not have sufficient reserve to cope. Decreased liver capacity also explains why medications that are inactivated by the liver are metabolized more slowly in the elderly, often leading to higher drug levels in the blood than the same dose causes in a younger person.

The capacity of the *rectum* to store stool increases with age, a disadvantageous development. While it sits in the rectum, the stool becomes dehydrated and hard. If it becomes too dry, the stool can clog the rectum, an uncomfortable condition known as *rectal* or *fecal impaction*. Even when impaction doesn't occur, passing hard, dry stool is uncomfortable and requires excessive straining, which can cause hemorrhoids and diverticulosis (both of which are discussed later).

CONSTIPATION

Constipation is hard to define because people differ: some go to the bathroom several times a day while others do so only a few times each week. Just because you move your bowels infrequently does *not* mean that you are constipated.

Why Does Constipation Develop?

Even though constipation is difficult to define, it is obvious when it occurs. The frequency with which you have bowel movements decreases; it becomes difficult to pass stool—you strain to do so; your stool becomes harder and drier. When constipated, you may experience cramps, lose your appetite, or feel nauseated.

Although constipation is not a normal part of aging, it is common in older people for at least five reasons: age-related changes in the parasympathetic nervous system; medical conditions affecting the intestines; use of medications affecting the GI system; lack of exercise; and a low-fiber diet.

As you get older, your parasympathetic nervous system becomes very sensitive to a variety of influences. If this system becomes inhibited—slowed—your peristaltic action slows down, decreasing the muscular contractions that move food and water through your GI system. The resulting increased transit time allows more water to be absorbed from food and waste as they pass through the colon, in turn making the stool harder and drier. Many factors inhibit the parasympathetic nervous system. For example, a strong emotional state such as depression has such an effect, as do all anticholinergic medications. (Anticholinergic drugs are discussed in chapter 2.)

Many commonly used medications have an anticholinergic effect. If you are taking antihistamines for allergies, an over-the-counter sleeping pill containing diphenhydramine (Benadryl), an antidepressant, an antipsychotic, an antispasmodic, or a muscle relaxant, you are likely to develop constipation unless you act to prevent it.

Certain medical conditions can also cause constipation. For example, *hypothyroidism,* a condition in which the thyroid gland is underactive, slows the function of the intestines. If you do not have a history of constipation but develop it over several weeks or months, your doctor will want to determine, through blood tests, whether you are hypothyroid.

Growths or narrowings in the colon, sometimes called *polyps,* can block the movement of stool. Some polyps are benign and can be removed by simple surgery. Others, unfortunately, may be malignant. Because cancer of the colon, discussed in detail in chapter 11, can be cured if caught early, it is important to determine quickly whether a growth in the colon is cancerous. If you suddenly become constipated, do not jump to the conclusion that you have cancer: colon cancer is one of the least common causes of constipation. However, if the constipation continues for more than a few days and if laxatives, a change in diet, and increased activity do not return you to regularity, promptly mention the change to your doctor.

Any medication that slows the colon, hardens stool, or draws water from the GI system can cause constipation. Medications with anticholinergic side effects (discussed above) and all narcotic painkillers, such as morphine, propoxphene (Darvon, Wygesic), codeine (Tylenol #3, Hicodan), and oxycodone (Percocet, Percodan) constipate because they slow peristaltic action in the colon. Iron supplements, especially if taken more than once a day or in large doses, constipate because they make the stool hard. Diuretics ("water pills"), which remove water from the body, will cause you to urinate more than usual and thus can constipate because they rob water from your stool, making it drier.

One reason why you may be troubled by constipation is a sedentary lifestyle lacking adequate exercise. Exercise stimulates movement in the GI tract and keeps the muscles of the abdomen strong, making it easier to move the bowels. You do not need to climb mountains or run marathons to get enough exercise to keep your GI system in gear; a few minutes of walking, swimming, or other aerobic exercise several times per week may be sufficient.

Lack of exercise is a special problem if illness or injury confines you to bed or if your mobility is otherwise limited. If you can, do some exercise, even if it is only to move between your bed and chair several times a day. If you can't, one of the gentle laxatives, described later in this chapter, may help to prevent constipation until you can become more active.

Bulk, also called *fiber,* is vital to the proper functioning of the intestines and plays an important role in maintaining regularity. Bulk is the part of food that the GI system can't digest. Low-fiber foods are almost entirely digested, leaving little waste or bulk; high-fiber foods leave large amounts of undigested bulk in the colon. Bulk stretches the walls of the colon, stimulating the movement of stool. Bulk also keeps stool soft, making it easier to eliminate.

By increasing your intake of fiber, you may prevent constipation. There is evidence that fiber has the additional benefit of reducing your risk of developing colon cancer, possibly because bulky stool protects the walls of the colon from cancer-inducing substances. A high-bulk diet will also reduce your risk of developing diverticulosis (the formation of pockets in the intestinal wall) and may be helpful to people who suffer from irritable colon, both of which are discussed later in this chapter.

Many foods contain fiber. Unprocessed grains—oat, wheat, and rice bran—are particularly good sources. Certain beans, nuts, and vegetables are high in fiber. Some high-fiber foods are also high in calories, so, if you increase the amount of fiber in your diet, do it carefully. It is not necessarily a step toward better health to gain weight because you increase fiber in your diet! If you need advice, ask your doctor to put you in touch with a dietitian or nutritionist.

Evaluating Constipation

If you experience chronic constipation, develop it suddenly, or if chronic constipation suddenly worsens, discuss the problem with your doctor. Constipation may be relatively harmless; on the other hand, it can be a sign that a serious illness exists. As with any such condition, your doctor will want to evaluate what, if any, treatment is appropriate.

Give your doctor a full history: have you experienced constipation for years; is it a recent development; have there been other changes in your health, medications, diet, or activity associated with the change in your regularity?

If constipation has been with you for a long time, your doctor may recommend nothing more than a change in diet or medication, the use of laxatives, or more exercise. However, if it has suddenly started or worsened, your doctor will want to learn more. Constipation can be a symptom of various diseases and conditions such as colon cancer, an intestinal blockage, or an underactive thyroid. Depending on what your doctor suspects, he or she may want more than a history of the problem and may recommend one of several examinations or tests.

The chief purpose in performing a rectal examination is to detect abnormalities such as hemorrhoids, tumors in the rectum, or blood in the stool. Your doctor will ask you to lie on your side, with your knees bent, and will examine your anus for problems. Wearing a rubber glove and using a lubricant, the doctor will gently insert a finger to feel for problems and to expose a strip of specially treated paper to stool. When developed chemically, this strip will indicate if there is blood in your feces, a warning sign of cancer. Because blood in the stool often cannot be seen, it is called *hidden* or *occult blood*. A rectal exam does not require you to prepare in any way and really is quite painless.

Blood tests are sometimes necessary to diagnose or rule out several medical conditions that can cause constipation. The tests can show, for example, whether the function of your thyroid gland is too low (that is, if you have hypothyroidism) or if the level of calcium in your blood is too high, two causes of constipation. A blood test can also show whether you have anemia, a sign that you might be passing occult blood.

If your doctor suspects that you have an abnormality in your rectum or sigmoid colon, he or she may perform a *sigmoidoscopy* (sigmoid means the lower part of your GI tract, -oscopy means to look around) or send you to a specialist, a *gastroenterologist,* for the test. During a sigmoidoscopy, a *sigmoidoscope,* a thin tube, is inserted into your rectum. Sigmoidoscopes gained a nasty reputation years ago when they were constructed as rigid rods and were often called "proctoscopes." Now, the instrument is a flexible, hollow, fiber-optic tube and causes little discomfort. The doctor looks through the scope to locate any abnormality, such as a growth, and can even take a sample (a biopsy) of any suspicious tissue directly through the scope. Although the GI tract has nerve endings that sense stretching, it lacks the kind of nerves that can sense cuts. You will not experience pain if the doctor snips a sample of tissue.

Although a sigmoidoscopy is no fun, it is not painful, and it can be of enormous help in determining whether you have a serious problem in your lower colon. The worst you may experience from a sigmoidoscopy, even if the doctor takes a tissue sample, is discomfort from the stretching of the muscles around the anus and the stretching of the rectum and sigmoid colon.

To prepare for the sigmoidoscopy, your doctor will ask you to administer an enema just before coming to the office. If you cannot easily give yourself an enema, you will need assistance from a family member, friend, or visiting nurse.

If your doctor suspects that there is a problem in your GI tract beyond the sigmoidoscope's reach or wants a permanent record of the condition of your lower GI tract, he or she may recommend that you have a *barium enema,* also know as a *lower GI* or a *lower GI series.* In the radiologist's office, you will be given an enema containing barium, a liquid which can be seen by x-rays. Using a fluoroscope, a type of x-ray machine, the radiologist will follow and take detailed pictures of the barium as it flows through your colon.

Your entire lower GI tract must be free of stool when you go to the radiologist's office. Usually, your doctor will recommend that you eat only liquid food for one or two days before the test. Additionally, you will need to take a laxative the night before and, immediately before going to the doctor's office, have an enema to cleanse any remaining stool. Again, if this preparation presents difficulties, you will need assistance. Discuss with your doctor well in advance how to prepare and be certain that you understand what you must do. Happily, the most difficult part of a barium enema is preparing for it; the test itself should cause little, if any, discomfort.

Another method for examining the colon is known as a *colonoscopy*. A *colonoscope* is similar to a sigmoidoscope but, because it is longer, it permits the doctor to view the entire length of your large intestine. As with a sigmoidoscope, your doctor can biopsy suspicious tissue directly through the colonoscope. In fact, because the colonoscope is somewhat wider than a sigmoidoscope, it is possible to remove some growths (polyps) entirely through the end of the scope. Thus, a colonoscopy can sometimes cure a GI problem as well as diagnose it.

A colonoscopy is usually performed at a hospital on an outpatient basis. It requires the same type of preparation as does a barium enema, described above. Although the test does not usually cause sharp pain, it can make you feel quite uncomfortable. Accordingly, you may be given sedatives to help you relax during the procedure. In that case, you will be sleepy after the test and will need help getting home. If you are frail, your doctor may recommend that you stay overnight at the hospital to prepare for, or to recuperate from, a colonoscopy.

Laxatives

Laxatives, also called *cathartics,* are medications that help you move your bowels. Even though most laxatives are sold over-the-counter, they are drugs and can cause side effects. Although laxatives are not an acceptable substitute for the proper exercise and good diet needed to keep your digestive system running smoothly, they do, at times, serve an important role.

There are several kinds of laxatives, including softeners,

bulking agents, osmotics, stimulants, oils, and enemas. Some treat constipation; others prevent it. Each has particular advantages and disadvantages. In selecting a laxative, match the right type to your specific need. That is more important than a choice based on a favorite taste or a dazzling television commercial. All laxatives generally work best if you take them with large quantities of water.

Stool softeners, such as dulcosate (Colace), are commonly used in hospitals and nursing homes to prevent constipation in persons confined to bed. They contain a chemical that holds extra water in the stool, making it less dry and hard. They are the gentlest laxatives, are good preventatives, but are not useful in treating constipation once it occurs. Stool softeners can be obtained without prescription for home use.

Because they produce larger, softer stools, *bulk* or *fiber laxatives* are the best medicine for preventing chronic constipation. They are not, however, the best treatment if you are already constipated. Although you can obtain fiber or bulk in the foods you eat, many people find purified bulk such as psyllium (sold under brand names such as Metamucil and Konsyl) more convenient and less fattening. Typically, these products are mixed with water or juice and then drunk. Some people do not mind such mixtures, but others find them unpalatable. As an alternative, there are now effervescent (bubbly) mixtures like Metamucil Effervescent that taste a little better. There also are bulk laxatives, such as Perdiem and Fibermed, which do not need to be mixed with liquid. These products contain bulk that has been pressed into small pellets or cookies that are swallowed or eaten and are then chased down with water or juice. Some bulk laxatives contain large amounts of sugar, added to improve taste; if you have diabetes or are on a sugar-restricted diet, ask your pharmacist to recommend a sugar-free bulk laxative.

Osmotic laxatives provide excellent treatment when you are constipated and can also be used to prevent constipation. Common osmotic laxatives include milk of magnesia and citrate of magnesia (also called Mag Citrate), both of which have been used for many years, and newer over-the-counter medicines, like lactulose and sorbitol. Osmotic laxatives contain special salts or sugars that are neither digested in the intestines nor absorbed into the body but rather attract water to the stool and keep it there. The water produces a softer stool that gently stretches the colon, stimulating the transit of waste. Osmotic laxatives are a good choice for people who have chronic constipation. It is usually best to take them at bedtime so that they can work while you sleep to stimulate a bowel movement in the morning.

Stimulant laxatives, the strongest kind, work by irritating the lining of the intestines, stimulating peristalsis. Prolonged use of stimulant laxatives can lead to an addiction—*laxative abuse*—in which, without these drugs, a normal bowel movement is very difficult to achieve. As a rule of thumb, try not to use stimulant laxatives for more than a few days at a time. Stimulant laxatives are particularly useful if a medical condition requires you to take a constipation medication. For example, if you are recovering from surgery and must use a narcotic painkiller, a stimulant laxative will counteract the constipating action of the narcotic.

The gentlest of the stimulant laxatives are cascara and senna, both of which can be bought over-the-counter at drug and health food stores. Senna makes a pleasant tea. Prunes and prune juice are also gentle stimulant laxatives that combine the effect of an osmotic and a stimulant laxative. Occasionally adding prunes to your daily bran is an excellent way to obtain stimulation. Bisacodyl (Dulcolax), as tablets or suppositories, is stronger; the tablets work overnight while the suppositories will stimulate a bowel movement in just a few hours. Castor oil (Neoloid) is very potent and can cause severe cramping. Use it only under the direction of a doctor and only if you have first tried gentler remedies.

Mineral oil is an unusual stimulant laxative because it also has a lubricating effect on the GI tract. It is, however, the most dangerous laxative, causing severe chemical irritation to the lungs if you accidently inhale it while swallowing. Use mineral oil only under the direction of a doctor, for very severe constipation. Never take it unless you are fully awake and completely able to swallow without difficulty.

TYPES OF LAXATIVES

Type	Examples	Use
STOOL SOFTENERS	Dulcosate (Colace) Pericolace (has a gentle stimulant also)	Prevention
BULKING AGENTS	Bran Psyllium (in Metamucil and Konsyl); Perdiem, which also has a gentle stimulant	Prevention
OSMOTICS	Milk of magnesia Magnesium citrate Sorbitol Lactulose	Prevention & Treatment
STIMULANTS	Bisacodyl (Dulcolax) Cascara Senna Neoloid (castor oil) Phenophthalene (in Ex-Lax)	Prevention, especially from medication-induced constipation, & Treatment
ENEMAS	Fleet brand or home-prepared, with or without soap	Treatment

Impaction

Sometimes constipation occurs because of *impaction*—when too much hard stool accumulates in the rectum, the end part of the colon. Impaction can be particularly uncomfortable and difficult to relieve. If you are impacted and take laxatives orally, food and waste in the upper part of the intestines may move, but the blockage in the rectum may not. This can result in painful cramping without relief of the problem. Thus, enemas are usually the best treatment for impaction.

Although you can use a commercially available enema, such as Fleet brand, it is preferable to prepare the enema yourself with a reusable enema bag, which can be bought at the pharmacy. Because the capacity of the rectum increases as you get older, you generally need a larger volume enema than the commercial brands contain.

When you prepare the enema, start with one to two pints (two to four cups) of tap water that is neither hot nor cold but, rather, neutral to the touch. Try to keep the water inside you for several minutes. It may take several enemas to clear the impaction. If this treatment doesn't work, add a small amount of purified liquid soap (available at the pharmacy) to the enema water. Soap is a gentle stimulant that causes the colon to contract. If it is too difficult for you to prepare and administer the enemas, you will need assistance from a family member, friend, or visiting nurse.

If the impaction does not break up after several enemas, a doctor or a nurse will need to clear the impaction manually. Never attempt manual disimpaction yourself. If you cannot remove the blockage with gentle enemas, call your doctor.

Problems Related to Constipation

If constipation persists for years, it can cause abnormalities in your lower GI tract such as diverticulosis, diverticulitis, and hemorrhoids.

If you strain when moving your bowels, you increase the pressure on the wall of your colon, which can lead to the formation of *diverticula,* small pouches on the walls of the colon. If the diverticula become filled with stool, they stretch, causing you pain and cramping in your abdomen, or bleeding into your stool, a condition called *diverticulosis*. Sometimes the pain is so severe that medication is needed, but narcotics, the strongest pain relievers, themselves cause constipation, which worsens the diverticulosis.

Sometimes diverticula become infected, a condition called *diverticulitis*—a serious problem causing fevers and pain. Usually, diverticulitis must be treated with intravenous antibiotics administered in the hospital. Until the infection is controlled, it is not safe to eat, so you will receive nutrition and fluids intravenously. Rarely, an abdominal abscess can form around one of the infected pouches, requiring surgery to drain the abscess.

Preventing diverticular disease is much easier than treating it, and eating a high-fiber diet or regularly using bulk laxatives are the best preventive measures. Once you have developed the symptoms, a change in diet is necessary but not sufficient to cure the problem. If you suffer from diverticulosis or diverticulitis or think you may, you must be under the care of a doctor.

Straining also tends to make the blood vessels in the anus bulge and dilate. These enlarged veins are called *hemorrhoids,* and as any sufferer will tell you, hemorrhoids can hurt, itch, and bleed. If the hemorrhoids are mild, you should be able to treat them yourself; more serious or long-lasting hemorrhoids need medical or surgical care.

If you develop hemorrhoids, use a stool softener or bulk laxative to decrease the amount of straining necessary to pass stool. The less the strain, the greater the chance that your hemorrhoids will heal and not recur.

Warm soaks are essential to the treatment of hemorrhoids because they relieve the pain and itching and increase blood flow, fostering quicker healing. Soaks also keep the area clean so that infections are less likely to occur. A *sitz bath* is one good way to accomplish warm soaks. Fill a tub with six inches of hot water and squat (do not sit) in the water for five or ten minutes. Repeat the sitz baths two to four times a day. If you cannot get in and out of a tub safely, use a special soaking basin, available at the pharmacy, that fits into a toilet seat.

Medications known as topical steroids can also be helpful. They are available at the pharmacy without a prescription, either in a tube (for example, a hydrocortisone cream) or as a suppository (for example, Anusol-HC). The creams are applied directly onto the hemorrhoids; the suppositories are inserted into the rectum.

If these simple treatments do not help, if a hemorrhoid becomes infected, or if the condition is chronic, your doctor may prescribe a stronger steroid or may recommend simple surgery. Surgical removal of hemorrhoids usually is done under local anesthetic without an overnight stay in the hospital. However, following surgery, your doctor may recommend a pain medication. Because of the sedating effect of such medicines and the pain you may experience, you should not drive after the procedure. Further, you may need assistance at home for a day or two. Of course, if the pain medicine is a narcotic, remember that it will have the unwanted side effect of causing constipation, the last thing you want following hemorrhoid surgery! Here is one of the occasions when a stimulant laxative is appropriate: use them for the day or two that you are taking the narcotic.

Although advertisements would have you believe that every older person suffers from constipation, it is not an inevitable part of growing old, and laxatives need not—indeed, should not—become a standard part of your life. With a sensible diet, rich in fiber, and a regular program of exercise, you should be able to maintain regularity. But if medication or illness confines you to bed and constipation does occur, choose your laxative carefully and be mindful of the complications it may cause.

GI PROBLEMS UNRELATED TO CONSTIPATION

The Esophagus

The *esophagus* is the tube that connects your mouth to your stomach. You will feel pain if anything irritates or stretches your esophagus. For example, if the contents of the stomach flow back into the esophagus, a condition known as *reflux* or *regurgitation,* you will feel a burning pain in the chest or throat that usually passes as soon as the esophagus clears. Food sticking in the esophagus or gas distending it can trigger chest pressure similar to the chest pain caused by a heart problem. If you are not absolutely sure that the chest pain you are experiencing is from your GI system, seek medical attention immediately.

If the esophagus does not contract properly, it will not move food smoothly from mouth to stomach and you will feel an uncomfortable sensation of fullness and pressure, called *dysphagia* (dys- means "abnormal" and -phagia refers to swallowing). When no other cause can be found for abnormal contractions of the esophagus, the condition is sometimes called *presbyesophagus* (presby- means "old"), a term I dislike because it has little meaning. The condition is not a normal part of aging, and the name does not explain why it develops. In fact, doctors don't understand what causes the problem; they can only suggest ways to deal with it. The recommendations are obvious: eat slowly, chew food well, moisten it with plenty of water, and avoid anticholinergic medications (discussed in chapter 2), which slow the muscular contractions in the esophagus.

Blockages in the esophagus also can cause pain when you swallow. For example, a *Schatski's ring*—that is, a localized area of narrowing—can block the proper passage of food. Or, a pouch, called a *Zenker's diverticulum,* can form in the wall of the esophagus, trapping food. Sometimes, a part of the esophagus loses the ability to contract, a problem called *achalasia,* preventing food from passing properly through that section. All of these problems are easy to diagnose and are usually treated successfully without surgery. Unfortunately, sometimes esophageal cancer causes the blockage.

By the time *esophageal cancer* causes the symptoms of blockage, it is usually advanced, having already grown deeply into the tissues in and around the esophagus. If discovered early, esophageal cancer can sometimes be cured with surgery. Later stages of the disease may be treated with radiation therapy and chemotherapy but, sadly, a cure is rare.

The Stomach

The *stomach lining* is uniquely suited to withstand harsh acids and enzymes. It protects the muscles of the stomach, which would otherwise be easily damaged by exposure to stomach contents. If the lining becomes damaged, however, you may experience symptoms of burning pain in the upper stomach or lower chest, nausea, or loss of appetite. Eating may reduce or eliminate the pain, because food buffers stomach acids, but relief is temporary, the pain returning shortly after eating.

If the irritation of the lining remains superficial, the problem is called *gastritis* (gastr- refers to the stomach and -itis means "inflammation" or "irritation"). However, if the irritation develops into an erosion deep into the lining, it is an *ulcer* or a *peptic ulcer* (peptic also means "stomach"). Ulcers are generally more serious than gastritis and take longer to heal.

Both ulcers and gastritis may bleed, and blood in the GI system that comes from the stomach may cause black stools, called *melena*. Sometimes an ulcer becomes so deep that it erodes through the stomach wall, a medical emergency called a *perforated ulcer*. Since both gastritis and ulcers have many similar symptoms, I will discuss them together.

Many medications—aspirin, nonsteroidal antiinflammatory drugs (NSAIDs) such as ibuprofen (Motrin, Advil), and steroids (such as prednisone)—often irritate the stomach lining. Stress stimulates your stomach to produce higher amounts of acid and may also cause gastritis and ulcers. Experiencing a serious medical illness is stressful, which is why some people develop ulcers when they are sick. Gastritis and ulcers often occur without any identifiable cause. Although spicy foods may upset your stomach, there is no evidence that eating them causes ulcers.

If you have symptoms of gastritis or an ulcer, see your doctor. After asking you about the problem, your doctor will examine your abdomen to see if it is tender and will do a rectal examination to test your stool for occult blood. If your symptoms warrant it, your doctor may suggest one of two types of study, an *upper GI* or a *gastroscopy* (discussed later), to evaluate the exact nature and extent of the problem. Unless the problem is severe, I do not usually recommend either of these tests until after my patients have tried to treat the problem for several weeks.

The first step in treating gastritis and ulcers is to determine what is causing them. For example, if you suspect that a medication is the cause, ask your doctor if the medication can be stopped or an alternative medicine substituted. If the cause is stress, discuss with your doctor ways to reduce stress.

Sometimes short-term counseling with a psychologist or social worker is very helpful.

In the process of identifying and eliminating the root cause, your doctor may recommend a medication to promote the healing of your stomach lining. There are four types of medications to consider: medications that neutralize stomach acid; medications that stop the stomach from producing acid; medications that coat the ulcer; and prostaglandin inhibitors.

Antacids are the oldest and safest treatments for gastritis and ulcers, and they work very well. Antacids are mineral salts, usually containing magnesium, aluminum, or calcium, that neutralize stomach acid. Since they do not prevent acid production but merely neutralize the acid that is produced, they must be taken frequently, generally every few hours. However, since food also buffers stomach acids, it is not necessary to take antacids at mealtimes. Your doctor will probably recommend that you take antacids every two to three hours between meals. Antacids containing magnesium (such as Mylanta and Maalox) tend to cause diarrhea; antacids containing aluminum (such as Alternagel and Amphojel) tend to cause constipation. You may want to alternate between the two types or take a brand that contains both magnesium and aluminum. (The active ingredients will be listed on the outside of the container.) Be aware that antacids containing bicarbonate, such as Alka-Seltzer and Briosche, are rich in salt (sodium) and, if taken often, can raise the bicarbonate level in your blood. You will probably need to take the antacids for six weeks.

Another approach to treating ulcers is to reduce acid production in the stomach. Although this goal used to be achieved surgically, it is now accomplished by using medicines that short-circuit the system responsible for acid production, a system of histamine receptors. Drugs known as *histamine-2 blockers,* such as cimetidine (Tagamet), rantitidine (Zantac), and famotadine (Pepsid), reduce acid production and allow ulcers to heal. (Histamine-2 blockers differ from the antihistamines used to treat allergies and colds.) Although histamine-2 blockers are effective and more convenient than antacids, since you take them only once or twice a day, they do have more side effects, interacting with other drugs and sometimes causing mental confusion.

Newer medications, such as omeprazole (Losec), are even more potent in blocking acid production. They prevent acid secretion through a different mechanism than blocking histamine. Omeprazole is powerful, but its safety in the elderly has not yet been adequately established.

Although doctors disagree on the best way to use histamine-2 blockers and omeprazole, I feel that older people should take them for no longer than six weeks and only if an ulcer is serious, does not respond to antacid therapy, or if you cannot take antacids frequently.

Sucralfate (Carafte) coats the stomach and protects its lining. It is neither an antacid nor a histamine-2 blocker; rather, it works by directly protecting irritated surfaces. Sucralfate is effective and appears to have few side effects, although it tends to cause constipation.

Misoprostal (Cytotec) is a new medication known as a *prostaglandin inhibitor*. It interacts with the chemicals in the stomach that play a role in the formation of ulcers. Misoprostal may be particularly useful in preventing ulcers and gastritis caused by the use of nonsteroidal antiinflammatory drugs (NSAIDs). Although misoprostal appears to be relatively safe in younger adults, it commonly causes nausea and diarrhea, and we don't yet fully know its side effects in the elderly.

If these treatments fail to cure the problem, your doctor may recommend further studies to determine the seriousness of the situation. The two most common tests are an upper GI series and a gastroscopy.

An *upper GI series* refers to a series of x-rays taken of your stomach and small intestine. The procedure is performed at a radiologist's or a gastroenterologist's office. You will be asked to drink a liquid containing barium, a substance that shows up under x-ray. The doctor or a technician will then take x-rays of your stomach. Ulcers will fill with the barium and thus show up on the x-ray. Other than fasting overnight before the test, there is no particular preparation necessary for an upper GI. Because barium is constipating, drink plenty of water after the test and take an osmotic laxative such as milk of magnesia to help your body pass the barium. Do not be concerned if your stool turns white: that is normal after drinking barium.

Alternatively, your doctor may recommend a *gastroscopy,* a procedure in which the doctor passes a flexible tube (a gastroscope) through your mouth and into your stomach. To make the test less uncomfortable, your doctor will first numb the back of your throat with an anesthetic spray. This study is more expensive (and more uncomfortable) than an upper GI series but has several advantages. Through the gastroscope, your doctor can study the lining of your stomach in great detail. If there is any suspicion that an ulcer might be cancerous, he or she can perform a biopsy directly through the scope. Just as with a biopsy taken during a sigmoidoscopy or colonoscopy, described earlier, you will feel no pain from a biopsy performed during a gastroscopy. As with an upper GI, there are no preparations for a gastroscopy other than fasting for twelve hours before the test.

Despite the fact that these two tests are relatively safe and painless, most people with symptoms of gastritis or ulcers need not have either one. Most often, a few days or weeks of treatment with antacids or other medications will make the problem go away. These tests are recommended only if symptoms persist or if you continue to have occult blood in your stool.

Older people can experience all of the GI problems that younger people do and several that usually occur only later in life. Fortunately, most GI problems that you may develop will not be serious. However, because GI cancers occur more commonly in the elderly and are best treated if discovered early, consult your doctor whenever you notice a change in the way your GI system is working. Remember that pain in the stomach or chest, blood in the stool, or black stools are never normal. If they occur, bring the symptom to your doctor's attention promptly.

If you didn't have problems with your GI system when you were younger, you shouldn't expect to develop them now. If you eat a diet that is rich in fiber and keep yourself on a program of regular exercise, you need not fear that age itself will bring with it new and unexpected GI problems.

11

CANCER

C ancer is often associated with old age, but to persons of all ages, the disease is frightening, conjuring up visions of suffering and death. The topic is not cheerful. Although many cancers can now be treated and some can even be cured, others cannot.

The good news about treating cancer is for those who are careful (or lucky) enough to discover it early. As you will learn in this chapter, cancer, if detected early, is often curable. You must know the warning signs of cancer and what your role should be in checking for these signs.

WHAT IS CANCER?

Normal cells obey strict rules of behavior. For reasons that we do not fully understand, cancer cells become transformed and violate those rules. They grow too quickly, do not stop growing when they should, divide too often and thus produce more and more cancerous cells, spread to distant parts of the body, consume large amounts of the body's energy, and produce toxic substances.

184

Carcinoma and Sarcoma

Doctors often speak of two distinct types of cancer: carcinoma and sarcoma. *Carcinoma* starts in the glands and surface tissues of the body. Breast, colon, prostate, and skin cancers are examples of carcinoma. *Sarcoma* starts in connective tissues such as bone, muscle, and cartilage. Cancer of the lymph glands, called *lymphoma,* is a form of sarcoma. Carcinomas are much more common than sarcomas.

Why Older People Get Cancer More Often

There are probably many reasons why normal cells become cancerous. Certain substances called *carcinogens*—toxic chemicals, radiation, viruses, and even chronic irritation—alter normal cells. For two reasons, most of these alterations do not lead to cancer. First, the changes tend to kill cells rather than make them cancerous. Second, when cells do become cancerous, your body usually recognizes and destroys them before they can grow and cause harm. Unfortunately, your body's immune system is not fool-proof, and when it fails, cancerous cells can grow.

Why then are you more likely to develop cancer than a younger person? First, you have experienced longer exposure to many carcinogens. Some carcinogens do their damage slowly; the changes they induce do not lead to cancer for years or even decades. Second, some cancers grow very slowly at first, taking many years before they become large enough to cause problems. Thus, it is not until later life that they are recognized. Finally, there is evidence that your immune system becomes less capable of recognizing and destroying cancer cells as you get older. Therefore, if cancer cells form, your body is less able to recognize and destroy them, allowing them to grow.

DISCOVERING CANCER EARLY

At first, cancerous cells grow in a clump within normal tissue. This growth is often called a *tumor.* Not all tumors are cancerous, however. Cancerous tumors are called *malignant tumors,* and noncancerous ones are called *benign tumors.* With time, the cancer enlarges into adjacent tissues, destroying and replacing the normal cells. Eventually, it enters the blood vessels and lymphatic system and then spreads *(metastasizes)* to other, often distant parts of your body. The distant cancerous growths are called *metastases,* and in time they too will grow, destroy and supplant healthy tissue, and spread.

In its earliest stages, cancer is a localized problem: remove the tumor and the problem is gone. If your cancer is discovered early, a surgeon may be able to remove all of it and cure you. Obviously, this kind of cure is what we all hope for, and that is why it is critical to discover cancer early. However, once metastases have occurred, the problem is no longer local, and, sadly, local treatment will not cure it.

If your doctor discovers that you have cancer, he or she will want to determine its stage—how big it has grown and whether it has spread. This is not always an easy task: metastases may be very tiny at first and can't always be detected, even with the most sophisticated tests and equipment. Blood tests, scans, examination of the cancerous tissue under a microscope, and your physical examination all provide your doctor with clues, but do not always permit a correct determination.

SCREENING FOR CANCER

Usually your doctor recommends a physical examination or laboratory test to confirm or exclude the existence of some disease. These examinations and tests are called *diagnostic tests.* However, even if your doctor has no particular reason to suspect that you have a disease, he or she may recommend *screening tests,* which help us as doctors to discover problems early, before symptoms occur. For some diseases—degenerative arthritis, for example—there is no particular advantage in early detection because treatment need not be started until symptoms occur. But for cancer, early detection—discovering the cancer before symptoms develop—is the goal.

Unfortunately, very few laboratory tests are appropriate or useful in screening for cancer even though they may be excellent diagnostic tests. If a test is too risky or uncomfortable, it should not be used to screen for cancer. If a test is too sensitive, it may generate positive results when you do not have cancer, making you undergo further testing that could be harmful.

Examination by Your Doctor

During your regular physical examination your doctor will check for signs of cancer. In particular, if you are a man, your doctor will screen for prostate cancer (discussed later in this chapter). He or she will gently insert a gloved, lubricated finger into your rectum to feel for nodules in the prostate gland. If you are a woman, your doctor will carefully examine your breasts for lumps or nodules, a screening test for breast cancer. Your doctor should also teach you how to examine your own breasts, and you should do so every month. Your doctor will also perform a pelvic examination to examine your ovaries and uterus and perform a Pap smear to screen for cervical cancer.

Younger women should have a Pap test every year, but many older women do not need it so often. If you have not had yearly Pap smears or if you have had abnormal ones, you should have one every year. Otherwise, having a Pap smear every three to five years is probably sufficient.

In both men and women, colon cancer often causes small amounts of blood to escape into your stool. You can't see this blood, but your doctor can test for it. He or she may do this by performing a rectal examination or by giving you several small stool-testing kits to use at home, which you then return to the doctor for analysis.

Your doctor and your dentist should carefully examine the membranes of your mouth and throat, looking for signs of oral cancer, a problem discussed in detail in chapter 7. If you wear dentures, be certain that your dentist and doctor examine the tissues under your dentures.

Your doctor should examine your skin for growths that

might be cancerous. Although most skin cancers occur on the surfaces exposed to the sun, such as the head, face, and shoulders, your doctor should examine all of your skin. If your doctor finds a suspicious growth, he or she can perform a biopsy or recommend that you see a dermatologist. Skin cancer is discussed in detail in chapter 6.

Laboratory Tests

Your doctor may recommend laboratory tests to screen for cancer. One important screening test for women is *mammography,* an x-ray of the breast. It uses extremely small doses of radiation, poses very little risk, and can detect breast cancers while they are still too tiny to feel. If you are a woman between the ages of 65 and 75, you should have a mammogram every year. Experts disagree on how often women over the age of 75 should have mammograms. If you or any woman in your family has ever had breast cancer, your risk of developing breast cancer increases, and you should continue to have a mammogram every year; if not, every second year may be often enough. Currently, Medicare pays for screening mammograms only every two years.

A second test often recommended to screen for cancer is the *sigmoidoscopy,* an examination of the lower part of the intestines that can detect colon cancer. A sigmoidoscope is a flexible tube that allows your doctor to see if you have polyps or other growths that may indicate cancer. (Sigmoidoscopies are described in detail in chapter 10). Many doctors feel that this test should be performed every few years, while others feel that the discomfort and cost associated with sigmoidoscopies make it a poor screening test. If you have had polyps or a previous colon cancer, or if others in your family have had colon cancer, you should have a sigmoidoscopy every year or two.

Considerable research has demonstrated that *chest x-rays* are not useful in screening for lung cancer. The test doesn't reveal lung cancer in its earliest stages, delivers a dose of radiation, which, although small, is not necessary given the information provided, and is expensive. Chest x-rays are useful for many purposes (as in diagnosing pneumonia) but not as a screening test for lung cancer.

Recently, several new blood tests have been proposed as useful screening tests for cancer. To date, most of these have not turned out to be very good. For the moment, I recommend none of them.

Early Warning Signs of Cancer

You must be aware of the early warning signs of cancer. If you spot one, don't panic. Call your doctor. Much more often than not, your doctor will find that you are well, and together you and your doctor can decide whether anything more needs to be done to assure that you do not have cancer.

Cancer and myriad other illnesses (including the common cold) can cause very vague symptoms, such as fatigue, nausea, loss of appetite, sudden sweats, and weight loss. Cancer can also cause specific symptoms. For example, if you develop a new growth, sore, or black spot on your skin that does not go away in a few weeks, ask your doctor to look at it—it might be skin cancer. If you develop a sore or change of color in a localized area of your mouth, have your doctor or dentist examine it to rule out oral cancer. Blood in your stool may be a warning sign of colon cancer, and a cough, shortness of breath, or a hoarseness to your voice that persists for several weeks or more may be signs of lung cancer. If you notice a lump in your breast, have your doctor feel it and schedule a mammogram. If you develop pain in your stomach that is not cured with antacids, ask your doctor if you need further treatment or tests.

Throughout this chapter you will learn more about the specific early-warning signs of several types of cancer. Don't be obsessed by them, but do be aware of the signals your body gives you.

Treatment of Cancer

The effort to find a cure for cancer remains far from its goal. Although doctors can slow the growth of many cancers and cure some, effective treatment for others still eludes us. The type of cancer, where in the body it is growing, and the extent to which it has grown and spread are all factors that determine the success of treatment.

Understanding the Goal of Treatment

Sometimes the goal of treatment is to remove or kill all of the cancer so that you can be cured. When that isn't possible, your doctor may recommend *palliation,* an attempt to reduce the size or slow the growth of the cancer. Unfortunately, doctors don't always communicate clearly or honestly whether the treatment they recommend is likely to cure or only to palliate. It is up to you to ask whether the proposed treatments have a probability of a cure for you or whether they can only delay the onset of debilitating symptoms and, ultimately, death.

Knowing the goal of treatment will allow you to decide what kinds of therapy you are willing to accept. All cancer treatments cause side effects, many of which are extremely unpleasant, and treatment requires you to spend time at the doctor's office or in the hospital. If the chance of cure is high, you may be willing to tolerate certain side effects and time in the hospital. If there is little chance of cure, you may choose to avoid time-consuming therapy with debilitating side effects. If palliation can delay the onset of symptoms and prolong your life for many months or years, it may be worth it. If, on the other hand, the treatment is likely to have only a brief effect, you may not be as inclined to go forward with it. A diagnosis of cancer is very frightening, and it is difficult to make careful decisions when you are scared. But the decisions to undergo treatment and which form of treatment to choose are crucial.

Cancer Specialists—Oncologists

If you develop cancer, your primary-care doctor probably will refer you to an *oncologist,* a doctor who specializes in cancer treatment. I recommend that most persons with cancer obtain opinions about treatment from two oncologists, because cancer doctors differ widely in what they recommend. Some are very aggressive, recommending treatment that causes severe side effects even when there is only a small hope of curing or slowing the cancer. Others won't recommend those treatments unless there is a realistic chance of substantial benefit. Some oncologists provide experimental treatments that might be beneficial but whose effectiveness and side effects are still under study. By obtaining two opinions, you will have a better idea of what is available. After consulting the oncologists, discuss your thoughts and the specialists' recommendations with your primary-care doctor and with your family or others close to you.

Deciding About Treatment

Just as your doctors differ in their recommendations, each cancer patient differs in what he or she is willing to undergo for the chance to be cured or to live longer. A diagnosis of cancer forces you to think about such things, to discuss them with your family and loved ones, and to talk about them with your doctors. If you don't reach a decision about these difficult issues, other people may make the choices for you.

Decisions like these are complicated, and it is very important that you have as much information as possible. Ask your doctors to explain the extent of your cancer and the options available to you. Ask them to explain the advantages and disadvantages of each type of treatment and how likely each is to cure you, make you feel better, or prolong your life. They should also tell you if the treatment itself will make you feel worse and, if so, in what ways and for how long. Your role is to explain to your doctors what you want and what you don't want. Together, you can plan the treatment that is best for you.

There are three different types of treatment for cancer: *surgery, radiation therapy,* and *chemotherapy.* Sometimes only one of these modalities, as they are called, will be recommended, but often several may be used. Each has certain advantages and disadvantages.

Surgery for Cancer

The best way to treat cancer is to remove all of it from your body, and that is the goal of surgery. Unfortunately, surgery can't always accomplish that goal. If, however, the cancer has not spread and is in a place that a surgeon can reach without damaging vital organs, surgery can often effect a cure.

For example, if you have a cancer growing in your lung, your doctors will perform tests to help determine, as closely as possible, its exact position, the extent of its growth, and whether it has metastasized. They will then measure how well your lungs function to determine whether you can survive if a portion of one lung is removed. If the results of all these tests are hopeful, the surgeon will likely recommend an operation to remove the cancer. If, however, the tumor has grown too close to your heart, if it has grown too large, if it has already spread to other parts of your body, or if the function of your lungs has been seriously compromised by other diseases, your doctors will not recommend surgery.

Even when a cure is not possible, surgery may be helpful. For example, a cancerous tumor in the colon may grow so large that it blocks the passage of stool, causing pain, nausea, inability to eat, and bleeding. Even if colon cancer has already spread to other parts of your body, an operation to alleviate the blockage is likely to make you feel better and may be worthwhile.

Radiation Therapy

Radiation is a form of energy that destroys all tissues; however, cells that grow rapidly are most susceptible to its effects. Since cancerous tissue grows much more quickly than normal, radiation can destroy cancer cells while having considerably less effect on normal tissues. In addition, radiation therapists can focus a beam of radiation directly on cancer tissue, doing their best to protect healthy tissue. These efforts concentrate the radiation's effects on the cancer and minimize its effects on healthy cells.

Not all cancers can be reached easily with beams of radiation without harming other tissues. If the cancer is close to the surface of your body, beaming the radiation is easier. If the cancer is deep, it may not be possible to treat it with radiation. Radiation therapists sometimes use creative methods to get radiation to a cancer without harming healthy tissues.

One such approach uses *radioactive implants,* tiny beads of radioactive material that your surgeon and radiation therapist place directly into the cancerous growth. After the beads have had time to kill the cancer, they are removed. Such implants are sometimes used to treat prostate cancer.

Radiation therapy does, however, cause side effects. You may have nausea and vomiting and feel weak and tired after each treatment. You may have to travel to the treatment center every day, tiring you even more. However, many people tolerate radiation therapy with little discomfort and do not find the treatments burdensome.

Radiation therapy may be used to cure your cancer or to reduce its size and slow its growth. In an attempt to cure cancer, it is often used together with other forms of treatment. For example, radiation is sometimes used before surgery to reduce the size of a tumor or after surgery to destroy any bits of cancer that may have escaped the surgeon. When used as the sole form of treatment, radiation therapy is often a palliative measure and not intended as a cure.

Chemotherapy

Because of the peculiar properties of cancer cells, some medications can destroy them while having less toxic effects on healthy cells. Medications that kill cancer are called *chemotherapeutic agents,* and the course of treatment with such drugs is called *chemotherapy.* Often, doctors combine several chemotherapeutic agents to increase their effectiveness in killing cancer cells while trying to minimize their effects on healthy cells, a process known as *combination chemotherapy.*

Chemotherapy has dramatically changed the extent to which doctors can treat cancer. Through careful research, oncologists have developed combinations of chemotherapy that can be very effective. However, chemotherapy doesn't always succeed, and many cancers don't respond to it. In addition, chemotherapy always poisons healthy tissue, often causing serious side effects that many people are not willing or able to bear.

It is not possible to describe the many successes of chemotherapy in this book. However, it is important to mention a few. For example, both breast and prostate cancer can now be treated with chemotherapy based on the use of hormones. Some kinds of leukemia can be treated remarkably well with combination chemotherapy, and the growth of one kind of lung cancer (called *oat cell*) can be slowed dramatically with chemotherapy even after it has spread throughout the body. A frank discussion with your oncologists and primary-care doctor will help you determine whether chemotherapy is likely to have a major or minor effect on your cancer and your comfort.

If the Cancer Cannot Be Cured

Many people ask, "What will happen if my cancer cannot be cured or if I'm not willing to undergo the recommended treatment?" The question arises not just from a fear of dying but from a fear of suffering. Death from cancer is rarely swift, and most of us dread the prospect of prolonged pain, illness, and debilitation. Even if your cancer can't be cured, don't lose hope. Doctors can control pain and do a great deal to reduce suffering.

In order to provide you with the care you want, your doctors must know your wishes. Do you want to forge ahead with treatments even when the outlook is bleak? Are you willing to forgo the possibility of living a few days or weeks longer in order to avoid the pain and discomfort caused by some treatments? You must tell your doctors what you want. In chapter 19 you will learn about what are called *advance medical directives* such as living wills and durable powers of attorney for health care (DPAHC). If you have cancer, it is critically important to complete these documents. They record your instructions about what you want done if you have an incurable disease, and allow you to name someone to speak for you if you become incapacitated. Completing these forms and sending copies of them to each of your doctors is necessary but not enough. You must also discuss your wishes with your doctor first. If he or she isn't comfortable following your instructions, find a doctor who is.

Of all the hardships of cancer, most people are concerned about *pain*. Pain can almost always be controlled by drugs. Usually the drugs work effectively when taken by mouth, but if need be, a special pump can be set up to deliver larger doses of the pain medication to you intravenously. If you have cancer and need pain medications, you need not fear becoming addicted to them. If your pain subsides, you will be able to stop taking the medications. Specialists use other helpful techniques to control pain in severe situations, including hypnosis, injecting or cutting nerves so that they do not sense pain, and using electrical stimulators that block the transmission of painful sensations.

Often, doctors can also use medications to control the *nausea* caused by some treatments (or by the cancer itself). If the standard medications prove ineffective, your doctor may prescribe a derivative of marijuana. This medication is entirely legal and is often very effective. It may even stimulate your appetite, which is frequently diminished by cancer. Again, don't fear addiction; if you need this medication, use it.

Cancer treatments can exhaust you, in which case you'll need extra help or additional care. You can get that assistance in your own home or in a nursing home, hospice, or hospital. Home care can provide nurses, equipment, and nurses' aides. Alternatively, you may choose to obtain your care in a nursing home. If your cancer cannot be cured, hospice services may provide the best care, since a hospice's goal is to provide comfort to dying persons. Hospice workers may be available to come to your own home, or you may prefer an inpatient hospice service. If you need more intensive nursing and medical attention than any of these sites can provide, you may need to be hospitalized. Discuss all these options with your doctor, who should be able to refer you to a social worker to determine which of these services are covered by your medical insurance and are available in your area.

COMMON CANCERS OF LATE LIFE

Cancer can arise anywhere in the body but is much more common in some tissues than in others. For example, cancer rarely occurs in muscle but often occurs in the skin. In older people, cancer occurs most commonly in the skin, breast, prostate, lung, and colon.

Skin Cancer

Skin cancer is by far the most common kind of cancer. Happily, it rarely causes death or even serious illness and can almost always be cured. Skin cancer differs in many important respects from other cancers and is discussed in detail in chapter 6.

Breast Cancer

After skin cancer, breast cancer is the most common cancer in women of all ages: each year, 50,000 American women over age 65 are found to have breast cancer. Women who discover their breast cancer early can frequently be cured, but a complete cure is rarely likely in those who discover it at a later stage. The best way to survive breast cancer is to find and treat it early. Frequent examinations of your breasts, yearly examinations by your doctor, and periodic mammograms are essential.

Breast cancer grows initially as a small, firm nodule or lump within the breast. You or your doctor may be able to feel the lump. A *mammogram* will provide further clues as to whether the lump is cancerous, but most lumps should be biopsied to be sure. A breast biopsy is a simple procedure usually done with local anesthesia, often in the office of a surgeon specializing in breast cancer.

Untreated breast cancer spreads quickly because the breast has a rich network of lymphatics throughout which the cancer spreads. (The lymphatics are a system of tubes and nodes that drain fluid from many tissues of the body.) After moving into the lymphatics in the breasts, the cancer can reach the armpit and then spread throughout the body to the bones, brain, and lungs.

If discovered at an early stage, a surgeon may be able to remove all of a breast cancer and cure you. A limited operation to remove only the tumor, called a *lumpectomy*, may be possible, although the surgeon will likely also remove lymph nodes to be sure that the cancer has not spread. If the cancer has grown large or spread locally, a more extensive operation, called a *mastectomy*, which removes the entire breast, is needed to eliminate all of the cancer. A *radical mastectomy* is even more extensive, involving removal of not only the breast but also part of its underlying muscle. This operation is rarely performed today and is reserved for unusual circumstances. Before undergoing any operation for breast cancer, discuss with your surgeon which operation is planned and why it is being recommended.

In addition to surgery, your doctors may recommend radiation therapy, which can often kill the small amounts of cancer that the surgeon cannot remove. Radiation therapy can also be helpful in treating the skin ulcerations that sometimes occur with breast cancer.

Several different kinds of chemotherapy are used to treat breast cancer. The most common is hormonal treatment, usually with tamoxifen (Nolvadex). Many breast cancers grow more quickly when exposed to estrogen, a naturally occurring female hormone, and some breast cancers require estrogen to grow. Tamoxifen blocks the action of estrogen, thereby slowing or even destroying the breast cancer cells. Fortunately, tamoxifen causes far fewer and less severe side effects than do most other chemotherapies. More potent chemotherapy is available to treat breast cancer that has metastasized. Unfortunately, these medications are rarely successful in curing the disease once it has spread, and they cause serious side effects.

When discovered early, breast cancer is curable, but finding it early requires vigilance. Examine your breasts every month and get to the doctor quickly if you feel or see anything out of the ordinary. If you don't know how to examine your breasts, ask your doctor or your doctor's nurse to teach you. Be certain to have mammograms regularly—yearly or every other year. With careful, frequent self-examinations of your breasts and periodic mammograms, you'll be doing everything possible to detect breast cancer when it is most treatable.

Prostate Cancer

The prostate gland, found only in men, produces the fluid in semen. The gland is located just behind the base of the penis; it extends up to the bladder and surrounds the uretha, the tube through which urine passes out of the bladder. (See Figure 12, in chapter 16, which shows where the prostate is located.) In older men, cancer of the prostate is the most common cancer, after skin cancer.

Prostate cancer grows very slowly, usually causing no symptoms until it has metastasized. Like breast cancer, prostate cancer in its early stages is curable, but often it isn't detected until after it has spread, at which point it is difficult, if not impossible, to cure.

Prostate cancer forms a nodule in the otherwise smooth surface of the gland. The nodule can be detected during a rectal exam when your doctor feels your prostate by inserting a finger into your rectum. Although some people find it embarrassing or uncomfortable, you should have this extremely important and simple screening test every year.

If your doctor finds a nodule in your prostate, he or she will refer you to a *urologist,* a doctor who specializes in the urinary tract system, penis, and prostate. Blood tests will help determine if the nodule is cancerous, but the urologist will perform a biopsy to be certain. A prostate biopsy, a safe procedure that rarely causes much pain, is usually performed in an outpatient surgical suite, using local anesthesia.

If the nodule is cancerous, your doctors will try to determine whether the cancer has metastasized. Blood tests, an ultrasound (an examination performed using sound waves), a CAT scan, and a bone scan (because prostate cancer usually metastasizes to bones) may be necessary. If your doctors are reasonably sure that your cancer has not spread, the urologist can perform a *prostatectomy,* an operation in which the prostate gland is removed. This operation can cure you if the cancer has not yet metastasized.

Many people know about the *transurethral prostatectomy (TURP)*, used to treat noncancerous enlargement of the prostate (described in chapter 17). The kind of prostatectomy used to treat prostate cancer is a much more extensive operation because, unlike the TURP, it must remove all of the prostate. One of the unfortunate complications of this operation is that it almost always causes impotence, although newer surgical techniques are better at preserving sexual function. If you are sexually active, tell your doctor so and have your surgery performed by a urologist familiar with these newer techniques. Radiation therapy, particularly radioactive implants, may also be useful in treating prostate cancer and is usually done in conjunction with surgery.

Prostate cancer can spread to many parts of the body, most often to the bones. After it has metastasized, a cure is generally not possible. Prostate cancer grows slowly, so that even if it has spread, it may not cause symptoms for a year or longer. If you have prostate cancer, hormonal therapy may slow its growth, delaying substantially the development of debilitating symptoms.

Prostate cancer requires male hormones to grow. Therefore, reducing the amount of these hormones in your body or blocking their actions slows the cancer's growth. Unfortunately, the loss of male hormones will affect other tissues that depend on them, leading to impotence, a decrease in body hair, enlargement of the breasts, and sometimes noticeable changes in personality such as depression and loss of energy.

There are two approaches to hormonal therapy. You can block the action of the male hormones or you can prevent them from being produced. Two medications, diethylstylbesterol (DES) and leuprolide, reduce or block the action of male hormones. Some doctors are reluctant to prescribe these medications, however, because they increase your risk of developing heart problems. To prevent the production of hormones requires surgical removal of the testicles, where *testosterone,* the principal male hormone, is produced. This operation, called *castration,* can cause profound physical and psychological changes. Before agreeing to the operation or even agreeing to take DES, understand fully what you can hope to gain and the side effects that you are likely to experience. Some older men decide that the side effects of both therapies are simply unacceptable.

Lung Cancer

Lung cancer can occur in all adults. Before so many women began smoking, it was found almost exclusively in men. Although on rare occasion nonsmokers develop lung cancer, for the most part the disease afflicts smokers.

Lung cancer can grow for a long time without causing symptoms. Eventually, however, it causes a cough, shortness of breath, or blood in your sputum. Sometimes it enters the nerves that run near the lungs, causing a hoarseness of voice.

There is no good way to screen for lung cancer before symptoms develop. Usually lung cancer is first detected on a chest x-ray as a spot, but by this time it is already well developed. If your doctor discovers a spot on your x-ray, stay calm; many other, less serious conditions may be responsible. If you do have a suspicious chest x-ray, you will need further tests, generally either a needle biopsy or bronchoscopy, to determine whether you have lung cancer.

A *needle biopsy* is performed by a radiologist. Using a CAT scan, a type of specialized x-ray, or other sophisticated x-ray equipment, the radiologist will determine the exact position of the spot, anesthetize the skin of your chest with an injection, and insert a needle through your skin and into the spot, taking a sample of it. Because your skin and chest wall will have been desensitized by the injection of local anesthetic and because your lung can't feel the needle, the procedure doesn't cause much pain, although it can be somewhat frightening. Complications can occur from a needle biopsy, including bleeding into the lung and collapse of the lung, but the procedure is often the safest way to find out if you have lung cancer.

Spots that are located deep within the lung are better reached with a *bronchoscope,* a long, flexible, fiber-optic tube that allows your doctor to look directly into your lungs. *Bronchoscopy* is generally performed in the hospital by a lung

specialist, a *pulmonologist*. The pulmonologist will anesthetize the back of your throat with a spray, then pass the tube
into your mouth, down your throat, and into your lungs. When
the doctor finds the area with the spot, he or she can take a
biopsy directly through the bronchoscope. As with the needle
biopsy, the lung does not feel any pain from the biopsy, and
the same complications can occur.

Once your doctor has obtained a tissue sample by either of
these methods, a pathologist will examine it under a microscope to look for cancer and to identify the kind of lung
cancer it is. The two most common types of lung cancer are
squamous cell and small cell.

Squamous cell carcinoma is the most common kind of lung
cancer and the one most closely associated with smoking.
This cancer often does not metastasize until it has grown
large, and so, if discovered early, a surgeon may be able to
remove all of it. Unfortunately, once it has spread, neither
radiation therapy nor chemotherapy is likely to cure it. *Small
cell carcinoma,* also called *oat cell,* is the other common type.
Unlike squamous cell carcinoma, small cell carcinoma metastasizes very early, going to many organs of the body, including the brain and the bone marrow. Therefore, an operation
usually cannot remove all of it. Unlike squamous cell cancer,
however, it does respond to chemotherapy. Although a cure is
not often possible, chemotherapy may allow you to live with
the cancer and feel better for considerably longer.

Colon Cancer

Colon cancer occurs in adults of all ages, but older people
are at greatest risk. Colon cancer arises in the lining of the
large intestine and often starts in polyps, which are very
similar to the moles or tags that grow on your skin. All polyps,
except the smallest, should be removed because of the possibility that they may be cancerous.

Age is not the only risk factor for colon cancer. The disease
runs in some families and occurs frequently in persons who
suffer from particular illnesses such as inflammatory bowel
disease. People who eat more red meat and those who eat a

low-bulk diet also have an additional risk. However, there is no evidence that a change in diet after reaching old age will substantially decrease your chance of developing colon cancer.

Sometimes colon cancer announces itself in its early stages, presenting an opportunity for discovery. For example, colon cancer often leaks tiny amounts of blood into the stool. Your doctor can test for that blood, even though it cannot be seen, by performing a rectal examination or by giving you a package of stool-test kits that you use at home and return in person or by mail. Either way, have your stool tested for blood every year.

Colon cancer may cause constipation, diarrhea, cramps, loss of appetite, or a change in the color or size of your stool. As you well know, many things besides cancer can cause all of these symptoms. You should be concerned only if you experience a change from what is normal for you and if the change persists.

If your doctor suspects colon cancer, he or she will recommend one of two tests: a colonoscopy or a barium enema, both of which are described in detail in chapter 10. The colonoscopy uses an instrument called a colonoscope to examine your colon, while the barium enema uses x-rays to outline your colon. In short, both tests allow your doctor to see any abnormal growths in the lining of your colon. If a growth is found, your doctor, or a specialist called a *gastroenterologist,* will perform a biopsy to determine if it is cancerous.

If colon cancer has not yet grown deeply into the wall of the colon, a surgeon can probably remove all of it. Sometimes, if the cancer is localized in a polyp, it can be removed in a relatively minor procedure performed through the hollow colonoscope. Unfortunately, once colon cancer grows deeply, it spreads quickly through the veins and arteries that supply the colon, often metastasizing to the liver and other organs. Colon cancer is classified into stages, called "Dukes stages," by how far it has spread. The classification ranges from Dukes stage A, the earliest, when the cancer remains on the surface of the lining of the intestine, to Dukes stage D, the most advanced, when the cancer has spread throughout the body. The stage of your cancer is the best predictor of whether it can be cured.

Some oncologists recommend chemotherapy for metastatic colon cancer. Since the cancer spreads earliest to the liver, the chemotherapy is sometimes administered into that organ directly, thereby concentrating its effects. Despite such treatments, the effectiveness of chemotherapy for colon cancer is poor, and its side effects are considerable. For many people with metastatic colon cancer, there is little to be gained from chemotherapy. When you are deciding whether to try chemotherapy for colon cancer, make your decision carefully. Get opinions from two oncologists and discuss your thoughts frankly with them, your primary-care doctor, and your family.

Cancer remains one of the most frightening diseases of late life, and the harsh reality is that cancer kills many people. We have come a long way in treating cancer, and there is no doubt that many cancers, if discovered early, can be cured. Yet, many cancers cannot be cured, and the treatments that are sometimes proposed have serious side effects. Some people are willing to experience those side effects, and others are not. You can make the right decision about treatment by obtaining several opinions, discussing your options with your doctors, and talking frankly about your wishes and goals with those you love. Whatever your choice, if your cancer can't be cured, your doctor and the health-care system will work hard to keep you free of pain and as comfortable as possible.

You have an active role to play in discovering cancer early: know the warning signs of cancer and keep up with the appropriate screening tests. Be vigilant in watching for indications of cancer. In fighting cancer, the best defense is an early offense.

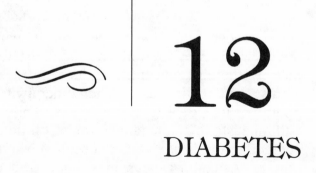

DIABETES

Diabetes is an elevation of blood sugar caused by inadequate amounts of insulin in the body. Although diabetes is not a geriatric disease—persons of any age can develop it—it is one of the most common chronic diseases of late life. Approximately 18 percent of people over age 65 and 25 percent over age 85 have it.

As your body digests a meal, the sugars in what you have eaten—from simple sugars such as table sugar or the sugar in fruit, to the complex sugars such as starch found in bread and pasta—enter your bloodstream. This process normally stimulates your pancreas to produce insulin, which in turn allows the cells of your body to take in and use sugar from your blood. Once the sugar moves from your bloodstream into your cells, the cells use it as a source of energy for their normal functions. When diabetes is present, the pancreas does not produce enough insulin, and the system of moving sugar from the blood into the cells does not function properly. As a result, cells are not able to use sugar normally and the level of sugar in the blood becomes too high, causing several serious problems.

WHAT IS DIABETES?

Diabetes is actually more than one disease. Children and young adults get a kind of diabetes called *juvenile onset* or *Type I diabetes.* In Type I diabetes, the pancreas, the gland that normally produces insulin, stops producing insulin entirely. The amount of sugar in the blood therefore rises suddenly, yet the cells are not able to take in an adequate amount of sugar to meet their energy needs. The body begins breaking down fat in order to supply some energy to the cells, but this process leads to a serious, acute medical emergency. This form of diabetes is very rare in older persons.

Older persons get *adult onset* or *Type II diabetes.* In Type II diabetes, the body fails to use insulin properly and thus requires more insulin than the body can produce. Although the pancreas continues to produce insulin, it does not produce enough to meet the body's increased needs. This abnormally poor response to the effects of insulin, called *insulin resistance,* results in blood sugar levels that increase gradually without the sudden complications that mark the onset of Type I diabetes in younger persons. Because, with Type II diabetes, there is still some insulin present, cells are still able to take in sugar, and the body does not begin breaking down fat to obtain energy. The elevated sugar levels in Type II diabetes cannot be ignored, however. If left untreated, they damage the blood vessels, resulting in chronic poor circulation, which in turn can cause severe complications including blindness, kidney failure, impotence, and the need for amputations.

Normal Age-Related Changes in Blood Sugar

If you do not have diabetes, your body produces enough insulin and your cells are so responsive to the effects of insulin that the level of sugar in your blood rises only moderately after eating. This increase, however, is greater than that which occurs in younger people; nevertheless, it is a normal physiological change associated with aging and doesn't constitute diabetes. In fact, your body will reduce this slight elevation in blood sugar to normal levels after several hours.

Before doctors learned about this normal age-related change in the body's response to sugar, many healthy older people were misdiagnosed as having diabetes.

Checking Blood Sugar

Blood sugar levels can be checked in two ways. The first is to sample blood randomly, that is, at any time of the day. This method is not the best because of the normal, age-related increase in blood sugar that occurs after eating. The better way is to measure blood sugar after fasting, no sooner than eight hours after you have eaten. If your fasting blood sugar level is over 140 milligrams per deciliter (mg/dl) on two separate days, you meet the criteria for diabetes and may need some form of treatment. If your blood sugar level is measured less than eight hours after eating and is very high, for example above 200 mg/dl, the test result indicates that your body does not produce enough insulin and that you have diabetes. Of course, since a test taken after you have eaten is so variable, the diagnosis should always be confirmed with fasting blood sugar tests.

RISK FACTORS FOR DEVELOPING DIABETES

There are three chief risk factors for developing diabetes: obesity, lack of exercise, and heredity.

Obesity

Fat cells use up insulin. If you have any predisposition to developing diabetes, excess weight may be just enough to bring on the disease. If you are overweight and have diabetes, losing weight may mean that you can reduce or eliminate the need for medications to control your blood sugar.

Exercise

If you do not exercise, you also have an increased risk of developing diabetes. Exercise facilitates weight reduction, of course, but, more important, it affects the way your body handles sugar. Vigorous exercise will cause some sugar to leave your bloodstream and to enter muscle cells even without using insulin, thereby decreasing the amount of insulin you need. The beneficial effects of exercise last all day. Just twenty to forty minutes a day of exercise—a brisk walk or swim, for instance—may reduce or eliminate your need for diabetes treatment.

Heredity

Adult onset diabetes often runs in families. If one or more of your close relatives developed diabetes after age 30, you are more likely to develop it. If this is the case for you, tell your doctor and have a fasting blood sugar test every year. Even if heredity predisposes you to developing diabetes, you can reduce your risk by keeping your weight under control and by exercising daily.

THE SYMPTOMS OF DIABETES

Almost half of older persons who have diabetes simply don't know it. Unlike younger people, for whom the onset of the disease is dramatic and often life-threatening, you can go for many years unaware that you have the disease. Thus, it is important to know the symptoms of diabetes so that if you develop any of them, you can be tested and begin treatment before serious medical complications develop. There are five common symptoms of diabetes, all easily recognized: frequent urination; thirst; blurred vision; development of frequent infections; and fatigue.

Frequent Urination

When the sugar in your blood becomes too high, you will urinate frequently; this condition is called *polyuria* (meaning more than usual urine). Polyuria occurs because the excess sugar passes into the urine, where your body tries to dilute it with more and more water. If you have polyuria, you may urinate very frequently, the quantity of each urination will be large, and your urine may be so diluted that it appears almost clear, like water.

Thirst

Frequent, large urination causes diabetics to become thirsty, called *polydipsia* (meaning more than usual thirst). Persons with high blood sugar often complain of a dry mouth and say that they can't satisfy their thirst even after drinking. Sometimes diabetics become abnormally hungry as well, but abnormal hunger, *polyphagia,* is more common in younger diabetics.

Blurred Vision

High blood sugar may affect your vision, too. When blood sugar is high, your eyes may not be able to focus well, and vision blurs. This symptom varies with the amount of sugar in the blood; it becomes worse when the sugar is high and disappears when the sugar level returns to normal. Sometimes high blood sugar also causes puffiness around the eyes.

Infections

High blood sugar levels may lead to infections. When blood sugar is high, your body's immune system, which fights infections, can't operate properly. High levels of sugar in the urine make it a perfect place for bacteria and fungus to grow. Bladder infections and fungal infections of the skin are more common, more serious, and often require more intensive treatment when they occur in diabetics.

Fatigue

High blood sugar levels often cause fatigue when water is pulled from some tissues—including your brain—into the blood. This in turn leads to a slight shrinkage of the brain, bringing on fatigue and weakness. If blood sugar gets too high and too much water leaves the brain, confusion and even coma can follow. Coma from high blood sugar, *hyperosmolar coma,* is not common but is extremely dangerous, requiring immediate hospitalization for insulin treatment, control of fluids, and close monitoring.

COMPLICATIONS OF DIABETES

What is so bad about a little extra sugar in the blood? What's wrong with being sweet? The problem is that through time, diabetes often seriously damages many organs of the body. High blood sugar not only causes thirst, urination, fatigue, and infections, but it can also damage blood vessels and nerves, destroy the kidneys, lead to blindness, and raise cholesterol. Persons with diabetes suffer twenty-nine times as much blindness, seventeen times as much kidney failure, five times as many amputations, and five times as much heart disease as people who do not have the disease. Diabetes also increases your likelihood of having a stroke. If your doctor badgers you to control your diabetes, it is because he or she knows about these complications and wants to help prevent them.

Poorly controlled diabetes has been compared to accelerated aging, as though people with high blood sugar age faster. Atherosclerosis, the accumulation of deposits in and the narrowing of the blood vessels, occurs more quickly, and the function of many organs deteriorates. Most diabetics don't live as long as other people. Controlling blood sugar reduces the bad effects of diabetes on most organs in the body, and some experts feel that very good control of blood sugar may even halt the complications of diabetes entirely. In older persons with recent onset diabetes, it is probably the elevation of blood sugar that does the damage and not some other aspect of the disease.

Atherosclerosis

Atherosclerosis in the large arteries of the body occurs more commonly in diabetics, in part because high blood sugar levels tend to increase cholesterol levels. The atherosclerosis may interfere with blood supply to your legs, inducing cramps when you walk, a condition called *claudication*. If the blood supply is severely impaired, further complications can occur. The muscles in the legs can die; infections can start easily and, without adequate blood supply, do not heal well. If blood supply is so poor that it can't maintain the muscles of the legs, or if an infection will not clear up, it may be necessary to amputate the leg or risk death.

Atherosclerosis also explains why older diabetic men often have problems with impotence. If the blood supply to the penis is affected by atherosclerosis, it impairs the ability to have or maintain an erection. Since this problem is not caused by a lack of sexual desire or by an inability to reach orgasm, there are several treatments that can help. These treatments are discussed in chapter 17.

Disease of Small Blood Vessels

Prolonged elevation of blood sugar also damages small blood vessels. The walls of the smallest arteries and capillaries thicken, and their lumen—the space in the vessels through which blood travels—narrows. The blood vessels no longer function normally, often supplying inadequate amounts of blood. Many different tissues in the body can be affected by changes in the small blood vessels. The brain can suffer tiny strokes, called *lacunar infarcts* (see chapter 13). The kidneys may sustain damage and incompletely purify the blood, a condition called *renal failure*. Small blood vessels also supply nutrients and oxygen to the skin. When the blood supply is inadequate, skin becomes infected and breaks down more easily, leading to skin ulcers, also known as bed sores. Diabetic skin ulcers are serious, and if the large arteries to the legs are partially blocked by atherosclerosis, the problem is compounded. Older diabetics should consider having their toenails cut by a podiatrist to help avoid problems with infection from ingrown nails. If you have diabetes, any infection of a limb, be it a foot, leg, or hand, is serious and must be treated by a doctor as soon as possible.

Nerve Damage

Sometimes the lack of blood supply to large nerves causes a sudden weakness in a limb, usually the leg, and may affect your ability to stand or walk. This problem, *mononeuropathy,* is usually temporary, and recovery can be expected. It is important, however, to get physical therapy as soon as possible so that the muscles do not tighten and waste away.

Smaller nerves can also be affected by high blood sugar. Usually, the affected nerves in the fingers and feet become noticeable first, with sensations of tingling or burning. This condition is called *peripheral neuropathy,* which for most diabetics is not serious, although some develop severe pain. Also, since peripheral neuropathy alters your ability to feel both light touch and pain, it is easy to damage your skin from burns or from sores when pressure on the skin isn't relieved frequently by a change of position.

Several medications may help peripheral neuropathy. The one that works best is carbamazepine (Tegretol), but you and your doctor should consider it only when the condition is very bothersome. Carbamazepine often causes side effects and necessitates a blood test every few weeks to be sure that it is not harming you. In addition, carbamazepine does not cure peripheral neuropathy, although it does usually relieve symptoms.

The Eyes

Diabetes can hurt your eyes and have drastic effects on your vision. The light-sensitive part of the eye, the retina, is served by a network of small blood vessels. When these are damaged by diabetes, *diabetic retinopathy* occurs, a leading cause of blindness in older persons. This problem is discussed in detail in chapter 8.

HOW TO AVOID PROBLEMS FROM DIABETES

The problems that diabetes causes are all related to high blood sugar. Evidence is accumulating that by keeping your blood sugar under tight control, you reduce your chances of suffering diabetic complications no matter what your age. Tight control means keeping your blood sugar levels as close to normal as possible.

Controlling Blood Sugar

Keeping your blood sugar in the narrow range of normal is difficult. If blood sugar becomes too low—for example, if you take too much insulin—many cells of your body, such as brain cells, can't function properly, a condition called *hypoglycemia*. Low blood sugar can make you feel nervous, shaky, weak, hungry, and confused, and it can cause severe headaches. Hypoglycemia, also called feeling "shocky," can occur very quickly, and is treated by eating something sweet, such as sugar or candy. Other foods have sugar in them as well—a glass of milk or a piece of fruit will also provide relief. Special glucose tablets (glucose is a kind of sugar) are also available and are especially convenient because they correct hypoglycemia more quickly than other forms of sugar. If you are not sure whether a "shocky" feeling you are experiencing is from low blood sugar, it is generally advisable to eat sugar and then test your blood sugar to be sure. You are unlikely to do yourself harm and you can correct any subsequent high level of blood sugar with a little extra insulin or by eating less later in the day. If your blood sugar is too low, it may continue to fall quickly, sometimes causing serious problems within minutes. If you don't do anything and the fall continues, you may become confused or pass out. A sudden, rapid drop in blood sugar severe enough to cause confusion or fainting is a serious medical emergency and must be treated without delay.

Although the normal blood sugar range is approximately 80 to 120 mg/dl, this range may not be an appropriate goal for you. Discuss with your doctor how tight your control should be and the target range for your blood sugar level. The degree of control and the target range will vary depending on your lifestyle, how willing you are to adjust your medication and diet, how much exercise you get, and your other medical problems. It's a challenge to maintain a normal blood sugar level, and you will expend considerable effort doing it. Nonetheless, the effort may save you from developing many complications from diabetes; it may even save your life!

Monitoring Blood Sugar at Home

Monitoring blood sugar levels has been made much easier in recent years by *home glucose* (sugar) *monitors.* These devices quickly measure the amount of sugar in your blood after you have pricked your finger with a fine needle mounted on a spring-loaded device. Fear not: the needle prick causes little pain. You then place a drop of your blood on a chemical strip that changes color in the presence of sugar. Some of these strips are read by comparing the color of the strip to the color on a chart, but because this comparison is not easy to make accurately, it is usually best to use a small electronic machine that accurately reads the color change or measures blood sugar levels in some other way. The machine then shows you your blood sugar level on a digital display; some will even record your blood sugar readings so that you can show them to your doctor or nurse. There are many blood sugar monitors on the market. The two that I find are easiest for my patients to use are the One-Touch and Exactech. Still, you shouldn't purchase any unit until you have tried it yourself at the pharmacy.

The major drawback with home glucose monitors is that they are expensive to use. The device itself costs between $100 and $200, and it is not always paid for by medical insurance. The chemical strips cost between 50 and 75 cents each. If you check your blood sugar two times a day, the cost runs to more than $60 a month. Despite their cost, however, they make it possible to monitor and thus to control your blood sugar levels much more accurately.

Home Urine Monitoring

Another way to measure sugar is to test your urine, since sugar passes into the urine if its levels get high enough in the blood. That is why sugar in the urine indicates high blood levels of sugar in the blood. The urine test, however, is not reliable and is no substitute for blood sugar measurements. Use it only if you can't test your blood.

TREATMENT FOR DIABETES

There are three basic ways to control blood sugar: diet, weight control, and medication. Some older people with diabetes will not need to take medicine, but all of them must adjust their diet, exercise, and maintain a healthy weight.

Diet and Weight Control

The diet you should follow is based on two simple concepts: (1) avoiding large amounts of fat and simple sugars, and (2) eating each food group (protein, carbohydrates, and fats) in balanced proportion. Simple sugars—in table sugar, honey, and fruits—raise blood sugar quickly and require large amounts of insulin to bring the blood sugar level back down to normal. Protein and complex carbohydrates supply energy without raising blood sugar precipitously. Protein is found in meat, fish, eggs, dairy products, and wheat and other grains. Complex carbohydrates are found in starch from flour, potatoes, and rice. Discuss your diet with your doctor. It is often helpful to talk also with a dietitian and to get more information from one of the helpful books that explain the diabetic diet.

If you have mild diabetes, you may be able to control your blood sugar by strictly following your diet. Most people, however, need additional treatment.

Medications

Fortunately, for most older diabetics, *oral hypoglycemic agents* work well. Oral hypoglycemic agents are pills that stimulate the pancreas to produce more insulin and may also increase your body's response to insulin. Generally, they are taken once or twice a day. Glyburide (Micronase, Diabeta) and glypizide (Glucotrol) are two commonly prescribed medications. Tolbutamide (Orinase) is also an effective medication, although many doctors prefer glyburide or glypizide. Most experts agree that an older medication called chlorpropamide (Diabenese) is generally not the best choice for older people. It lasts too long and can cause prolonged low blood sugar if for any reason you are unable to eat. Chlorpropamide can also make you retain water, resulting in swelling and changes in the salt content of your blood.

If oral hypoglycemic medications fail to maintain your blood sugar level in an acceptable range, you will need to take insulin, which must be taken by injection. Insulin can't be taken by mouth because the acid and other chemicals in your stomach destroy it. Happily, injecting insulin is not difficult, and very small disposable needles have made it nearly painless. Insulin injected under the skin is absorbed into the bloodstream, where it supplements your body's own insulin supply. The dose of insulin must be carefully adjusted so that you have enough to lower your blood sugar but not so much that your blood sugar falls too low.

Some insulin is extracted from animals and some is created in the laboratory by bacteria that have been genetically altered. Insulin produced in the laboratory is called *human insulin* not because it was actually obtained from humans but because it is identical to the insulin found in humans. Most people can use either kind of insulin; the only people who must use human insulin are those who are allergic to the animal insulins or who are resistant to its effects.

The many different preparations of insulin differ in the way they are absorbed. Some, such as Regular insulin and Semilente insulin, are made to be absorbed quickly, while others such as NPH, Lente, and Ultralente are absorbed more slowly and have longer-lasting effects. To give you the best day-long effect, your doctor may have you mix different insulins. Some people can take long-acting insulin just once in the morning while others must take insulin two or more times daily to maintain adequate control.

There is no reason to fear insulin therapy. If you have difficulty filling the syringe with the correct amount of insulin, several strategies may help. Magnifiers mounted on the syringe are available, making it easier to see the dose. Syringes can also be filled by a friend, nurse, or family member a week in advance and stored in the refrigerator for daily use. If injecting yourself frightens you, a spring-loaded device will do the injecting for you. If you are deeply disturbed by needles, a special insulin gun can blow the insulin under your skin using a strong burst of air without a needle.

Some pharmacies specialize in products for people with diabetes. The pharmacist can describe the many devices now available to help you take your medication and monitor your blood sugar.

If you take any medication for diabetes, wear a medical alert bracelet and carry a card in your wallet identifying yourself as diabetic.

Although diabetes is a chronic disease that can lead to serious complications, careful control of your blood sugar levels will help you avoid or delay the onset of many problems. Many of the difficulties that used to stop older people from being able to manage their diabetes carefully have been overcome. By taking advantage of these developments, you can do a great deal to help yourself and lead an otherwise normal and healthy life.

STROKE

Strokes, like earthquakes, start suddenly, without warning, and end quickly. They can be severe, leaving devastation in their wake, or so mild that little evidence remains that they ever occurred. Strokes, sometimes called "shocks" or CVAs (cerebro-vascular accidents), are among the most feared illnesses that can befall an older person. Fortunately, strokes occur less frequently than they used to.

In the past thirty years, the incidence of stroke in the United States has fallen by half, and stroke in the elderly has declined even more. This reduction is due primarily to better control of diabetes and hypertension, which, as you will learn, are risk factors for developing strokes. Yet, strokes remain an important concern: for all our medical progress, they are still ten times more common in persons over age 75 than in those under age 55 and are the third leading cause of death in the elderly.

What Is a Stroke?

A stroke is the death of brain tissue caused by inadequate blood supply. Some basic physiology will help you to under-

217

stand how strokes occurs. The brain is made of cells: cells require oxygen and nutrients to remain alive. If the blood supply is interrupted, even for a few minutes, those cells won't receive adequate amounts of oxygen and nutrients and will die. A stroke occurs when the blood supply to any portion of the brain is interrupted long enough for cell death to occur. Thus, doctors usually refer to a stroke as a *cerebro-* (meaning "brain") *vascular* (meaning "blood supply") *accident* (CVA).

Virtually all the blood that reaches the brain comes through a pair of arteries in the front of the neck, the *carotid arteries,* or through a smaller pair in the back of the neck hidden within the spinal column, the *vertebral arteries.* These arteries branch out into smaller and smaller arteries to supply the entire brain. This vascular system is similar to an irrigation system, feeding smaller and smaller canals, each of which ultimately brings water to a single plant. If an interruption of blood flow occurs in one of the main branches, a large portion of the brain may be left without blood, and a large stroke will occur; if the interruption occurs only in a small branch, a small stroke will result.

Unlike many other kinds of tissue—skin, muscle, and bone—brain tissue cannot regenerate; once it dies, it is lost forever. The area of brain that dies can never function properly again, but luckily, other parts of the brain may be able to take over some of the lost functions. Thus, after a stroke, many people can regain part or all of a function they initially lost, such as their ability to speak, walk, or use their limbs. That is why most people benefit from therapy after a stroke.

A stroke is usually marked by a sudden loss of some bodily function. Because each area of the brain controls a specific function or part of the body, the location of the stroke determines which functions are impaired or lost. For example, if the stroke occurs in the speech center of the brain, it will result in slurred speech; a stroke elsewhere may affect vision, strength, urination, swallowing, or the ability to maintain balance or feel sensation. A stroke can even result in loss of consciousness, confusion, a change in personality, dementia, and depression.

WHO IS AT RISK FOR HAVING A STROKE?

Anyone can have a stroke, but some people have conditions or diseases—hypertension and diabetes, for example—that increase the risk. Both of these ailments affect small arteries, making their walls thicker but weaker and reducing their capacity to carry blood. Because smoking also produces these changes in blood vessels, smoking dramatically increases the risk. These abnormal blood vessels become clogged and burst more easily than do healthy ones, and if a stoppage or break occurs in a blood vessel in or to the brain, a stroke will result. Atherosclerosis—the buildup of fatty deposits (called plaque) on the inner walls of blood vessels—also increases the risk of stroke, particularly when the plaque builds up in the carotid or vertebral arteries. Thus, stopping smoking and taking careful control of blood pressure, diabetes, and atherosclerosis will reduce the risk of suffering a stroke.

Sometimes a blockage occurs even in healthy arteries. For example, if a blood clot forms elsewhere in your body and travels through your arteries, eventually it will get stuck, blocking the blood flow. If the clot blocks an artery in your brain, you suffer a stroke. The circulating clot is called an *embolism,* and a stroke that occurs from an embolism is called an *embolic stroke.* Embolic strokes are unlikely to occur except under certain medical conditions, one of which is atrial fibrillation—irregular heartbeats that cause blood to pool abnormally in the heart. If you have had an artificial heart valve surgically installed, you also run an increased risk of embolic stroke. Thus, people with atrial fibrillation or artificial heart valves often need to take an anticoagulant, such as Coumadin, a medication that helps prevent blood from clotting (see chapter 3).

Finally, you run an increased risk of suffering a stroke if you have major surgery. During complex operations, sudden changes in blood pressure and heart rate can occur, and these changes, as well as the stress of surgery, sometimes result in a stroke. Fortunately, this complication is not common; nonetheless, if you have any of the risk factors for stroke, get a careful evaluation from your surgeon and anesthesiologist before any operation so that they can take precautions to increase your chance of getting through surgery without complication.

KINDS OF STROKES

Cerebral Infarction

The most common kind of stroke is called a *cerebral infarction* (cerebral means "brain," and infarction or infarct means "cell death resulting from lack of blood and oxygen"). A cerebral infarction occurs when an artery to the brain becomes clogged; if tiny accumulations of platelets (cells in the blood that often stick together) become lodged in the arteries, they further block the flow of blood. An embolism, as described earlier, can also cause a cerebral infarction.

Cerebral Hemorrhage

Another kind of stroke, *cerebral hemorrhage* (hemorrhage means "bleeding"), occurs when a blood vessel (usually an artery) in the brain ruptures, allowing blood to leak within the brain. Blood is useful to tissue only if it circulates through the vascular system of arteries, capillaries, and veins. When it pours directly into tissue, it cannot provide oxygen or other nourishment and in fact is harmful.

Only 5 percent of all strokes are cerebral hemorrhages, but cerebral hemorrhages are often more severe than other kinds of strokes, because the blood that leaks into the brain tissue destroys more brain cells than would have died from the loss of blood supply alone. It also causes *edema* (swelling), which can trigger other parts of the brain to malfunction.

When small blood vessels burst, they usually stop bleeding quickly because of the body's normal mechanisms for stopping internal bleeding. However, when bigger blood vessels rupture, enough blood may leak into the brain to cause destruction in large areas, areas critical to normal functioning.

All of these complications explain why 35 to 40 percent of those who suffer a cerebral hemorrhage die as a result of the stroke.

The brain is surrounded by different layers of tissue that support and encase it, and hemorrhage can occur within any of these layers. The outermost layer is the *dura;* then, closer to the brain itself, is the *arachnoid*. If the blood vessel that leaks is within the brain itself, the result is called an *intracerebral hemorrhage* (intracerebral means "within the brain"). If the blood vessel leaks just under the arachnoid, it is referred to as a *subarachnoid hemorrhage*. Finally, the bleeding can be just under the dura, and when this happens it is called a *subdural hemorrhage*. Subdural hemorrhages result in an accumulation of clotted blood called a *subdural hematoma*. Because this blood is physically separated from the tissue of the brain by the tough dura, it cannot directly damage the brain. However, if the accumulation is large enough, it may exert harmful pressure on the brain and result in symptoms similar to those of a stroke. Sometimes a subdural hematoma can produce more subtle changes that appear as confusion or dementia. Because, later in life, the veins that cross the dura grow fragile and break easily, you are particularly prone to subdural hematomas. Even a relatively mild trauma to the head may precipitate one. Therefore, if you hit your head and then experience headache, dizziness, confusion, or any other unusual symptom, contact your doctor immediately.

Lacunar Infarcts

A third kind of stroke is called a *lacunar infarct,* a tiny stroke that results from blockage in the smallest blood vessels in the brain. These vessels are so small that an individual lacunar infarct often produces no noticeable symptoms. However, this kind of stroke is usually not an isolated event: rather, lacunar infarcts continue to occur over months or years. When a sufficient amount of brain tissue has died, some loss of function is inevitable. Lacunar infarcts usually have their greatest effect on mental processes, leading to a kind of dementia called *multiinfarct dementia*. (This condition is discussed in more detail in chapter 15.) Lacunar infarcts are more likely to occur if you have poorly controlled diabetes or hypertension.

TRANSIENT ISCHEMIC ATTACKS (TIAS)

When the blood supply to part of the brain is interrupted only temporarily, the event is called a *transient ischemic attack* or a *TIA* (ischemic means "lack of blood"). A TIA may cause all of the symptoms of a stroke, but the symptoms disappear entirely within twenty-four hours. While a stroke is the result of a lack of blood and oxygen that is serious and long-lasting enough to cause the death of brain tissue, TIAs are caused by a brief interruption in blood and oxygen supply leading to only temporary dysfunction. In a TIA, brain tissue does not die, it merely malfunctions temporarily.

TIAs may be a warning sign that a stroke is likely to happen. After all, they indicate that a portion of the brain, for a short time, did not get enough blood. If the situation had persisted longer, the affected brain tissue would not have survived. If you think you may have suffered a TIA, seek medical attention immediately, and make sure you receive a complete evaluation from your doctor, including a discussion of the options for treatment.

PREVENTING STROKES

Once a stroke has occurred, the portion of brain that has died will never recover. Thus, it is better to prevent a stroke than to treat it. If you have hypertension or diabetes, make every effort to keep the disease under control. If you smoke, stop. If you assume that because you've been smoking for years it's too late to get any benefit from quitting now, you're wrong. Quitting will reduce your risk of developing a stroke no matter at what age you stop or for how long you have smoked. If you have atrial fibrillation or an artificial heart valve, ask your doctor about the risks and benefits of anti-coagulation medication. If you use Coumadin (warfarin), be sure to have the level of activity of the drug monitored regularly by your doctor.

Because approximately one-quarter of all strokes are preceded by a TIA, and 5 percent of all TIAs are followed by a stroke within one year, we know that TIAs are a warning sign that a stroke is more likely. Take this warning seriously, and make every effort to prevent subsequent problems. Some of the symptoms that might indicate a TIA (or a stroke) are: sudden weakness on one side or in one limb, slurred speech, fainting, loss of vision, or loss of sensation in part of the body. If you experience something that might be a TIA, contact your doctor immediately or go to the hospital emergency room without delay. Do this even if all the symptoms have gone away. Your body has given you a warning sign; heed it!

Of course, your symptoms may not have been caused by a TIA or a stroke. Very low or very high blood pressure, seizures, heart problems, or other medical disorders may mimic TIAs and strokes. That is why your doctor will check your blood pressure, perform a full neurological and medical examination, obtain an electrocardiogram, and carry out some basic blood tests. Further tests may also be necessary. For example, your doctor may check your heart for arrhythmias (irregular heartbeats or unusually fast or slow pulse); this test is often done with a Holter Monitor, a small device worn on a belt or strap from your shoulder, which records heart activity on an electrocardiogram for periods of twelve or twenty-four hours. It may be necessary to perform a CAT scan, a special x-ray of the brain that may show whether a stroke has occurred. A newer test, called an MRI (magnetic resonance imaging) can also be used for this purpose. I generally prefer the CAT scan, because the narrow, confining equipment used in an MRI can be somewhat frightening to patients.

If your symptoms were the result of a TIA, your doctor should discuss the possible causes and the measures that can be taken to reduce your risk of stroke. He or she may suggest that you start aspirin therapy. Aspirin, best known for its ability to lessen pain, also stops platelets (one of the types of cells in the blood that can block arteries) from adhering to one another, thereby reducing the chance that they will form clots or blockages. When used to block the clotting action of platelets, the recommended dose of aspirin is either one baby or one regular aspirin daily. Stronger anticoagulants, such as Coumadin or heparin, may be needed if you have already had a stroke or have had several TIAs within a short time. Even though most people who have TIAs do not require hospitalization, it is extremely important to see a doctor immediately for evaluation.

BLOCKAGE IN THE CAROTID ARTERIES

TIAs and strokes are sometimes caused by a partial blockage of the arteries in the neck, the carotid arteries. Even when TIAs and strokes have not occurred, doctors often listen to these arteries with a stethoscope. If the flow of blood through the arteries is normal, there will be no noise; if the flow is abnormal because of a partial obstruction, that obstruction may cause a *bruit,* a distinctive noise to your doctor's ears.

Two tests are commonly used to learn more about a bruit. One, a *carotid echo* or *Doppler study,* uses sound waves to measure blood flow and to determine whether plaque has narrowed the artery. A second test, *ocular plethysmography,* measures the flow of blood into the eye, which comes directly from the carotid artery. Both tests are painless and virtually without risk.

If you have a bruit and if either of these tests indicates a problem, you and your doctor will have to make a difficult decision, weighing the potential benefit of further investigation or treatment against potential harm. The test that gives the best view of any obstruction in the carotid arteries is called an *arteriogram* or *angiogram.* It is an uncomfortable and somewhat risky test performed by feeding a catheter (a thin tube) into a large artery of the arm or leg until it reaches the carotid artery. Dye that shows up on x-ray is then injected into the carotid artery through the catheter, and x-rays are taken. Because an arteriogram can lead to serious complications—bleeding, renal failure, allergic reactions, and strokes among them—this test should be performed only if absolutely necessary.

The operation performed to remove a blockage of the carotid artery, a *carotid endarterectomy,* is even more problematic and is in fact a very dangerous operation that results in a stroke or death nearly 10 percent of the time. A carotid endarterectomy should be performed only under very specific conditions. First, the vascular surgeon performing it should be experienced in the procedure and have a proven record demonstrating a low complication rate. Don't hesitate to ask your surgeon about his or her experience in performing the procedure. Second, be certain that the operation is absolutely necessary. Recent studies show that surgeons perform carotid endarterectomies more often than is appropriate. If the operation is suggested, obtain at least one additional medical opinion, preferably from a neurologist, a doctor who does not perform surgery. Discuss both opinions with your primary-care doctor before you reach a decision.

TREATING STROKES

If a stroke, rather than a TIA, has occurred, you probably will need hospitalization. During the first few days after suffering a stroke, several complications can occur, and you will need close monitoring and treatment, which are best done in a hospital. For example, the stroke may progress, leading to further impairments. Sometimes the brain swells in response to a stroke, causing further damage. Certain medications, given intravenously, can help treat the swelling, but if the problem is more serious, a neurosurgeon may have to operate to allow closer observation or to relieve the swelling.

Another reason for hospitalization is that a stroke may lead to the loss of essential bodily functions. For example, a stroke can impair your ability to swallow food without choking, and it may be necessary to feed you intravenously or via a nasogastric tube (a small plastic tube that is inserted into the nose and down to the stomach) until you can swallow again.

Sometimes a stroke can be so serious that virtually all bodily functions need assistance. No one can predict when or if any of these functions will return. Therefore, following any serious stroke, it is essential to decide whether to aid these functions—including breathing, eating, and adjusting your heart's functioning—artificially. Taking over these functions may require a respirator, nasogastric tubes, intravenous feedings, and potent medications that affect heart rate and blood pressure. In reaching a decision, the wishes of the stroke victim regarding his or her care should be paramount. However, if your stroke is severe, you may not be able to speak or write or even move, so doctors will usually rely on your next of kin for instructions. The section in this book on advance medical directives in chapter 19 describes how to record your wishes in advance so that others may follow them if you become incapacitated.

STROKE REHABILITATION

If you have had a stroke, you and your family should discuss with your doctor and a social worker what special help you will need during recovery. The first question is where rehabilitation should take place and approximately how long it should continue. As you will learn, rehabilitation can be done at home, in outpatient centers, in nursing homes, and in specialized rehabilitation hospitals.

Stroke rehabilitation therapy involves retraining and strengthening. Although brain tissue killed by a stroke does not regenerate, undamaged portions of the brain may in time take over some functions previously carried out by the damaged portions. Rehabilitation targets whatever deficits were caused by the stroke and seeks to improve lost functions such as walking, writing, speaking, swallowing, coordination, controlling the bladder, and reading. When brain function can't be recovered, using alternate muscles and strategies to avoid injuries may help you function more successfully. Rehabilitation should begin as soon as a stroke victim is medically stable, but everyone should be realistic about what such rehabilitation can accomplish. It will likely help you improve, but it may not be able to restore all of the functions that the stroke took away.

The first goal of rehabilitation is to prevent complications from lack of movement or weakness. Therapists and nurses will turn a patient frequently to prevent bed sores, move the limbs to prevent blood clots, and stretch the limbs or use braces to prevent contractions caused by tightened muscles.

Next, doctors and therapists will identify the long-term rehabilitation needs and the potential for recovery of the lost functions. Some people may need only minor instruction, while others will require extensive retraining. If you can cooperate and maintain a vigorous course of retraining, you are most likely to benefit from intensive rehabilitation. Although the goals of rehabilitation must be adjusted to your needs and individual abilities, too often the plans for rehabilitation are not ambitious enough: a few tough weeks of intensive rehabilitation often can result in the regaining of much of your independence.

Rehabilitation is often a slow process. Although it begins in the hospital it must continue beyond discharge. In fact, rehabilitation is generally better accomplished in several settings other than the hospital. Your doctors, working closely with a social worker, should advise you about which facilities will best suit your needs.

If you require the most intensive rehabilitation, a stay in a rehabilitation hospital is often appropriate. There, you can receive training two to three times daily in an environment designed specifically to be safe and beneficial for you. Rehabilitation hospitals are staffed by *physiatrists* (doctors who are expert in rehabilitation), nurses, and physical and occupational therapists who are experienced in caring for persons who have had strokes.

If you need somewhat less intensive rehabilitation, a nursing home equipped and staffed for rehabilitation therapy can provide the necessary environment. It is important to choose the nursing home carefully because not all provide adequate rehabilitation services.

Rehabilitation can also be accomplished on an outpatient basis for those who can return home safely. Outpatient rehabilitation may mean regular visits to a rehabilitation center or perhaps having a therapist come to your home. In either case, determine whether you will need help with your normal activities when you return home and whether your helpers will need special training. Also find out what equipment you will need at home so that you and those helping you can be trained properly in its use before you leave the hospital.

Naturally, you would rather return home than spend time recovering in a rehabilitation hospital or nursing home. A premature return, however, may be unsafe and may inhibit your rehabilitation. If you need therapy more than once daily, it probably can't be provided at home, and rehabilitation in a hospital or nursing home is preferable. Further, if you can't get from your bed to a chair, walk, or eat without assistance, living at home is usually not a feasible option. Take advantage of the several weeks of intensive, inpatient rehabilitation if your doctor recommends it. It is an investment that will pay you dividends for the rest of your life. Agreeing to go to a rehabilitation hospital or nursing home doesn't mean that you will be confined there forever. The purpose of a temporary stay is to help you regain your independence, not to limit it.

Whether rehabilitation is provided at home or elsewhere, it is organized around two related specialties, physical therapy and occupational therapy. *Physical therapy* is concerned with basic functions—muscle strength, walking, and relearning to get from a bed to a chair. *Occupational therapy* is concerned with more specialized functions such as speaking, eating, reading, washing, dressing, and using the bathroom. Both forms of therapy work together to meet your needs.

Physical and occupational therapists may suggest equipment to make tasks or even just the training easier for you. For example, braces may help you walk or prevent your muscles from contracting. Arm rails, stools, or steps may make it easier and safer for you to get into bathtubs, and a raised toilet seat can help you use the toilet more easily. Special utensils, combining the function of a fork and a knife, make it possible to cut food and eat with one hand. Large-button telephones, large-handled combs, and Velcro closures on clothing are examples of aids that may make daily life less of a challenge.

Canes are one of the most important pieces of equipment for a person who has had a stroke: they can prevent falls and can help get you up and about safely. Don't be embarrassed about using a cane. If you need one, use it! It can be your passport to independence. The famous anthropologist Margaret Mead, who always used a cane, said that she wouldn't consider sitting on a stool with only two legs, so why should she walk with only two legs?

There are many kinds of canes, and your therapist will suggest the best one for you. The traditional cane looks like a stick with a curved top. However, a cane may have a broad-based bottom with four legs, called a four-point cane. Canes can even be built with an underarm support that combines the features of a crutch and a cane. Regardless of which kind you use, make certain that it's the correct height for you—so that when holding it your arm is partially bent at the elbow. If a cane doesn't provide sufficient stability and safety, your therapist may recommend that you use a walker. A walker—in effect a hand rail that moves with you—is very stable, an excellent aid to mobility. For some people, a walker with wheels may be preferable to one without wheels.

A stroke is a feared and frightening occurrence. Although strokes can be devastating, many people who suffer them recover substantial function through rehabilitation. Nonetheless, it is far better to prevent a stroke than to recover from one. If you have diabetes or high blood pressure, keep it under control. If you smoke, stop. If you do have a stroke, take advantage of rehabilitation to help yourself recover as quickly and fully as possible.

14

TREMOR AND PARKINSON'S DISEASE

We take for granted the ability to control our muscles. Yet, even simple movements require a complex series of coordinated actions between the brain, muscles, tendons, and bones. For example, to reach for a dish in the kitchen cabinet, your brain must determine the current position of your arm and hand, stimulate the muscles in your shoulder and arm to contract, monitor changes in your arm's position as it moves, alter the tension of the muscles that push and those that pull so that the whole process proceeds smoothly, and stop the movement at precisely the correct position.

Much can go wrong during this process. This chapter discusses two such problems: tremor and Parkinson's disease. Tremor—that is, shaking—occurs commonly in older persons. Most tremors are more embarrassing than harmful. However, some tremors can limit your ability to accomplish simple tasks. Parkinson's disease, an illness that occurs in the elderly, causes a constellation of symptoms (including tremor); when advanced, Parkinson's disease can lead to profound debilitation.

TREMOR

What Is a Tremor?

Normally, the movement of an arm, leg, or any muscle group appears smooth. In fact, motion is accomplished by a series of imperceptibly small alterations of contractions in muscles that oppose one another. If that alteration becomes exaggerated to the point that it can be seen, we call it a tremor.

Most people have experienced a tremor at some time. Perhaps when you were very nervous, angry, or upset, you noticed your hand or even your entire body shaking. These transitory tremors last only a few moments and stop when the disturbance ends. Tremors that persist regardless of your emotional state are produced by other causes. These persistent tremors commonly afflict the elderly and can interfere with the most basic activities. For example, tremor makes simple tasks, such as eating soup, sewing, using small tools, and writing difficult or impossible. Tremor can force you to abandon a profession or hobby. It also tends to embarrass you, partly because other people often perceive shaking as a sign of nervousness, agitation, or fear. Thus, tremor tends to socially isolate those who suffer from it.

Tremors are not a normal part of aging although they are common. Most tremors are mild and remain so; they are more an annoyance than a serious health problem and require no treatment. Sometimes, however, tremor is a symptom of another medical problem. If your tremor interferes with the things you want to do, treatment may be able to control it. Always bring to your doctor's attention any new or worsening tremor to determine what is causing it and what treatment, if any, you should consider.

One consequence of tremor—embarrassment—can almost always be avoided. Many people become very embarrassed by a tremor unnecessarily, and well-meaning friends and relatives often aggravate matters. Although you might encourage a friend or relative to seek medical attention, there is no need for constant reminders: the consequences of the tremor are clear enough to those who suffer from it. The spilled soup, rattling dishes, and difficulty in manipulating a button are signs of a medical condition, not of nervousness, agitation, or fear. Never make fun of someone's tremor.

Senile Tremor

The most common tremor affecting older people is called a *senile tremor.* (Remember, *senile* just means "old age"; it does *not* indicate dementia.) When younger adults develop this tremor, it is often called an *essential tremor;* an identical tremor sometimes runs in families and is called a *familial tremor.* Senile tremor results from the exaggeration of normal muscular movements, but no one knows why so many older people develop it.

Because senile tremor is an exaggeration of normal muscle movements, it occurs only when you use a muscle, not when a muscle is at rest. The tremor is most noticeable when a muscle is used at its greatest extension, for example, when you stretch out your arm to reach for something, because the balance between opposing muscle groups is most accentuated at the point of farthest reach.

Doctors describe a tremor by its *frequency* (the speed at which it occurs) and its *amplitude* (how big it is). Senile tremors have a high frequency and generally a low amplitude. Thus, senile tremor is described as a *fine tremor.* Other tremors, like those caused by stroke or damage to the brain, have low frequency and high amplitude, which doctors refer to as a *coarse tremor.*

Senile tremor usually affects the arms and hands most noticeably. It may occur more on one side of your body or on both sides equally. Muscles other than those in your arms can be affected. For example, senile tremor may lead to a slight bobbing of the head. Bobbing occurs because your neck muscles position and hold your head in place even when your head is still. Your voice may develop a vibrato or "shaky" sound because muscles move your vocal cords. The actress Katharine Hepburn developed both of these conditions. She also showed the world that a senile tremor need not interfere with a profession or cause embarrassment. Senile tremor usually remains a mild condition, although sometimes it worsens slowly over years.

Senile tremor can ebb and flow from mild to severe shaking for several reasons. Just as nervousness, fear, or excitement can cause a transitory tremor in persons who usually do not shake, these strong emotions may temporarily exacerbate a senile tremor. Often, people become embarrassed by their slight tremor, and the embarrassment makes them self-conscious and nervous, which accentuates the tremor. Many stimulants, such as caffeine (in coffee, tea, dark sodas, and some over-the-counter drugs), worsen senile tremor.

Alcoholic beverages are effective treatment for tremor but have well known, dangerous side effects. Katharine Hepburn is reported to have observed, "One drink will stop the tremor; several drinks stop everything else." Put another way, in appropriate circumstances, a small amount of alcohol may be sensibly used to treat senile tremor. For example, if you occasionally perform fine needlework or model building in the evenings and find that your tremor interferes, a small drink may calm your shaking sufficiently to permit you to continue your hobby. Of course, you must be careful not to drink if even slight intoxication might be harmful or if alcohol interacts with medications you are taking, and you shouldn't drink alcohol so often as to become dependent on it.

There are other treatments for senile tremor. A group of medications called *beta-blockers,* frequently used to treat other medical problems such as high blood pressure and angina, are often successful in controlling tremors of several types, including senile tremor. Interestingly, actors sometimes take them to prevent shaking from stage fright. Beta-blockers useful in tremor treatment include propranolol (Inderal), nadolol (Corgard), and atenolol (Tenormin). Although even small doses will often control a tremor, these drugs can't be used by everyone because of their side effects, which include slowing of the heart, lowering of blood pressure, and decreasing the pumping action of the heart. If your tremor really bothers you or interferes with your chores and hobbies, ask your doctor if you can use a beta-blocker safely.

There are several other ways to reduce a senile tremor and

its effects. First, look at your diet and habits. If caffeine makes you shake more, stay away from coffee, tea, and dark sodas, which generally contain caffeine. Many nonprescription pain medications also contain caffeine, so read the labels before taking them. Be careful not to reach for things in ways that are awkward or cause strain; hold things close to your body rather than at arm's length. When fitting a tray with dishes, put doilies or napkins between cups and saucers to reduce rattle and the embarrassment it might cause.

There are also specially designed and adapted everyday utensils that can help you. For example, to make eating soups or cereals easier, use spoons that have deep bowls rather than shallow ones. There are even rocker-spoons—spoons with a hinge that allows the bowl to swing a little; the system works like a shock absorber for a tremor, making it easier to eat. Comfortable, large handles on combs and cups make them easier to hold, thereby calming a tremor. Adding Velcro patches to your clothing may be useful if a tremor makes snaps and buttons difficult to use. If you need help finding such aids, ask your doctor to put you in contact with an *occupational therapist,* a specialist in adapting equipment, who will advise you about modifying common tasks. Above all, don't be embarrassed by your tremor. Be honest about it with your doctor, family, and friends and work with them to minimize its effects.

Other Kinds of Tremor

Although the senile or essential tremor is the most common tremor in older people, other kinds can occur. For example, weakness can cause you to shake. At all ages, you probably have noticed that a muscle will begin to tremble when you strain it vigorously. For example, if you press your arms against each other as hard as you can and hold the strain, you will begin to shake. If you are weak, either because of illness or lack of exercise, the challenge even of routine tasks may bring on this kind of tremor.

Medications can cause tremor, too. For example, many of the medications used for lung or breathing problems, such as theophylline (Theodure), metaproterenol (Alupent), and iso-ethrane (Bronkosol), can cause a fine tremor, especially if the dose is too high. Theophylline, very similar to caffeine, is also found in tea, which is why you may shake after drinking tea. Diet pills and other strong stimulants may have the same effect. Lithium, a medication used to treat psychiatric illnesses such as manic depression, causes a very coarse tremor (low frequency and high amplitude).

People who drink large amounts of alcohol often shake when they are not drinking. That tremor may be a sign of alcohol withdrawal. A more serious form of tremor, called *asterixes,* occurs when the liver has been damaged, often from years of alcohol abuse.

Strokes, brain tumors, and other diseases that damage brain tissue can also lead to tremor. The part of the brain called the *cerebellum* coordinates muscle movements. Thus, tremors that occur from damage to that part of the brain are sometimes called *cerebellar tremors.* Cerebellar tremors are coarse and differ from senile tremor, which is a fine tremor.

Evaluating Tremor

When you tell your doctor about your tremor, he or she will ask you when it started, whether it is getting worse, if it occurs when your limbs are at rest or only when you lift or reach, and if other members of your family have ever had it. Your doctor should also review your medications to see if any of them could be causing or aggravating the problem. If you use certain medications, such as theophylline, your doctor may check the level of the drug in your body by taking a blood sample.

Your doctor will also examine your tremor, first by watching your hands and arms as they rest quietly by your side. Then you may be asked to hold your hands straight out. Finally, your doctor will test the movements of your muscles. You may be asked to touch your nose or other objects, to write, or to follow instructions that put your arm and hand muscles through several different tasks. By this physical examination, your doctor will be able to determine if your tremor occurs at rest, with action, or only at the end of a movement, and to characterize its frequency and amplitude.

If your doctor thinks you have senile tremor, it is unlikely that any further tests will be needed. In that case, you should discuss whether medication, such as a beta-blocker, is appropriate for you. If your doctor is at all concerned that an illness is the cause, you may be referred to a neurologist for further examination, or your doctor may suggest a CAT scan or MRI scan of your brain to be sure that nothing more serious is wrong. Remember, however, that the vast majority of tremors occurring in older people are mild senile tremors and require neither medication nor further evaluation.

PARKINSON'S DISEASE

Many people wrongly think of Parkinson's disease whenever they notice a tremor. Parkinson's disease has many symptoms other than tremor, and even its tremor is distinct from the senile tremor of older people.

Parkinson's disease was first described by Dr. James Parkinson in 1817 and was first called the Shaking Palsy. The disease is not rare: nearly 1 million Americans suffer from it, most of whom were first afflicted while in their fifties or sixties. Parkinson's disease starts insidiously, and at first it is often difficult for doctors to determine exactly what is wrong. Unfortunately, the symptoms invariably get worse, eventually making the disease easy to recognize. The rate at which the disease progresses is very variable, however, and not everyone goes on to develop the most serious forms of parkinsonism. In addition, doctors now have several medications that help control the disease.

What Causes Parkinson's Disease?

Parkinson's disease is caused by degeneration of the part of the brain that produces a chemical called *dopamine*. Dopamine is a neurotransmitter—that is, a chemical that allows brain cells to communicate with one another. We don't know why this part of the brain degenerates, although some experts have speculated, but not proved, that a virus causes the disease. A large number of people who survived the encephalitis epidemics between 1919 and 1926 (which were caused by a virus) developed Parkinson's disease many years later, and this observation suggests that a virus may be involved. Other experts have suggested exposure to toxic substances as a cause. This theory has gained some weight recently with the discovery that a chemical—accidentally manufactured by people trying to produce illegal drugs—can cause the disease and with the discovery of the high incidence of Parkinson's disease on a South Pacific island where the inhabitants commonly eat a toxic seed. In short, doctors can't yet identify for certain the cause or causes of Parkinson's disease and thus can recommend little in the way of prevention.

The Symptoms of Parkinson's Disease

Your brain relies on dopamine to coordinate many kinds of movement; lower than adequate levels of dopamine lead to abnormal movements. The features of parkinsonism are slowed movements *(bradykinesia),* a lack of movement *(akinesia),* tremor, stiffness, and an odd way of walking. A person with Parkinson's disease appears almost to be frozen in place before beginning any new movement.

Persons with Parkinson's disease move slowly and respond slowly. Even when startled, a person with Parkinson's disease may not respond immediately. Between the time that someone with the disease decides to move a limb or stand up and the time that his or her body actually responds, there may be a noticeable lag of a second or more. The limbs also become stiff; shaking hands with someone who has Parkinson's disease may feel like trying to bend soft metal, which is why doctors call this *lead-pipe stiffness.* The slowed and stiff movements often make a person seem as though he or she has lost the ability to move freely.

Early in the disease's course, two particularly noticeable features sometimes occur. The first involves facial appearance. Normally, the muscles of your face alter your expression, from a smile to a frown and everything in between. The muscles around your mouth and eyes contract frequently and quickly to highlight what you are saying and thinking. With Parkinson's disease, these expressive changes may disappear, making a face seem flat and emotionless. Too often, families and doctors misidentify this condition as depression, because without facial expression people appear withdrawn and without joy.

The second noticeable change is in the way the disease affects walking. Since it becomes difficult to initiate movement, walking slows, but, even more dramatically, the ability to start and stop walking and to change direction are affected. What you see is a person who can't easily get started walking, but once going tends to run with short, shuffling steps, all in a line, without altering direction.

Parkinsonism may also affect handwriting. If your doctor suspects Parkinson's disease, he or she may ask for a sample of your past and present writing to see how it has changed. Often, people with Parkinson's begin writing with very small letters, called *micrographia* (micro- means "small" and -graphia refers to writing).

The tremor associated with Parkinson's disease does not always occur in someone stricken with the illness, but when it does, it is distinctive. The tremor differs from the senile and other tremors described above: it occurs at rest—for example, when your arm is lying quietly on your lap or on a table. The tremor usually disappears as soon as the arm is lifted or moved, only to start again when the arm comes to rest. The tremor of Parkinson's disease is sometimes called a *pill-rolling tremor* because it appears as a slow rocking back and forth, as though a person were rolling a pill in the palm of the hand. Both the frequency and the amplitude of the tremor are low.

As Parkinson's disease progresses, all of these symptoms worsen, eventually interfering with or preventing activities that require strength and coordination. Even the muscles that coordinate swallowing may become involved, making choking more likely. Equally devastating is a form of dementia that occurs in nearly one-third of people with Parkinson's disease. Usually, the dementia does not develop until the disease has been present for many years.

Diagnosing Parkinson's Disease

There is no laboratory test for Parkinson's disease. Your doctor diagnoses the disease by taking a history of your symptoms and by examining you. The presence of brady-kinesia, resting tremor, stiffness, and lack of movement identifies the disease. If it is very mild and your doctor is not sure about the diagnosis, he or she may nevertheless recommend treatment. If you improve with treatment, the change will help your doctor to be certain of the diagnosis.

Treatment for Parkinson's Disease

Despite our inability to determine what causes the disease or to prevent it, doctors can treat Parkinson's disease. There are useful medications and several experimental surgical procedures that offer promise. Each type of medication has a particular advantage and disadvantage, and it is important that you and your doctor choose and monitor your treatment carefully. Additionally, physical and occupational therapy helps many people with Parkinson's disease.

The most commonly used medication to treat Parkinson's disease is Sinemet. Sinemet actually contains two drugs: the main ingredient is L-dopa, a chemical that is converted in the brain to dopamine, the neurotransmitter whose decreased levels lead to the symptoms of Parkinson's disease. The second component is carbidopa. Carbidopa can't penetrate into the brain; elsewhere in your body it prevents L-dopa from becoming dopamine. Without carbidopa, dopamine levels outside the brain would be very high, causing serious elevation of blood pressure and abdominal cramping. Thus, Sinemet works by increasing the level of dopamine in your brain without increasing the level of dopamine elsewhere in your body.

At first, it would seem sensible that by replacing the lost dopamine in your brain, Sinemet would provide a perfect cure. Unfortunately, your body and brain aren't so simple, and Sinemet can't provide a complete solution. As Parkinson's disease progresses, your brain becomes less sensitive to the effects of dopamine, and you can't replace enough of it to reverse the symptoms of the disease. In fact, some experts believe that starting treatment with Sinemet accelerates the loss of responsiveness to the drug. Therefore, many doctors who specialize in the treatment of Parkinson's disease recommend that you delay dopamine-replacement therapy with Sinemet until the symptoms of the disease become intolerable. Other experts disagree, and, relying on recent scientific reports, suggest that this medication can be started early in the course of the disease without negative effect.

Sinemet's many side effects provide more important reasons to delay treatment with the drug as long as possible. Sinemet can cause high blood pressure, flushing, dry mouth, nausea, gastrointestinal upset with cramping and diarrhea, and several other problems. The L-dopa in Sinemet can also cause agitation, paranoia, confusion, hallucinations, nightmares, and depression. If you use Sinemet and experience side effects, tell your doctor. Changing your dose or the ratio of carbidopa to L-dopa in the Sinemet may alleviate the side effects.

Amantadine, a medication often used to treat or prevent influenza, ameliorates the symptoms of Parkinson's disease, especially stiffness. Some doctors, myself included, often begin treatment with amantadine. Although it too has side effects (it can cause agitation and, rarely, seizures), patients often find amantadine more tolerable than Sinemet. Amantadine is a less powerful treatment than Sinemet. In advanced stages of the disease, it rarely works well enough on its own and may need to be used in conjunction with Sinemet.

Benztropine (Cogentin) and diphenhydramine (Benadryl) are sometimes prescribed either alone or in combination with other drugs. Although these medications can alleviate parkinsonism, in older people they tend to produce severe side effects because of their anticholinergic properties. (Anticholinergic properties of medications are described in detail in chapter 2.) At the doses needed to treat Parkinson's disease, they are likely to cause confusion, blurred vision, dry mouth, constipation, urinary retention, and light-headedness.

Several other medications can be useful, especially if Sinemet is inadequate to control your problems. These include bromocriptine (Parlodil) and selegiline (Deprenyl). Pergolide is a medication that has recently been released for the treatment of Parkinson's disease and has shown great promise for people with advanced stages of the disease.

An experimental new surgical treatment for Parkinson's disease is currently under investigation. It involves the implantation of tissue from the adrenal gland of human fetuses directly into the brain. The adrenal gland produces dopamine, and fetal tissue, when transplanted, is more likely to grow and develop properly than is tissue obtained from any other source.

Although there have been reports of the operation's success, it has been tried in very few people, and it is not yet clear whether this surgical treatment is safe or generally effective. Because it involves the implantation of foreign tissue directly into the brain, the procedure poses risks that very few people should consider until more is known. Nevertheless, this new approach to treating Parkinson's disease may someday offer a surgical cure, not just a temporary control. The current debate over the ethical issues involved in fetal-tissue research can be expected to affect scientific study of this new procedure.

In conjunction with medication, many people with Parkinson's disease will also benefit from physical and occupational therapy. For example, your physical therapist may suggest that you use a walker fitted with front wheels to make walking easier and safer and will instruct you on exercises to keep up your strength. An occupational therapist can teach you how to reduce the risk of choking when eating, fit you with braces to help you move about, and suggest safety equipment that may help you stay as active as possible. Discuss the role of physical and occupational therapy with your doctor.

Parkinson's Syndrome

Certain medications can cause symptoms which mimic those of Parkinson's disease. When parkinsonism is caused by one of these medications, or by any cause other than the disease itself, we call it *Parkinson's syndrome* rather than Parkinson's disease.

The class of medications called *antipsychotics*—haloperidol (Haldol), thioridazine (Mellaril), thiothixene (Navane), for example—block the action of dopamine in certain areas of the brain, producing Parkinson's syndrome. Usually, the symptoms disappear within several days of stopping the medication, but occasionally they persist. If you or someone you care for is receiving an antipsychotic medication, be alert for parkinsonism. Since this side effect can be grave, ask your doctor to explain why the antipsychotic medication is needed, and, if it is not essential, ask your doctor about stopping it. (See the discussion of antipsychotic medications in chapter 2.)

Most tremors that you may experience are not serious, require no treatment, and don't get markedly worse as you get older. But tremor can be a sign of illness and therefore should be discussed with your doctor. If your tremor is troubling to you, there are medications and practical steps that will help. Parkinson's disease is a much more serious medical problem. Fortunately, Parkinson's disease can be treated, although it can't be cured, and the treatment generally controls the disease for many years.

15

DEMENTIA AND ALZHEIMER'S DISEASE

To many people, dementia is even more frightening than death. Dementia is a condition marked by serious loss of memory and an inability to think and to understand information; it is *not* a normal part of aging. It does, however, occur commonly: one in twenty Americans over the age of 65 suffers from some degree of dementia.

A person with dementia has a life expectancy only one-quarter as long as a person the same age without it. Because demented people are likely to spend some of their final years in a nursing home, dementia robs them not only of years but also of their independence. Nearly half of all persons entering nursing homes suffer dementia. Dementia is not, however, always an irreversible condition. There are many causes of dementia, only one of which is Alzheimer's disease. Some of the causes of dementia can be treated successfully, leading to an improvement in memory, thought, and understanding.

243

How Dementia Differs from Normal Memory Changes of Aging

The brain, like every other organ, undergoes normal changes of aging that lead to normal changes in brain function. For example, you may find it more difficult to learn new things—a new language, for example—or to recall quickly the names of acquaintances or public persons. You may tell the same story or joke more than once to the same person. These changes don't mean that you're ill; they are common and normally occur as you get older. They are *not* symptoms of dementia. As the writer Dr. Samuel Johnson observed in the eighteenth century: "There is a wicked inclination in most young people to suppose an old man decayed in his intellect. If a young or middle-aged man, when leaving company, does not recollect where he laid his hat, it is nothing; but if the same inattention is discovered in an old man, people will shrug up their shoulders and say, 'His memory is going!'"

Dementia is characterized by a much more serious decline in intellectual capacity, a decline that interferes with a person's ability to work or to participate in social activities. Demented people forget whole events, not just the details. It is not that they forget if they locked the door or turned off the stove (which we all do), but rather that they don't think even to do these things. Thus, houses remain unlocked, stoves stay lit, food goes uneaten, checks go uncashed, and bills go unpaid.

By definition, dementia is a condition that affects memory and causes at least three of the following additional changes: impaired ability to recognize people, places, or objects; problems in finding words; difficulty in working with numbers or performing mathematics; disorientation of time and place; and alterations in personality.

People suffering from dementia may get lost, be unable to describe events or medical complaints, make errors in balancing checkbooks or paying bills, or become withdrawn, angry, depressed, confused, or paranoid. Peculiar personality traits sometimes become more pronounced: a person who always worried about money becomes obsessed with finances; a person who always put things away now hides (and loses) them; and a person who was messy becomes completely disorganized.

Dementia is a chronic condition, beginning slowly and worsening over time. In its early stages, dementia may be subtle, and the changes it causes may be easily overlooked. Eventually, however, the deterioration in mental capacity becomes apparent and undeniable.

When older people experience changes in their mental status or become confused, the word *dementia* is sometimes bandied about too quickly and wrongly. Be careful to use the word correctly, for it is, after all, a diagnosis that is feared. It implies an imminent and inexorable decline. If your doctor or other health-care professional uses the word *dementia,* ask if he or she is sure that the condition being described *is* dementia and not some other abnormal mental state.

Many names have been used incorrectly to describe dementia, such as *senility* and *hardened arteries to the brain*. These terms are inaccurate and misleading. *Senile* merely means "old" and *senility,* "old age"; referring to dementia as senility falsely implies that dementia is normal or inevitable. Hardening of the arteries suggests that dementia is caused by atherosclerosis, which it is not. Some people, including doctors, incorrectly use the term *Alzheimer's disease* to describe all dementia, but, as you will learn, Alzheimer's disease is only one of several causes of dementia.

DEMENTIA VERSUS DELIRIUM

Delirium is an acute confusional state characterized by the inability to pay attention to the environment and surroundings. Its hallmark is confusion rather than memory loss, as is the case for dementia. If you become delirious, you may not understand where you are; what day or month or even year it is; what is being asked of you; or why people are paying so much attention to you. It is not that your memory is functioning abnormally, it is that your brain is unable to perceive and understand properly. Although these same characteristics may occur late in the course of dementia, in delirium they occur suddenly, at the very onset of the problem.

Delirium is usually caused by an illness or a reaction to a medication. Unlike dementia, which begins almost imperceptibly and progresses slowly, delirium begins dramatically and progresses rapidly. It is often easy to tell the exact date and sometimes even the exact time when the delirium began.

Delirium is a grave sign of serious illness and requires immediate medical care. If confusion or disorientation strikes someone suddenly, get help right away. The doctor will try to determine the cause of the delirium and treat it. Treatment is often successful, in which case the delirium will end.

DEMENTIA, DEPRESSION, AND PSYCHOSIS

Depression can look like dementia and may fool even the experts. If you suffer from depression, you may become withdrawn and quiet, stop paying attention to appearance, appointments, or anything else, and seem to lose the ability to remember or understand. Depression may begin subtly, just as dementia does, or it may appear suddenly, associated with some terrible event such as the loss of a loved one, the anniversary of such a loss, the development of some disease, a move, or a financial setback. Depression can mimic dementia and leave you mentally paralyzed.

If depression is suspected as a cause of mental impairment, a thorough evaluation by a geriatrician, internist, psychologist, or psychiatrist is essential. Your advanced age should never deter you or your family from seeking treatment for depression or inhibit your doctor in offering it. Your age will not prevent you from responding well to all of the therapies used to treat depression, including the use of antidepressant medications.

Psychosis, a mental condition marked by delusions, hallucinations, paranoia, or an altered sense of reality, is occasionally confused with dementia. Although psychosis sometimes occurs in association with dementia, it may develop independently. Sometimes, psychosis is caused by medical illness or occurs as the side effect of a medication. Whatever the cause, psychosis can often be effectively treated, often with anti-psychotic medications.

CAUSES OF DEMENTIA

The principal cause of dementia is *Alzheimer's disease*. Although doctors and the public sometimes use the terms as if they mean the same thing, the two are not equivalent. Dementia is the condition, and Alzheimer's disease is *one* of its causes. Not all dementia is caused by Alzheimer's disease; in fact, in one in three cases of dementia the cause is something other than Alzheimer's disease.

Alzheimer's Disease

In 1906, Alois Alzheimer described the medical history and condition of a 51-year-old woman who had lost her ability to remember and think. Although these symptoms of dementia are as old as history, the disease that is one cause of them was named after Dr. Alzheimer because he first recognized and systematically described the illness. Note the age of Dr. Alzheimer's patient. If she had been ten or fifteen years older, the doctor might have incorrectly attributed her symptoms to old age, a mistake that many doctors still make. It is hard for many people, doctors included, to understand that dementia is *not* a normal part of aging but rather an abnormal condition.

Because Dr. Alzheimer described the disease in a relatively young person, the disease was originally called presenile (meaning, "before old age") dementia. We know now that the disease is the same, regardless of the age at which it appears; it is just rarer in young people. Today, doctors often use the term *Senile Dementia of the Alzheimer's Type* (SDAT) or just *Alzheimer's disease,* regardless of the age of the afflicted individual.

The medical profession knows a great deal about Alzheimer's disease, even though doctors can't yet cure or control it. For example, after the death of an Alzheimer's victim, at the time of an autopsy, doctors can recognize the features of the disease in brain tissue: unusual formations called Alzheimer's plaques, neurofibrillary tangles, vacuolar degeneration, and Hirano bodies. The media have widely reported on a theory that aluminum causes Alzheimer's disease and that aluminum levels are high in the brains of those afflicted with it. Most experts, however, no longer believe that aluminum has anything to do with the illness, and there isn't the slightest evidence that you should avoid aluminum in any form.

The diagnosis of Alzheimer's disease can be made with absolute certainty only by performing an autopsy, after death. During life, doctors can be sure about the presence of dementia but can only suggest Alzheimer's disease as its cause. Alzheimer's disease can't be diagnosed by CAT scans, MRI scans, or any other test. Scans are useful, however, to determine whether there might be other causes of dementia—pressure on the brain from subdural hematomas (see page 221), or brain tumors, strokes (see chapter 13), or hydrocephalus (an obstruction of the normal flow of the fluids that bathe the brain, leading to increased pressure on the brain). Blood tests may be useful to exclude other illnesses as well, but blood tests don't diagnose either dementia in general or Alzheimer's disease in particular.

Researchers are investigating promising new tests, performed on spinal fluid, to diagnose Alzheimer's disease with certainty during life, but for the moment this work is still in its preliminary stages. Thus, today, doctors can diagnose Alzheimer's disease only by recognizing its signs and symptoms and by excluding the possibility of other causes of dementia.

Multiinfarct Dementia

Multiinfarct dementia is the second most common cause of dementia and generally occurs in persons who have a history of high blood pressure or diabetes. In multiinfarct dementia, tiny strokes, *lacunar infarcts,* destroy vital brain tissue; when enough brain tissue has died in critical areas, mental function declines, causing the symptoms of dementia. Even though multiinfarct dementia generally is not reversible, it is important to recognize it because the careful control of diabetes or high blood pressure may slow or even stop progression of the condition (see chapter 13).

It used to be said that "hardening of the arteries" (atherosclerosis) in the brain causes dementia. This is false. The small strokes that lead to multiinfarct dementia are not caused by atherosclerosis, a buildup of fatty deposits in the arteries. Atherosclerosis may lead to the more common type of stroke, in which people develop weakness of a limb or slurred speech, but it does not lead to lacunar infarcts and dementia.

Other Causes of Dementia

Together, Alzheimer's disease and multiinfarct dementia cause over two-thirds of all cases of dementia. There are, however, other, rarer causes. Table 6 lists most of the conditions that can lead to dementia. (Several of these causes are not discussed in the text.) For example, some people with Parkinson's disease develop dementia, and there also is a rare viral disease—Creutzfeld-Jacob disease—that can cause dementia. Too, some alcoholics develop a form of dementia.

While the conditions discussed above that cause dementia generally are not curable, others can be treated. Treatable causes of dementia include abnormal thyroid gland function, abnormally high or low levels of salt in the blood, certain vitamin deficiencies, syphilis, brain tumors or other structural problems of the head, such as subdural hematomas or hydrocephalus, and toxic side effects from medications. These diseases may cause dementia, but with treatment the dementia usually reverses. Since there is always the possibility that one of these treatable diseases or abnormal conditions is causing dementia, if your mental condition changes, see a doctor experienced in evaluating dementia. Your primary-care doctor may be able to help you or you may need to see a geriatrician.

T A B L E   6
CAUSES OF DEMENTIA

NONREVERSIBLE CAUSES OF DEMENTIA	
CAUSE	COMMENT
ALZHEIMER'S DISEASE	The cause of Alzheimer's disease is unknown. It is the most common cause of dementia.
MULTI-INFARCT DEMENTIA	MID is caused by small strokes, called *lacunar infarcts,* and occurs most commonly in persons with hypertension and diabetes.
PARKINSON'S DISEASE	The cause of Parkinson's disease is unknown. It causes people to become stiff, slow moving, and tremulous. Many people with Parkinson's disease also develop dementia.
ALCOHOL ABUSE	Chronic alcohol abuse can lead to dementia.
CREUTZFELD-JACOB DISEASE	This disease is caused by a viral infection of the brain and is rare. It can cause dementia.
AIDS	Dementia sometimes occurs in persons with AIDS.
HUNTINGTON'S CHOREA	Huntington's chorea is a genetic disease characterized by bizarre, abnormal movements. Later in its course, dementia occurs.

| POTENTIALLY REVERSIBLE CAUSES OF DEMENTIA | |

CAUSE	COMMENT
SYPHILIS	Syphilis, if left untreated, infects the brain and can cause dementia. Syphilis, a bacterial infection, must be treated with antibiotics.
SUBDURAL HEMATOMAS	A subdural hematoma is a collection of blood under the skull that can put pressure on the brain, causing dementia.
MENINGIOMAS	Meningiomas are slow-growing tumors that occur under the skull and can put pressure on the brain, causing dementia.
BRAIN TUMORS	Occasionally, brain tumors can cause confusion and memory problems that can seem like dementia.
NORMAL PRESSURE HYDROCEPHALUS	This condition occurs when the fluid that bathes the brain cannot escape and pressure develops on the brain, leading to dementia, urinary incontinence, and a characteristic abnormality of gait.
FOLATE AND VITAMIN B_{12} DEFICIENCY	These vitamins are essential for proper functioning of the brain. Severe deficiencies can lead to dementia.
MEDICATION TOXICITY	Many medications can cause older people to become so confused and sedated that they appear demented.
DEPRESSION	Depressed older people can appear demented; this condition is sometimes called *pseudodementia*.

CAUSE	COMMENT
THYROID DISEASE	Both underactive and overactive thyroid function can cause a condition that looks like dementia in the elderly.
ABNORMALITIES OF CALCIUM AND OTHER ELECTROLYTES	Electrolyte abnormalities (*e.g.,* abnormal levels of calcium, sodium and magnesium) can occur from medications, dehydration, or many diseases and can cause confusion and sedation, symptoms that may mimic dementia.

THE CHARACTERISTICS OF DEMENTIA

The characteristics of dementia are similar regardless of the cause. At first, people may cover up their lost abilities, sometimes very effectively. For example, if you ask a man with dementia what he is watching on television, the reply may be, "I'm watching my favorite program." In fact, he can't remember the show's name. With time, however, it becomes difficult to hide the signs of short-term memory loss—that is, the memory of recent events. Soon after hearing or reading something, the information is forgotten. A person suffering from dementia will ask the same questions repeatedly, unable to remember the answer or even to recall asking the question. Demented persons find it increasingly difficult to learn anything new. Trying to get somewhere they have not been before or to cook an unfamiliar dish becomes difficult, if not impossible. As the disease progresses, long-term memory—memories from the distant past, such as names of friends, addresses of family members, and recollections of familiar places—begins to fail. Eventually, it becomes impossible to hide the dementia.

With advancing dementia, personality changes may also occur. The worst or best characteristics may become exaggerated as the person loses the ability to keep those characteristics in check. Thus, one demented person may become hostile, fearful, or sexually uninhibited, whereas another may become docile, overly friendly, and talkative.

It is impossible to predict accurately whether dementia will progress slowly or rapidly; it often depends on the cause. Alzheimer's disease, for example, usually causes dementia to worsen at a steady rate. An old theory held that if a person developed Alzheimer's disease when relatively young, the deterioration progressed more quickly, but recent studies have shown that this is not so. People who worsen slowly during the first year of the disease will probably continue to lose mental capabilities at that same slow rate, and those who have a rapid early decline will probably continue to worsen precipitously. Multiinfarct dementia causes dementia to worsen in steps rather than continuously, as each small stroke takes its toll on the brain's ability to function.

EVALUTING DEMENTIA

The advanced stages of dementia are easy to recognize. Even ancient writers were able to describe the condition long before doctors understood anything about it. In early stages, dementia frequently goes undiagnosed. If you have noticed problems with your memory or with that of someone you love, consult your doctor or a specialist in geriatric medicine. To evaluate your mental status and diagnose dementia, your doctor will need to talk to you and collect medical information, perform a physical examination, and order laboratory tests.

Medical Interview

The evaluation begins with an interview, which should be conducted in quiet and nonthreatening surroundings. The environment in which the interview takes place is very important. For example, if you have poor hearing or eyesight, an interview conducted in a noisy or bustling place (such as an emergency room) may easily lead your doctor to erroneous conclusions. During the interview, your doctor will try to determine all of the following:

- Your ability to function in social or work situations
- Your ability to reason
- Your ability to recognize the current time, location, and people present at the interview
- Your ability to remember both recent and remote events
- Your ability to perform mathematical calculations and verbal exercises
- How good your judgment is
- Your emotional state
- Your ability to perceive, recognize, and copy objects
- Your other medical conditions, including your use of medications, alcohol, or other drugs

Your doctor must evaluate you with an understanding of your ethnic and educational background. If you could never add and subtract in your head, you can hardly be faulted for not knowing how to do it in old age! A person who never reads newspapers or who avoids TV cannot be expected to know about current events. On the other hand, if you made your living as a mathematician, you should be able to do more than simple arithmetic.

Physical Examination

Your doctor will also perform a physical examination to look for signs of disease or conditions that might affect your brain. In particular, your doctor will examine the function of your neurological system, searching for abnormalities that might indicate the need for special diagnostic tests. For example, he or she will check your reflexes, coordination, and sensation, looking for differences between one side of your body and the other.

Laboratory Investigation

Laboratory evaluations must also be performed. The tests most commonly needed are:

- Thyroid function (to check for overactivity and underactivity)
- Vitamin B_{12} and folate (two vitamins needed for proper brain function)
- VDRL (a test for syphilis, one cause of dementia)
- Calcium levels in your blood (which, when abnormal, can cause confusion)
- Kidney function (to look for renal [kidney] failure, which can cause abnormal brain function and lethargy)
- Glucose (sugar) levels in your blood (untreated diabetes can lead to changes in brain function)
- Sedimentation rate (a test that screens for the possibility of some rare diseases that can occasionally cause confusion and memory changes)

Sometimes, but not always, additional tests such as a CAT or an MRI scan of the head are needed. The CAT or MRI scans are most appropriate if your memory problem is less than two years old, if your symptoms are in some way atypical or unusual, or if your doctor found some abnormalities on your neurological examination, such as muscular weakness, abnormal sensation, or changes in your ability to walk. A lumbar puncture (spinal tap) is rarely part of the evaluation of dementia, although it generally is part of the evaluation of delirium and other acute changes in mental status.

TREATMENT OF DEMENTIA

If your doctor discovers one of the treatable diseases causing dementia, you can anticipate improvement. For example, if your dementia is the result of an underactive thyroid gland, thyroid hormone replacement will help you. If your dementia is caused by increased pressure on your brain (a subdural hematoma), an operation to relieve it may help. Unfortunately, for the vast majority of people with dementia, treatment holds only limited promise.

Medications

Although there is no good treatment for most people with dementia, there are medications that are sometimes used in the attempt to try anything that might be helpful. Hydergine, once the world's most prescribed medication, has recently been shown to be ineffective in treating dementia, and there is no reason to use it. Antipsychotic medications, such as Mellaril (thioridazine) and Haldol (haloperidol), are often used to control agitation, violent or unruly outbursts, or the paranoia that may accompany dementia. However, they don't directly improve the memory or learning problems of dementia and are frequently overused and misused. All of the antipsychotic medications can cause severe side effects. If your doctor prescribes antipsychotic medication, ask whether they will lead to some improvement and whether they cause side effects. A second opinion from a geriatrician may be beneficial. (See also the discussion of antipsychotic medications in chapter 2.)

Other medications that have been shown to be of no help include lecithin, cyclospasmol, high-potency vitamins (including shots of vitamin B_{12}, unless a deficiency of B_{12} has been found), and special diets. If your doctor has prescribed any one of these treatments, ask why, what results the doctor expects, and whether the treatment has achieved a demonstrable benefit.

Recently, new medications have shown some promise in experimental trials and are being studied in large national trials. None is yet available for general use.

Care of the Person with Dementia

Despite the lack of useful medications, the medical profession can help demented persons and their families. Accordingly, after the doctor has diagnosed dementia and has offered his or her opinion as to whether it is caused by Alzheimer's disease or something else, arrange a second interview to discuss what needs to be done.

As a caregiver to someone with dementia, first, know what

not to do. Many medications, some of which can be purchased over-the-counter without a prescription, worsen dementia. Medications with anticholinergic side effects and those that cause sedation are usually the riskiest (see chapter 2). Try to avoid changing the person's environment, if possible. A move to a new home or city or even repainting or rearranging furniture may prove very disruptive. Above all, never scold or punish a person with dementia; this response is as futile as it is cruel. Frustration is inevitable, but misdirected anger can only aggravate matters. If you are stressed by delivering care to someone with dementia, speak with your own doctor and obtain additional help at home. Often, medical insurance and Medicare can cover the cost of some home care. Alternatively, daycare and senior centers may be able to provide some relief.

It is also important to think about how dementia will change your needs as the condition worsens. Consider whether you will need to move to a nursing home or hire attendants to make it possible to remain in your own home. The best nursing homes have long waiting lists, and to be admitted, you must plan well in advance. Doctors and especially geriatric social workers can provide much of the information necessary for you to make these decisions intelligently. If you have not yet spoken to a social worker, ask your doctor to put you in contact with one, or call your local social-services agency or area agency on aging; their numbers should be listed in the phone book. In confronting the challenges of caring for someone with dementia, the social worker is one of the most important persons on your professional team.

Often it is important to obtain legal advice, especially if you must manage money or property. These arrangements should be made as early as possible. Once dementia progresses, it may not be possible for a dementia victim to make his or her wishes and instructions known or to document them in a legally enforceable way. (See chapter 19.)

Be certain to explicitly and legally document your desires and instructions for your own medical care before the dementia gets severe. While some people want aggressive medical treatment, such as respiratory support, cardiac resuscitation, and feedings through tubes if they fall grievously ill and are not expected to recover, others want none of that technology. The presence of dementia often makes a difference in deciding such issues. In some states, a *durable power of attorney for health care* or a *living will* are recognized by law (both are discussed in detail in chapter 19). If you complete these documents while you are competent, they will be legally binding in accordance with your state's laws. In addition to the legal paperwork you complete, be certain to discuss with your primary-care doctor your wishes regarding the aggressive use of medical technology. If you and your doctor disagree substantially on this important issue, find a doctor sympathetic to your position, whatever it may be.

Once dementia progresses, your physician, nurse, and social worker will help coordinate your care in the safest and most helpful way. Because you will have unique needs, the services you will require must be tailored to you. If you remain in your home, it may be necessary to turn off or disconnect gas stoves and other potentially dangerous appliances. Timers can be placed on electrical equipment for automatic shut-off. Neighbors or doormen can be asked to keep an eye out for you, or alarms can be placed on doors to alert your family if you wander from the house. Post emergency phone numbers near the phone, and help orientation with large, easily read calendars and clocks. You may need to stop driving. In many states, your doctor has a legal obligation to report your dementia to the appropriate state agency so that it can assess whether you can keep your license.

There are many additional services to make care at home easier. Visiting-nurse services can be arranged, or special health aids can be obtained as needed; in some cases, you will need the service of full-time attendants, a solution that is, unfortunately, expensive. In many communities, meals can be delivered and supervised transportation obtained with a phone call. A case manager may be able to help your family arrange and coordinate all these services. It is of prime importance to find out what options you have and to contact people and agencies who can provide, often free, the services you need. It is the creativity of your doctor, social worker, family, and friends all working together to find the right solutions that can allow you to remain in your own home. If you prefer to go to a nursing home, choose it carefully. A few excellent books are now available to help the families of those with dementia. One of the best, and the one that I recommend, is *The 36-Hour Day,* by Nancy L. Mace and Peter V. Rabins.

Doctors have described dementia for centuries and have had a name for its principal cause, Alzheimer's disease, for nearly eighty years, but we still know very little about either. Although our ignorance is great, there are several areas in which we are making progress. It is clear that neither dementia nor Alzheimer's disease is a normal part of aging. Dementia differs from delirium, depression, and other treatable medical problems that cause changes in mental function. Occasionally, dementia can be treated successfully. More often, it can't, and the condition will worsen with time. Nevertheless, even when dementia cannot be treated, there remains a great deal that all of us can do to provide comfort and care to those who suffer from it.

16

URINARY INCONTINENCE

I ncontinence is the inability to properly control the function of your bladder or bowel. If you are incontinent, you can't control when or where you urinate and defecate. Urinary incontinence, discussed in this chapter, is much more common than fecal incontinence, affecting between 5 and 10 percent of people over age 65—approximately 2 million people!

Urinary incontinence can become extremely difficult for you or your family to handle. In fact, the burden of incontinence is the most common reason why elders enter nursing homes. Even in nursing homes, incontinence continues to affect happiness and health, taking up half of the time nurses spend caring for patients. Patients need to be cleaned, their clothing and bed linen have to be changed, and the medical complications, including rashes, infections, and bed sores, demand attention. All told, we spend nearly $8 billion each year on incontinence and its associated problems.

Despite the widespread occurrence, the high cost in terms of dollars, time, the quality of life lost, and the medical complications of urinary incontinence, many people are reluctant to discuss this problem with their doctors. As doctors, we are not blameless either; we often fail to ask about incontinence, and some doctors are not well informed about the many ways

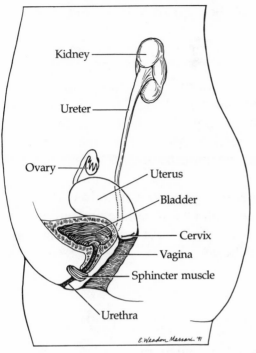

FIGURE 11
Female Urinary Tract

Kidney

Ureter

Ovary

Uterus

Bladder

Cervix

Vagina

Sphincter muscle

Urethra

E. Weadon Massari '91

FIGURE 12
Male Urinary Tract

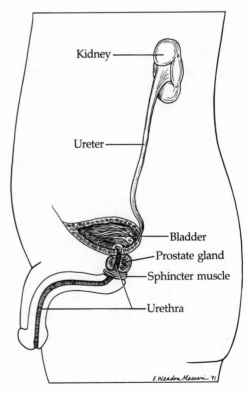

Kidney

Ureter

Bladder

Prostate gland

Sphincter muscle

Urethra

E. Weadon Massari '91

in which incontinence can be controlled or successfully treated.

Incontinence is not a normal part of aging and can often be completely cured. When it can't, incontinence can often be brought under control. There is always something that can be done to prevent it from ruining your life. The first thing you should realize is that you are not alone in your suffering—millions experience the same embarrassment, the same fears, and the same dread. Never hesitate to discuss your incontinence problem with your doctor. There is almost always something that can be done to improve the situation.

To understand incontinence and what can be done about it, you first need to know something about how your bladder works and how it passes urine.

WHAT IS INVOLVED IN URINATION?

The process of passing urine, called *micturition,* is more complex than you might think. Follow Figures 11 and 12 to help you understand the anatomical features involved.

Your kidneys produce urine and pass it through the *ureters* to the *bladder,* where it is stored. Your bladder is primarily a muscle and must squeeze to empty itself. Your body has several mechanisms to help hold urine in the bladder. Two round muscles, called *sphincters,* at the base of the bladder remain tight, providing a muscular barrier. In addition, normally your bladder is positioned within your abdomen so that pressure from your abdominal muscles is applied on the sphincters and not on the bladder itself. Your *urethra,* the tube that leads from your bladder and through which urine passes out of your body, also has some built-in resistance to help hold back urine.

Nerves in your bladder measure when it is full and signal your brain to say that the bladder needs to empty. Another part of the brain, however, allows you to hold your urine until you get to the bathroom. When you are ready to urinate, your brain sends signals to the sphincter muscles, causing them to relax, and to the muscles in the walls of the bladder, causing them to contract and squeeze the urine out.

To control your urination, all parts of this complex system must work in a coordinated and cooperative way. Problems in different parts of the system lead to different kinds of incontinence. Doctors talk of four types of incontinence: urge incontinence, stress incontinence, overflow incontinence, and spontaneous bladder contractions. Each type of incontinence can be caused by several different problems, including medication use, atrophic urethritis, dementia, diabetes, and several other diseases.

URGE INCONTINENCE

With aging, the part of the brain that inhibits urination is less able to delay urination; the time between feeling the warning urge to urinate and the necessity to actually do it shortens. If you can feel the need to urinate but can't hold back long enough, you suffer from the most common type of incontinence, *urge incontinence*.

What could be worse? A young person might be able to run the distance as soon the urge is felt, but you are probably less swift, especially if you have had a hip fracture, arthritis, or are ill in some other way. With urge incontinence, the need always to be close to a bathroom may force you to stay in your house rather than venture out. The fear of being caught too far from a toilet may mean that you exercise less, isolate yourself socially, and become depressed.

The Causes and Treatments of Urge Incontinence

Urge incontinence may be caused by a sudden illness or a chronic problem. Bladder infections, for example, can irritate the lining of the bladder and cause urge incontinence. When infection is the cause, the onset usually is sudden and may be accompanied by pain with urination. Other sudden changes, some of which are quite obvious, may cause urge incontinence. For example, if illness or injury makes it difficult for you to get out of bed and walk to the bathroom quickly, you may experience urge incontinence. Fortunately, you can expect to become continent once you become mobile again. Some other causes are not so obvious.

Medication can cause urge incontinence. For example, diuretics ("water pills") increase the amount of urine you produce. The strongest diuretics, furosemide (Lasix), ethacrynic acid (Edecrin), and bumetanide (Bumex), are sometimes prescribed to treat congestive heart failure, while milder diuretics such as hydrochlorothiazide (HCTZ and Dyazide) are used to treat hypertension (high blood pressure). These medications increase the production of urine, placing additional stress on your bladder. If you take them at night, you may experience incontinence, because when you are asleep you are less aware of a full bladder and will have even less time to get to the bathroom.

If a medication is causing or worsening your incontinence, ask your doctor about changing your medication or the time when you take it. If a diuretic is the culprit and causes you difficulties at night, consider taking it in the morning. If you like to go out in the morning, ask your doctor if you can take your diuretic after you get home.

Urge incontinence frequently develops in people with dementia because of deterioration in the part of the brain that inhibits urination. However, incontinence is not necessarily a sign of dementia. Urge incontinence may occur in any older person. You shouldn't fear that because you have urge (or any other kind of) incontinence, you are developing dementia.

If you have urge incontinence, several practical steps may help you. Place a commode, chamber pot, or bedpan near your bed; empty your bladder before going to sleep, before taking a nap, and before venturing out of the house; wear clothing equipped with snaps, zippers, or Velcro rather than buttons and laces so that it is easy to undress quickly. These tactics may lessen or even completely control your problem.

If not, you may have to be creative to remain continent. Charting how often you are incontinent will help determine how often you need to urinate. (If you care for someone with incontinence, especially someone suffering from dementia, do this for them.) If you find that you become wet every 4 hours while awake, set an alarm clock or wristwatch to go off every 3-1/2 hours to remind you to empty your bladder.

There are also medications to treat urge incontinence. They work in one of two ways. Some cause the muscles in the wall of the bladder to relax. When these muscles squeeze, they cause the bladder to empty; relaxing them gives you a little more time before your bladder must empty. For example, all anticholinergic medications (discussed in chapter 2) relax the muscles of the bladder. However, anticholinergic medications have many unwanted side effects, such as constipation, blurred vision, or confusion. Nonetheless, if used carefully, anticholinergic medications such as bethanechol (Urecholine) can be helpful and safe. Another medication, flavoxate (Urispas), relaxes the bladder without strong anticholinergic side effects. It is safer although weaker than bethanechol; I often start treatment with this medication.

Other medications (for example, ephedrine, pseudephedrine, and imipramine) increase the tightness of one of the sphincter muscles that blocks the flow of urine. These medications may increase the time between feeling the urge and the start of urination just long enough to make the difference between continence and incontinence.

STRESS INCONTINENCE

If you lose urine when you cough, laugh, pick up heavy objects, or get up from a bent-over position, you have *stress incontinence,* which is caused by the inability to sufficiently tighten the sphincter muscles that shut off the flow of urine.

Stress incontinence is much more common in women than in men. Although it can affect women of any age and sometimes occurs after giving birth, it is most commonly a problem for elderly women. Stress incontinence is particularly vexing because it occurs when you are most active, often during recreational activities, and are particularly vulnerable to embarrassment. Fortunately, stress incontinence can often be cured or controlled.

The Causes and Treatments of Stress Incontinence

Stress incontinence has three causes: your abdomen may be putting pressure on your bladder rather than helping the sphincter hold back urine; your urethra may not be providing adequate resistance; or your pelvic muscles and sphincters may be weak.

Some older women develop stress incontinence because their bladder has shifted position so that the muscles of the abdomen press on it. If this is your problem, a *pessary,* a mechanical lift inserted into the vagina, may help correct your bladder's position. If you are overweight, losing weight may help reduce the pressure on your bladder. One of several operations, generally safe and effective procedures performed by a *urologist,* may, however, be the best way to reposition your bladder and cure your incontinence.

One of the most common causes of stress incontinence in older women is *atrophic urethritis.* In atrophic urethritis, the tissue lining the urethra, the tube by which urine leaves the bladder, becomes thin. This change occurs after menopause because this tissue depends on estrogen, a hormone whose level in your body declines after menopause. With a thinner urethral lining, your urethra provides less resistance to the flow of urine and may allow urine to leak.

Your doctor can determine if you have atrophic urethritis by performing a vaginal examination and looking at the lining of your vagina and urethra. Atrophic urethritis is easily cured by applying topical estrogen cream directly onto your urethra or by taking estrogen supplements in pill form. (This use of estrogen is also discussed in chapter 17.)

Another factor that contributes to stress incontinence is weakness of the sphincters that are meant to hold back the flow of urine. Special exercises can strengthen the muscles of your pelvis that assist these sphincters. These exercises, which you can learn from printed hand-outs available from your doctor, are the same exercises that many women learned after childbirth to tighten the same muscles.

Your doctor may also prescribe a medication (such as ephedrine, pseudephedrine, or imipramine) to increase the tone of your sphincters. You can take these medications either regularly or just from time to time before situations that might present special awkwardness if you do become incontinent.

OVERFLOW INCONTINENCE

Overflow incontinence occurs if your bladder has become overdistended—that is, stretched with urine. Overdistention can occur because the flow of urine out of your bladder is obstructed in some way or because your bladder muscles can't squeeze properly. When your bladder overdistends, you urinate in frequent small amounts but don't drain your bladder completely. In some people, an overdistended bladder is painful, but others, especially those suffering with dementia or in whom the condition develops slowly, may feel very little discomfort.

Causes and Treatments of Overflow Incontinence

In men, an enlarged prostate, called *benign prostatic hypertrophy* (BPH), can obstruct the outflow of urine. A man's urethra passes through his prostate, and when the prostate is enlarged, it squeezes the urethra, making urination difficult. BPH that is serious enough to cause urinary obstruction or overflow incontinence will almost certainly require an operation. Surgery for BPH is discussed in chapter 17. In both men and women, constipation can distend the rectum (the last part of the colon), which puts pressure on the outflow of the bladder, making it difficult to urinate. Obviously, if you have incontinence from constipation, you will need treatment for the constipation (see chapter 10).

The muscles of the bladder are very sensitive to two types of medications: those with anticholinergic properties and narcotics (both of which are discussed in detail in chapter 2). Anticholinergic medications and narcotics weaken your bladder muscles. When you take these medications, you may feel that you have emptied your bladder completely and that you won't have to urinate again for hours. In reality, your bladder remains partly full, and you will need to urinate again in a very short time.

There are other, less common causes of overflow incontinence, such as injuries to the spinal cord and damage to the nerves of the bladder. The latter may occur if you have had diabetes for many years, because diabetes can damage nerves.

The treatment for overflow incontinence is always to identify and treat its cause. Sometimes, however, it is necessary for your doctor to take quick action to empty your bladder completely. To help you, your doctor may suggest a catheter—a tube inserted into the urethra and into your bladder. The catheter may be removed immediately after your bladder has been drained, or you may have a slightly different type of catheter, a *foley catheter,* left in place for a few days until normal bladder function returns.

Spontaneous Bladder Contractions

Remember that the bladder is largely muscle, a muscle that must squeeze to empty itself. If it squeezes when it shouldn't, you will become incontinent. For reasons doctors don't fully understand, in some older people the bladder occasionally squeezes briefly but forcefully, in what are called *spontaneous bladder contractions.* If you suffer from spontaneous bladder contractions, you don't even feel the urge to urinate, but rather may suddenly—and without warning—leak a small amount of urine. Usually your doctor can diagnose spontaneous bladder contractions from what you describe, but to be sure, you may need special urological tests to measure the contractions of your bladder.

This kind of incontinence can often be treated with the same medications as those used to treat urge incontinence. If you suffer spontaneous bladder contractions, one helpful trick is to urinate frequently, never letting your bladder get full. However, because your bladder may contract even when it is not full, this precaution will not entirely solve the problem.

T A B L E   7

MEDICATIONS THAT CAN CAUSE URINARY INCONTINENCE

Medication	*Why It Causes Incontinence*
DIURETICS (water pills)	Diuretics cause increased urine production and thereby may stress your bladder.
SLEEPING PILLS & TRANQUILIZERS	Sleeping pills may cause you to sleep so deeply that you don't sense a full bladder early enough. It is also more difficult to get to the bathroom quickly when sedated.
ANTIHISTAMINES (allergy pills)	Antihistamines are contained in many cold pills and in most over-the-counter sleeping pills. Most have anticholinergic properties and therefore affect your bladder's ability to squeeze properly. They may lead to an overdistended bladder and finally to overflow incontinence.
NARCOTIC PAINKILLERS	Narcotics, like antihistamines, affect the ability of your bladder to squeeze. Additionally, they can lead to constipation, which in itself can lead to overflow incontinence because of pressure on the outflow of the bladder. They also sedate you, making it more difficult for you to sense a full bladder and get to the bathroom quickly.
GASTROINTESTINAL ANTISPASMODICS (stomach cramp pills)	Antispasmodics are sometimes prescribed for abdominal cramping. These medications have strong anticholinergic effects. As with antihistamines, these medications can lead to retention and overflow incontinence.

INCONTINENCE CAUSED BY MEDICATIONS

Incontinence, particularly urge and overflow incontinence, may be caused or aggravated by certain medications. In addition to those already mentioned, such commonly used medicines as sleeping pills, antispasmodics, and scores of other over-the-counter and prescribed medicines may cause you difficulties. Your primary-care doctor should know all of the medications you take and should determine if any of them is causing your incontinence. Table 7 lists some of the medications that most commonly lead to incontinence.

EVALUATING INCONTINENCE

Your primary-care physician may know how to evaluate incontinence, or he or she may refer you to a geriatrician or a urologist, a doctor who specializes in treating problems of the bladder and urinary tract. Regardless, the evaluation will begin with a medical history. Your doctor will ask you when the problem began, whether it happens occasionally or frequently, whether you experience an urge to urinate when it happens, and whether the problem occurs only when you cough, sneeze, or pick up heavy objects. Your doctor should ask you about other medical problems such as diabetes, congestive heart failure, and hypertension and should review all the medications you are using, both prescription and over-the-counter. Your doctor will then perform a physical examination. For women, the examination should include an internal pelvic examination. In both men and women, the doctor should also do a rectal examination.

As part of the evaluation, your doctor may suggest what is called a *diagnostic catheterization*. This test is performed after you have tried to empty your bladder completely. It allows your doctor to measure how much urine remains in your bladder, the *postvoid residual*, and to test for infection in your urine. In a diagnostic catheterization, the doctor inserts a thin tube into your urethra and removes it just a few moments later. Although the test may be momentarily unpleasant, it generally is not painful.

You may need further tests to diagnose the cause of your incontinence. For example, *urodynamics* measure the tone and contractions of your bladder, using a catheter and a pressure gauge. A simplified version of this test can be performed by your primary-care physician; a more comprehensive version of urodynamics requires special equipment and is performed by a urologist.

CATHETERS

Sometimes, doctors suggest the use of a foley catheter for people with incontinence, especially for persons with dementia who live in nursing homes. A *foley catheter* is a tube that remains in place, draining urine into a bag. Although there are times when it is important to use this device, many nursing homes use them too frequently and for too long. Incontinence should be treated with a foley catheter only under special circumstances: when the skin of the thighs or back is getting damaged by constant contact with urine, and after other means of keeping the skin dry and healthy have failed, for example.

Foley catheters shouldn't be used routinely to treat incontinence because they greatly increase the risk of infection and can cause simple bladder infections to become serious illness; they are also just plain uncomfortable. They are convenient for the nursing home because they lessen the staff's work. Since catheters are often used inappropriately, if someone you care for is in a nursing home and has a foley catheter, ask the doctor whether all alternatives to a catheter have been tried and why the catheter must be used. Convenience for the nursing-home staff is not a legitimate reason to use a foley catheter.

INCONTINENCE PADS

Incontinence pads to absorb urine are now generally available. In the past, adults with incontinence had to use diapers to absorb urine, but now they can purchase inconspicuous, properly fitting, disposable undergarments that help protect outer clothing and prevent odor or stain from becoming apparent. Incontinence pads are particularly useful for people suffering from stress and urge incontinence.

If you hide your incontinence, you will miss the chance to cure or control it. This is a shame because so many of the causes of incontinence are easily diagnosed and treated. Even if your incontinence can't be completely cured, there are many ways to adapt to it, which will allow you to go on leading a full life. So, talk about the problem with your doctor and those close to you. If your doctor doesn't know how to evaluate incontinence, ask for a referral to a geriatrician or urologist who does. Although most older persons with incontinence can be evaluated through a careful and complete medical history and physical examination, some will need to undergo brief catheterization. In a few cases, the doctor may want to refer you to a urologist or geriatrician for further tests. No one enjoys these evaluations and your embarrassment is understandable. But your doctors can often work with you to cure or control your incontinence.

SEXUALITY, GYNECOLOGY, AND REPRODUCTIVE ORGANS

The ancient Romans used to say that for women, life begins at 40, the age when the priestesses of Vestal were freed from their vows of chastity. Since then, most of the world has come to feel that both life and sex begin somewhat earlier. Yet, many of us still labor under the ill-conceived notion that sexual desire and activity stop sometime before old age.

One of my professors had an interesting way of pointing out the fallacy of this notion to his college students. In the first class of our course on human sexuality, he would spy out a freshman, and, finger pointed, say, "So now you've gone off to college, leaving your parents alone for the first time in eighteen years. Do you know how relieved they are to have you out of the house? Do you know how they're celebrating being together without the kids? And do you know what they're doing right now? On your living-room couch?" Needless to say, each year the mortified student shrunk into his chair with horror, thinking, "Not my parents! They wouldn't; they couldn't!"

Many people remain sexually active into their eighties,

273

nineties, and beyond. Others do not. Normal aging leads to many changes in sexuality, but it doesn't lead to an end of sexual desire or the ability to fulfill that desire. Some people stop having sex as the result of changes in relationships or because they simply don't have a partner with whom to be sexual. For a few, illness does affect their sexuality. As with all physiological functions, people differ in the way their sexuality changes with aging. As with every other topic in this book, you shouldn't feel shy about discussing with your doctor your concerns or problems regarding sexuality.

Everyone, even the most sexually active elders, experiences changes in sexual performance with age. In this chapter I will discuss those changes and what they mean in relationships. You'll also learn about problems of the reproductive organs and about some of the abnormalities of sexual function and how they can be treated.

Physical Changes in Women

After a certain age, women can no longer bear children. With *menopause,* you lose your fertility, and fundamental changes occur in your reproductive organs and in the levels of female hormones in your body. When menopause began, your ovaries and uterus became less sensitive to the hormones that once stimulated them to *ovulate* (release eggs) and *menstruate* (bleed) every month. At menopause, your body responded by producing even greater amounts of those hormones in surges, and you may have experienced hot flushes and mood swings because of the sudden, high levels of hormones. Eventually, however, the surges stopped and your hormone levels fell, terminating the cycle of hormone production, ovulation, and menstruation that began at puberty.

Estrogen and Its Effects

The very low, postmenopausal levels of *estrogen* and *progesterone,* the two most important female hormones, cause a variety of changes in your body but don't affect your underlying sexuality. The low hormone levels affect your bones, causing them to lose strength, a problem discussed in detail in chapter 5. Your breasts change in size and shape because the low levels of estrogen can't stimulate the glandular tissue of your breasts to grow. The layer of fat below your skin has thinned, too, making your skin appear less robust, more vulnerable to injury, and more likely to show wrinkles. However, there is no evidence that the lower hormone levels affect your personality, make you less interested in sex, or less capable of enjoying it.

Other kinds of tissue besides breast tissue require the stimulation of high levels of estrogen to grow. The linings of the vagina and the urethra, for example, become thinner and dryer. If the lining of the urethra becomes especially thin, *atrophic urethritis* may result, leading to incontinence of urine (discussed in the preceding chapter). If the lining of the vagina becomes thin and dry enough to cause bleeding or to make sexual intercourse painful, the condition is called *atrophic vaginitis*. Both of these conditions may affect your sexual activity, but both can be treated successfully.

Estrogen Replacement

Fortunately, your doctor can give you the estrogen that your body no longer produces. This treatment, called estrogen replacement therapy, makes sense for many, but not all, older women. If you are bothered by the effects of low estrogen, discuss this therapy with your doctor. Estrogen replacement, when used at low doses, is quite safe and has many beneficial effects on your bones, heart, blood vessels, and skin, as well as on your breasts and the lining of your vagina and urethra. Estrogen replacement is not without side effects, however, and has been shown to increase slightly your risk of breast and uterine cancer. Some women also experience an uncomfortable enlargement of the breasts and a recurrence of monthly menstrual bleeding.

Estrogen replacement is safest when used at low doses, generally 0.625 milligrams of conjugated estrogen per day. Many experts recommend that you take the estrogen replacement for only three weeks of each month, to mimic the natural cycle that your body produced prior to menopause. There may even be benefit to taking the second female hormone, progesterone, during the week that you do not use estrogen; this schedule even more closely duplicates the natural cycle of hormone production before menopause. However, the recommendations for estrogen replacement are frequently revised, so be certain to revisit the issue with your doctor from time to time.

The way you take replacement estrogen depends on what you are trying to accomplish. For example, if you want to stimulate growth of the tissues of your urethra and vagina, you may prefer to use estrogen cream, which concentrates its effectiveness where you want it and helps avoid side effects. If you want to prevent osteoporosis (discussed in chapter 5), you must take the estrogen by mouth so that it can be absorbed into your bloodstream and reach your bones. Ask your doctor if estrogen replacement is appropriate for you. If you use it, ask for the lowest effective dose, and take it for only three weeks of each month.

Vaginal Lubrication and Engorgement

When you become sexually aroused, the blood flow to the vagina increases, leading to thickening of the tissues of the vagina and the production of lubrication. These changes make sexual intercourse more comfortable for both partners. As you age, these normal sexual responses occur more slowly, and the amount of natural lubrication produced often decreases. These changes may cause discomfort during sex, a condition called *dyspareunia.*

Therefore, many older women (and their sexual partners) find that they must allow more time for foreplay, such as kissing, caressing, and touching, in order to allow the vagina to engorge and to produce its natural lubrication, before attempting sexual intercourse. Some couples aren't used to extended foreplay and will need to speak frankly about what each partner needs to do for sexual activity to be comfortable and pleasurable. If this is difficult for you, talk with your doctor, who may be able to facilitate the conversation and further explain the physiological aspects to both of you. Your physical discomfort is probably coming from a normal change in your physiology and not from a change in your emotions.

If a little added time and foreplay aren't sufficient to permit comfortable intercourse, you may benefit from using a lubricant that helps eliminate vaginal dryness. Water-soluble lubricants, such as Johnson & Johnson's K-Y Jelly, are generally good, but ask your doctor or pharmacist for a specific recommendation.

Estrogen replacement, discussed above, may be the best solution. If you have discomfort during sexual intercourse, your doctor should perform a pelvic examination to determine if you have signs of atrophic vaginitis. If so, your doctor may recommend estrogen cream. Some people find the cream inconvenient, however, and prefer to take estrogen by mouth. Both forms work equally well. But don't expect to notice a change immediately; the treatment may take several weeks to be effective.

Physical Changes in Men

Men don't experience a menopause, and most remain fertile throughout life. Yet, men experience important physiological changes in their sexuality. These changes are, in many ways, just as dramatic as those that occur in women but may be much less noticeable since they occur more subtly, over many years.

Hormones

The major male sexual hormone is *testosterone,* and testosterone levels decline with age. Although this change probably has minimal effects on sexual interest or function, it may explain why certain illnesses and some medications more frequently cause impotence in older men.

Erections

When a man becomes sexually aroused, the blood flow through the penis increases, and a muscle at its base tightens, slowing the outflow of blood. The result is an erection. With age, several aspects of this process change. You don't get an erection as quickly as you did in your youth. You may have noticed that your erection softens faster, too. Finally, even at the peak of sexual arousal, the erection is not as firm as when you were young.

Happily, these changes do not normally interfere with your ability to have sexual intercourse. As with women, a little extra time spent in foreplay usually allows you to become fully erect. The use of a lubricant will facilitate penetration, even if your penis is not fully firm.

The most vexing problems occur when men and women become troubled by what are really just normal changes. Men may fear that getting erect more slowly or having a softer erection is a sign that they are losing sexual potency or are somehow less "virile." Women may be afraid that they no longer arouse their partner. Such fears can lead to psychological problems that in turn affect sexual performance and enjoyment. If you are concerned about your ability to develop an erection, talk with your doctor.

IMPOTENCE

Impotence is the inability to have pleasurable sexual relations. Although impotence is usually thought of as a man's problem, women can also suffer from impotence. There are three kinds of impotence: the loss of desire for sexual relations, the inability to perform sexually, and the inability to reach sexual orgasm.

Libido

Sexual desire is sometimes called *libido*. Your libido can be affected by both medical and psychological conditions. Many medications decrease libido, leaving you uninterested in sex,

T A B L E   8

MEDICATIONS THAT CAN CAUSE SEXUAL IMPOTENCE

BETA-BLOCKERS	(such as propranolol [Inderal], nadolol [Corgard], atenolol [Tenormin], metoprolol [Lopressor])
RESERPINE	(such as Serpasil, Sandril, Rauwiloid, Moderil)
GUANETHIDINE	(Ismelin)
METHYLDOPA	(Aldomet)
CLONIDINE	(Catapres)
ESTROGEN USE BY MEN	(such as DES, used for prostate cancer)
NARCOTICS	(such as codeine, propoxyphene [Darvon], oxycodone [Percocet/Percodan])
CIMETIDINE	(Tagamet)
BARBITURATES	(such as phenobarbital)

and many also affect a man's ability to have an erection. Table 8 describes some of the medications that have one or both of these side effects.

Virtually any serious medical illness can affect libido. And if you are weak and tired, you aren't likely to be interested in sexual activity. Liver and kidney diseases are particularly well known for decreasing sexual desire, and alcoholism commonly affects libido.

Psychological illness is another common cause of loss of interest in sex. One of the hallmarks of depression, for example, is a loss of pleasure of any kind, including sexual pleasure. If someone you love suffers from depression and loses interest in sex, consider this loss as a sign that the depression is worsening and seek medical advice.

Sometimes, relationship problems can affect your sexual desire. As a result, couples may lose physical interest in each other and simply stop having sex. Sometimes sexual interest dies when love dies, but that is not always the case. For some couples, old age brings a natural termination of sexual contact, while others remain sexually active. However, if one of you is interested in sex and the other is not, unhealthy resentment and anger can follow. Your doctor should ask about your sexual activity and whether it or its absence is causing difficulties for you or your partner. If need be, your doctor can direct you to counseling or other psychological treatment to resolve some of these questions.

Many older persons would like to have sex but do not have an available partner. What makes it hard for them to meet new people is a lack of social or relationship skills, especially if they have had one partner for many years and then found themselves once again single. Eventually, the lack of a partner may lead you to lose interest in sex altogether. Or, it may inspire you to develop the skills necessary to find a new partner and to rediscover fulfilling sexual relations.

Inability to Perform Sexually

In order for a man to have sexual relations, he must be able to get and maintain an erection; when he can't, doctors call the problem *erectile impotence*. For a woman to have sexual relations, she must be comfortable during sex; when she isn't, doctors refer to the problem as *dyspareunia.*

Many medications impair a man's ability to have an erection. Table 8 describes the more common ones. If you are concerned, ask your doctor about the medications you are using, especially those used to control high blood pressure. Alcohol, although not usually thought of as a medication, is well known for affecting erections. As Shakespeare noticed, alcohol provokes the desire but takes away the performance.

Two common illnesses, altherosclerosis and diabetes, can also cause erectile impotence. Atherosclerosis clogs arteries and decreases blood flow. If the artery that supplies blood to the penis is partially blocked, you will not be able to have an erection. Diabetes can also affect both the blood supply and the nerves to the penis.

Treatment is available for erectile impotence. If your doctor isn't familiar with the treatment or is uncomfortable talking about the subject, ask for a referral to another doctor, either an internist or a urologist who specializes in impotence.

Your doctor will determine if your problem is due to atherosclerosis, nerve damage, or a psychological problem. The tests are all simple and shouldn't be embarrassing when carried out by a concerned and sensitive physician. Once your doctor has determined the cause of your problem, he or she will be able to recommend treatment.

A ring or band that fits around the base of the penis often provides a solution; it prevents blood from leaving the penis but does not block the flow in, thereby causing an erection. These aids can be purchased in shops that sell sexual paraphernalia, or your doctor can help you order one. More sophisticated devices actually pull blood into the penis with a kind of pump. Your doctor will help you determine what aid is best for you.

If these devices fail, another option is surgery. Of course, surgery should not be considered by everyone, but if you want to be sexually active and can't because of this problem, discuss surgical procedures with your doctor. A urologist who specializes in treating impotence can insert a pump system into your penis to replace the natural mechanism for producing an erection. Although this may seem fantastic, the effect is quite natural and the implanted pump can allow you to lead an active sex life.

Women, like men, can also have problems performing sexually. Just as the penis engorges with blood to become erect, the vagina engorges with blood and the muscles of the pelvis relax to allow sexual penetration. If this doesn't happen, women experience pain during sex (dyspareunia). This condition can be due to both medical and psychological problems. As we saw earlier, atrophic vaginitis can cause it; surgery or radiation therapy that has narrowed the vagina or harmed its lining is another cause. Even vaginal infections can lead to dyspareunia, although treating the infection generally cures the problem. Many different types of psychological distress, including depression, anxiety, and distaste for sex or for your sexual partner, can contribute to or cause dyspareunia.

If atrophic vaginitis is the cause, estrogen taken by mouth

or applied to the vagina may help. If surgery or radiation is to blame, corrective surgery may be possible. Vaginal infections can always be treated with antibiotics, suppositories, or douches. Counseling and other forms of psychological therapy are helpful for many people, regardless of whether a medical condition is causing dyspareunia. Remember also that if you want to have sex but find it painful, you can be sexually intimate without penetration.

Orgasm and Ejaculation

Age alone does not affect a woman's ability to reach orgasm or a man's ability to ejaculate. The quantity of semen that men produce in old age diminishes and the sperm in the semen may not be as fertile, but men are physically able to ejaculate regardless of age unless medications or illness interfere. The medications that most often affect ejaculation are the same ones that affect libido and erections and are described in Table 8, above; most commonly, these are drugs used to treat high blood pressure.

GYNECOLOGICAL PROBLEMS

In older age, women can experience all of the gynecological problems that occur earlier in life, and several additional ones that in fact become more likely. Some are structural, such as uterine prolapse, and others are gynecological cancers, including cervical and ovarian cancer.

Uterine Prolapse

The uterus is normally held in place by ligaments—bands of strong, fibrous tissue. If these ligaments weaken, your uterus can shift its position. Most often, this change causes little or no problem, but occasionally it causes pain, interferes with urination, causing incontinence or difficulty in urinating, or puts pressure on the vagina, making sexual intercourse uncomfortable. When necessary, a gynecological surgeon can reposition the uterus and secure it in place. This operation is not a procedure to be undertaken lightly, but it is relatively uncomplicated and usually successful.

Gynecological Cancer

Cancer can occur in any part of the female reproductive system—one reason why your doctor should perform periodic gynecological examinations. Your doctor will look for cancer in the vagina, perform a Pap smear to screen for cancer of the cervix, and feel your ovaries to search for enlargements that might indicate a cancerous tumor. For some older women, yearly examinations are needed; others may need these examinations only every few years.

Vaginal cancer can start in the skin and membranes lining the vagina or the vulva. These cancers may be raised, appearing as warts or skin tags, or they may be ulcerated, like a sore that doesn't heal. These cancers can cause pain, swelling, or discharge, but often they cause no symptoms at all. If you develop any new growth or sore on, in, or near your vagina, see your doctor. As long as you discover the cancer early, a gynecological surgeon can remove it for a complete cure. These vaginal cancers and their treatment are similar in many ways to other kinds of skin cancer, described in detail in chapter 6.

Cervical cancer occurs most commonly in women between the ages of 50 and 70 but continues to be a potential problem throughout late age. When cervical cancer is diagnosed early, it can be cured with surgery. The operation, called a *hysterectomy*, removes the uterus and usually the cervix.

Cervical cancer grows slowly. After it has spread, however, it is very difficult to treat, and a complete cure for advanced cervical cancer is rarely possible. That is why it is important for women of every age to have a Pap smear regularly. A Pap smear, as you probably know, is a simple screening test for cervical cancer. Your doctor performs it by gently scraping the surface of your cervix with a wooden stick and placing the material on a glass slide. If you have had Pap smears regularly and they have always been normal, after age 65 you need to have the test repeated only every two to five years. However, if you have had abnormal Pap smears or have close relatives who have had cervical cancer, you should have a Pap smear yearly. Don't forget to have your Pap smear: it can save your life.

Ovarian cancer, fortunately, is not common. It is very serious, difficult to diagnose, and difficult to treat.

Ovarian cancer rarely causes early symptoms. Your doctor may feel an enlargement when performing a pelvic examination, but generally, small ovarian cancers are difficult to spot. As the cancer grows and spreads, you may experience abdominal pain, weight loss, nausea, and enlargement of the abdomen. If your doctor suspects ovarian cancer, you will probably have a CAT scan or ultrasound (a test that uses sound waves just like the sonar used in submarines) to see if your ovaries are abnormal. Currently, however, there is no good way to screen for ovarian cancer.

Ovarian cancer can be treated with chemotherapy, but the success rate is low. The drugs are very potent and will likely make you sick. If chemotherapy is recommended, ask your doctor about the likelihood that the treatment will cure you and what side effects you are likely to experience. (See chapter 11 for a discussion of chemotherapy.)

PROBLEMS WITH THE SCROTUM, TESTICLES, AND PROSTATE

Men too can experience medical problems with their reproductive organs. Some of these conditions, such as hernias, are not unique to old age but can happen throughout life. Others, such as prostate enlargement and prostate cancer, occur mostly in old age.

Hernias

A hernia, often called a "rupture," occurs when a portion of the intestinal tract pushes through a weakening in an abdominal muscle. Hernias can occur in several different locations, but the most common type is an *inguinal hernia.* The inguinal canal is the passageway through which your testicles passed from inside your abdomen to your scrotal sac when you were very young. After your testicles descended, your body closed off the inguinal canal so that your intestines could not slip through. On occasion, a piece of intestine manages to get caught in the canal, a condition known as an inguinal hernia.

Often, inguinal hernias cause little noticeable pain or other complications. You may develop a temporary hernia when you bend over or strain, but the situation resolves itself as soon as the piece of intestine pulls back out of the canal. If the hernia persists, you may notice a bulge in or near your scrotum. If, however, the piece of intestine gets caught, you can experience severe pain and damage the intestine.

If you have a recurring inguinal hernia and it causes you pain, or if your hernia may damage your intestines, you will probably need an operation. Fortunately, repair of an inguinal hernia is relatively simple. If you are particularly healthy, you may be able to have the operation performed as an outpatient. If not, expect to spend one night in the hospital. During the operation, the surgeon pulls the intestine out of the inguinal canal and tightens the canal by sewing it partially closed, so that the intestine can't slip through again.

Prostatic Enlargement

The *prostate* is the gland that produces the liquid part of your semen. As shown in Figure 12, it is located just below the base of your penis, and it can be felt as a small dome by inserting a finger into your rectum. Your doctor feels your prostate during a rectal examination. The prostate surrounds the urethra, the tube that brings urine from the bladder and through the penis.

As you get older, your prostate enlarges, but generally this change causes no problem. However, if your prostate gets too big, a condition called *benign prostatic hypertrophy* or, BPH, as it is called (benign means "not cancerous," and hypertrophy means "enlargement"), the prostate can block the flow of urine through the urethra.

If your prostate is causing a blockage of urine, you may find that it is difficult to start your stream of urine. It may also be difficult to empty your bladder completely, in which case it fills up again quickly and you have to go to the bathroom frequently. Prostatic enlargement may interfere with your sleep if you must get up periodically to urinate.

If prostatic enlargement leads to a serious blockage, you may need an operation to open up your urethra. This operation, a *transurethral prostatectomy* (often abbreviated *TURP*), is performed by a urologist in the hospital, either with general anesthesia or a spinal tap. The urologist removes part of your prostate by inserting a thin scope into your urethra. At the end of the scope a tiny knife cuts away part of the prostate and opens the urethra. You can expect to be in the hospital for only one day but for several days may feel some pain when you urinate.

Although this operation has become routine, you should have it only if necessary—if you must strain to pass urine or if a backup of urine is harming your bladder or kidneys. If you are experiencing only minor symptoms, consider delaying the operation. Although it is generally safe, having anesthesia and the stress of any operation always pose some risk. In addition, a small percentage of men become impotent after a TURP. If you are sexually active, discuss this possible complication with your doctor before you agree to the operation.

If you have prostatic enlargement, there are two precautions you must take. First, never use medications with anticholinergic side effects (see chapter 2). Anticholinergic medications weaken the bladder and may further diminish your ability to pass urine. Second, avoid letting your bladder get too full. Go to the bathroom frequently and take the time to empty your bladder as much as possible.

Prostate Cancer

Prostate cancer is remarkably common. Fortunately, it grows very slowly and generally does not spread until it has been in the prostate for several years. However, once it spreads it can cause terrible symptoms and is rarely curable. (Prostate cancer is discussed in detail in chapter 11.)

Many people remain sexually active throughout their lives. Yet, we all experience normal age-related changes in our sexual functions and must adapt to them. The organs of sex and reproduction age with you, and you must be aware of the few changes that might indicate a medical problem. If your doctor is uncomfortable discussing these issues or is not knowledgeable, see another doctor. Despite what many people may say or think (". . . at your age!"), be assured that age alone presents no barrier to having or enjoying sexual activity. An active sex life, for those who want it, can be maintained at any age. When you do have a sexual problem, talk it over with your doctor. Many such problems have a physical cause that can easily be treated, and if the cause is psychological, your doctor is often a good source of information.

18

PREVENTION

Doctors talk about three types of prevention. *Primary prevention* attempts to prevent an illness or injury from occurring—getting a yearly flu shot, for example. *Secondary prevention* involves discovering a disease early, when it can still be cured—for example, getting a mammogram for early discovery of breast cancer. *Tertiary prevention* attempts to minimize the bad effects of a disease or an accident. Keeping a wound clean and dressed to prevent infection is an example of tertiary prevention.

Not all diseases and disabilities can be prevented, especially in older persons. Additionally, many medical problems that could have been prevented would have required a change in your lifestyle decades ago, and none of us can go back in time. Yet, a surprising array of common health problems can either be prevented altogether or their effects mitigated if you discover and treat them early. Prevention is not always easy, and you may have to change your diet, take up exercise, or abandon bad habits. If you make those commitments sensibly, however, you are likely to be healthier. In this chapter I will discuss how pollution, diet, exercise, vaccinations, and periodic medical examinations affect your health and what you can do to prevent avoidable medical problems.

POLLUTION

Although pollution affects our air, water, and the foods we eat, we know very little about how most specific pollutants affect our health. Some substances in the environment cause illness rapidly, while others affect us only after many years of exposure. You may just now be suffering the consequences of pollutants to which you were exposed many years ago. Doctors are quite certain of the link between some pollutants, such as cigarette smoke and asbestos, and disease. For other environmental factors, our evidence is more ambiguous. Nonetheless, scientists are certain that many chemicals in the environment can harm your health, and avoiding the known risks is likely to help you avoid disease.

Smoking

One of the most common and harmful environmental pollutants is cigarette smoke. Cigarette smoke damages your lungs' ability to sweep out harmful bacteria, making you more susceptible to bronchitis and pneumonia. It causes a chronic irritation that destroys your lung tissue, eventually leading to emphysema and chronic bronchitis. Cigarette smoke also makes your arteries constrict, decreasing the blood supply to your legs, feet, and hands. Likewise, blood supply to the skin is also reduced, and some scientists believe that this reduction accelerates the formation of wrinkles. Cigarette smoke is also a *carcinogen* (an agent that causes cancer) and is directly responsible for most cases of lung cancer. A recent report indicates that more than 400,000 Americans died in 1990 as a result of smoking. The more you have smoked in your lifetime, the more likely you are to develop these problems.

Even inhaling the smoke of those around you can make you sick. There is good scientific evidence to show that sitting in a room with someone who is smoking exposes you to many of the harmful effects of the cigarette smoke.

But there is good news even for smokers. When you stop smoking, your body begins to heal itself, regardless of your age. Within weeks, your lungs' self-cleaning mechanism improves. After quitting, every year that you do not smoke further diminishes your risk of developing lung cancer, emphysema, and chronic bronchitis. Even if you already have lung problems, your breathing will almost assuredly improve if you stop smoking. The data from researchers are clear: if you smoke, no matter what your age, stop! If someone you love smokes, try your best to get him or her to stop. Don't allow others to smoke around you, especially if you have lung or heart disease.

Air Pollution and Industrial Pollution

Long exposure to air pollution may increase your chances of developing chronic lung disease and cancer, just as cigarette smoke can. Smog is an accumulation of toxic chemicals from cars and industry that gets trapped in the air. If you have lung or heart problems, smog is likely to make you short of breath. If you live in a large city or near a factory that spews toxins into the air, you may suffer frequently. Staying inside an air-conditioned building with the windows closed will help; however, even a sealed, air-conditioned room can't block out all the pollution. Some people with lung disease find that breathing is easier in desert communities, where the air is often cleaner and drier.

Many older persons have been exposed to intensely high levels of other forms of pollution in their workplace, a problem called industrial exposure. Although federal and state laws now offer better protection to workers, these laws are relatively recent. If you were a welder, metal worker, miner, or worked with asbestos, you may have inhaled toxic chemicals years ago that have remained in your lungs, where they can cause chronic irritation or cancer. If you worked with paint thinners and other organic chemicals, the skin of your hands and arms were probably in frequent contact with them. Such chemicals can be absorbed through the skin and may have damaged your bone marrow or liver. There is a long list of industrial chemicals that cause medical problems. If your job did expose you to chemicals, asbestos, coal dust, metal filings, or other potentially harmful substances, be certain to tell your doctor and ask if you should be checked for any special health risks.

We don't usually think of noise as a pollutant, but it is. Loud noise for long periods of time in a factory or from machinery elsewhere may have affected your hearing. (Hearing loss from noise and its treatments are discussed in detail in chapter 9.)

EXERCISE

Regular exercise does more to preserve and enhance your health than anything else under your control. In the chapters on osteoporosis, heart disease, and constipation we saw how exercise can prevent or minimize problems from those ailments. Unfortunately, too many people buy the one-liner that "disease is a small price to pay for not having to exercise." That attitude, if you hold to it, can make your later years difficult.

Exercise, above all, makes you more physically fit. Your muscles will be stronger and more limber, helping to prevent injuries. With time, exercise conditions your heart and lungs so that you can be more active without getting short of breath or becoming fatigued. Research studies clearly show that exercise protects you from heart attacks and strokes far more than a modest reduction in your cholesterol level! Put another way, if you were to spend as much effort exercising as you do worrying about cholesterol, you'd be much better off.

Exercise also burns calories, so that you can either lose excess weight or eat more without gaining weight. A good exercise program also helps you sleep better at night and stimulates your GI system, preventing constipation. And weight-bearing exercise—walking, jogging, and dancing—strengthens your bones, helping to prevent osteoporosis.

If you have been physically active all your life, strive to remain so. If you haven't exercised recently, see your doctor before you begin an exercise program to talk over what is appropriate for you. Start slowly and increase your activity every week or so. Starting too vigorously will only make you sore or cause injury; getting back into good physical shape takes time. Regardless of where you begin, you will feel better for the effort you put out.

When you exercise, aim to increase your heart rate and to keep your body moving. This kind of exercise—brisk walking, jogging, biking, and swimming—is called aerobic exercise. Aerobic exercise is better for your body than straining during weight lifting, because it conditions your heart and lungs and lets your body break down fat more efficiently. In order to get the most out of it, be sure to exercise for at least fifteen minutes at a time; your goal should be to condition yourself so that you can comfortably go for thirty minutes or more of sustained aerobic activity without stopping.

Your disabilities may limit the kind of exercise that you do, but everyone can participate. If you have heart or lung problems, you may need to start with the most gentle of activities, like slow walking or even stretching and reaching in place. If you have arthritis, you'll need to choose an activity that does not cause you pain, and if you have problems with your balance, you should exercise while seated.

Walking is one of the best forms of exercise. You may have to begin on level ground. If you are in better physical shape, you'll want to walk up and down hills to get a good workout. Jogging is more vigorous but is more likely to cause injuries to your joints, ligaments, and muscles. If you have arthritis, jogging may be painful.

Bicycle riding is a good alternative to jogging and can be as vigorous as you want while still remaining gentler on your joints. Consider using a stable, three-wheeled bike to reduce the risk of a fall if a two-wheeler feels risky.

If it is not easy for you to exercise outdoors because of bad weather, safety concerns, or problems with your sight or balance, a stationary bicycle may be the solution. Most of these exercisers look very much like a typical bicycle but are constructed so that you can adjust the amount of force required to ride. If you have a balance problem, you might prefer an exercise bicycle with a low seat that has handles on either side, which provide added safety and ease in getting on and off.

Swimming in a pool is wonderfully healthy and vigorous for everyone and especially for people with arthritis. Because your body floats in water, exercising in the pool reduces the weight on your joints, minimizing the risk of injury. The water still provides resistance, however, allowing you to work your muscles and condition your heart. If you can't swim, consider walking in the shallow end of the pool. This activity allows you to enjoy all the benefits of exercising in water. Of course, make sure that the pool is supervised by a lifeguard and, if necessary, has proper rails or grips for your safety.

There is some form of physical activity that is right for you. You just have to try different things until you find it. Exercise need not be boring and in fact should be fun. If you have not exercised in the past, start wisely by first consulting your doctor on how best to begin.

DIET

You can prevent a number of medical problems just through healthier eating. We know that a balanced diet lessens the complications of several common medical conditions, such as diabetes, high blood pressure, and congestive heart failure. However, there is no one diet that is best for everyone. What is healthiest for you depends on your complete medical history and the changes that you are willing to make. Remember that every diet requires giving up something.

Protein and Carbohydrates

In general, you should eat protein, carbohydrate, fat, and fiber every day. Protein, found in meat, eggs, fish, milk products, and many legumes, is necessary for your body to build muscle, skin, and other tissues. Carbohydrates (sugars and starch), which supply your body with energy, are found in bread and pasta, in fruits, and in many beans. Fat is found in meat, dairy products, and many vegetables and nuts.

Fat and Cholesterol

Fat is not all bad, and some fat in your diet is absolutely necessary for your cells to function normally. Polyunsaturated fats, found in vegetables and nuts, don't raise your cholesterol. Other kinds of fat, such as the cholesterol and saturated fats found in meat and cream, tend to increase the cholesterol level in your blood. High cholesterol levels can in turn lead to coronary artery disease and atherosclerosis, the fatty buildup in arteries that reduces blood circulation. Therefore, many doctors recommend that younger persons avoid eating these kinds of fat. Whether avoiding these foods in later life is beneficial, however, has not yet been proved. Since mildly elevated cholesterol levels aren't likely to increase substantially your risk of atherosclerosis or heart disease for many years, it may not make sense for all persons in their eighties and nineties to give up eating animal fats. If you don't care for red meat and can easily cut it from your diet, it's probably a good idea to do so as long as you substitute other forms of protein.

Have your cholesterol level checked at least once. If it is above 260, your risk of developing coronary artery disease (CAD) is high enough to consider making changes in your diet. Discuss with your doctor what, if anything, you should do. If your cholesterol is between 200 and 260, a change in diet will decrease your risk of developing CAD so slightly that for many older people the long-term benefit is negligible. If you're lucky enough to have cholesterol below 200, there is little advantage to reducing animal fat in your diet. (See chapter 3.)

Fiber

As we saw in chapter 10, a high-fiber diet helps prevent constipation, bowel cancer, and diverticulosis. The American diet tends to be low in fiber, the undigestible matter in food that lends bulk to your stool. You can increase the bulk content of your diet by eating fibrous, fresh vegetables such as celery, and whole grains such as bran. You may prefer, however, to take purified fiber produced from plants and seeds and sold under such brand names as Metamucil, Konsyl, Perdiem, and Fibermed.

Sugar

As you grow older, you are less able to digest large amounts of sugar rapidly than when you were younger. This means that even if you don't have diabetes, your blood sugar climbs higher after eating sugar. Although we know that the very high blood sugar levels associated with diabetes can cause serious medical problems, doctors are not sure whether the normal age-related sugar intolerance is harmful. It doesn't make sense, therefore, to avoid sugar entirely. It is probably wise, though, to eat sweets in moderation. At your yearly physical exam, your doctor should determine whether you have any of the warning signs of diabetes, just in case.

Salt

You may have noticed that your taste for salt has changed—you want more of it. As you grow older, your ability to taste salt decreases, and other flavors prevail, making some foods taste bitter. For most people, adding a bit more salt to food presents no difficulty. However, if you have high blood pressure, congestive heart failure, liver or kidney problems, or swelling in your legs, avoiding salt may be very important for you. Salt substitutes contain potassium rather than sodium and may be safer. However, such substitutes also tend to be slightly bitter, a taste magnified by the normal age-related changes in your taste buds. Like many people, you may find that pepper, herbs, or other strong spices are better alternatives for salt than are potassium-based salt substitutes.

Vitamins

Many Americans take vitamin and mineral supplements, although very few need to. Usually, multivitamins contain relatively small amounts of many different vitamins and are unlikely to cause any harm; but they are expensive. If you can't eat a reasonably balanced diet or don't regularly get fresh vegetables and fruits, taking multivitamins may be useful. If you consume a regular balance of meat or dairy products, fresh vegetables, and fresh fruit, multivitamins are unlikely to be of any measurable benefit.

If you do use vitamins, never take high concentrations of any particular vitamin unless your doctor has specifically recommended it. Some vitamins, taken in high concentrations, especially vitamins A and D, can actually cause medical problems. Also, be wary of the extraordinary claims of what vitamins can do. Research studies clearly show that vitamin C can't prevent or cure the common cold. And no one has been able to demonstrate that mineral supplements prevent hair loss, that vitamin E prevents cancer, or that the B vitamins give you more energy. For example, vitamin B_{12}, which some doctors claim gives older people added vigor, will not help you at all unless you have a deficiency in the first place, something easily determined by a simple blood test. If you do have a vitamin deficiency, your doctor will recommend that you take supplements but at a dose that is safe and sensible.

VACCINATIONS

Vaccinations aren't just for children. Everyone over age 65 should receive a vaccination against pneumonia and an annual flu (influenza) shot.

Pneumonia Vaccine

A vaccination against pneumococcal pneumonia, the most common kind of pneumonia in older people, can help prevent the disease. Even if you do get pneumococcal pneumonia, having had the vaccine will protect you from the most serious complications. The vaccine carries virtually no risk and has been shown to reduce the death rate from this disease. You need to get this vaccine only once. If you haven't had it yet, tell your doctor. If you may have had it but aren't sure, there's no harm in being vaccinated again.

Flu Vaccine

Many people mistakenly use the word *flu* to describe the common cold; the real flu, or influenza, is a serious and often deadly viral disease. Nearly 20 percent of elderly people who get the flu die from it. Although it can be prevented with a vaccine, many people needlessly risk their lives by forgetting to have an annual flu shot.

In the United States, flu occurs only from late October through February, causing fevers, muscle aches, fatigue, and an infection of the lungs accompanied by coughing and shortness of breath. Although most people recover, you can expect to spend several days in bed feeling miserable, and many more days—or even weeks—might pass before you regain your full strength.

Influenza can be prevented *if* you get a flu shot every year. The influenza virus changes annually in subtle ways, so the vaccine to prevent the disease must be tailored to the specific strain of that year. Luckily for us, each new influenza strain causes illness first in the Southern Hemisphere, and scientists can manufacture a new vaccine before people in the Northern Hemisphere are affected. Because of these yearly changes in the virus and the vaccine, you must get a flu shot each year, early in the autumn.

A large scientific study has shown that, contrary to what some people have thought, you can neither catch the flu nor a cold by getting a flu shot. Although you probably don't like injections and your arm may well get a little sore from it, the flu shot poses extremely little risk, while protecting you from a deadly illness.

PERIODIC CHECKUPS

Even if nothing seems wrong, you should see your doctor at least once a year. Your regular checkup aims to discover problems early, before they become severe. You and your doctor will have the opportunity to discuss anything worrying you, and your doctor will have a chance to review your general health, diet, exercise routine, smoking, drinking, drug use (both prescription and over-the-counter drugs), and the safety of your home. He or she should be sure that you are emotionally well and that you are not having problems psychologically or sexually.

As part of your physical examination, your doctor will check your heart for unusual sounds or murmurs and your blood pressure to be sure that it is neither too high nor too low. He or she will examine your skin for cancerous lesions and will perform a rectal examination to check for blood in your stool, a warning sign of gastrointestinal cancer. If you are a man, the rectal examination will also include a prostate exam, because nodules or lumps in the prostate may indicate prostate cancer. If you are a woman, your doctor should examine your breasts for lumps to detect breast cancer early.

Your doctor may also suggest some laboratory tests, not necessarily because he or she thinks you have a medical problem but rather to discover any abnormality before it becomes a problem. When a test is used for this purpose, it is called a *screening test*. For example, if you have never had your cholesterol level measured, your doctor may check it. Your doctor may also suggest a CBC (complete blood count) to determine the number of red blood cells, white blood cells, and platelets, and the proportion of cells to liquid in your blood. Your doctor can use the CBC to screen for anemia and other blood problems. Many older people don't need to get a yearly CBC, however, and your doctor will use your medical history to decide if it is appropriate for you.

Another blood screening test measures sugar in your blood. Diabetes is common in older people, and there is evidence that the sooner your doctor detects it and begins treatment, the better off you will be. For a blood sugar test to be an accurate measure of early diabetes, however, you must fast for at least eight hours before your blood sample is taken (see chapter 12).

Women may need two additional tests, although not every year. All women, even those over age 65, should have a pelvic examination and a Pap smear, a simple test for diagnosing cervical cancer. If you have had Pap smears regularly in the past and they have always been normal, the Pap smear may be repeated every five years or so. If, however, you have not been tested regularly or have had some abnormal tests or abnormal findings from pelvic examinations in the past, you may need such tests yearly.

Mammograms are also important for older women because they detect breast cancer in its earliest stages, when it is most likely to be curable. Every woman younger than age 75 should have a yearly mammogram, and many doctors believe that even older women should, too. If you have a family history of breast cancer or have ever had breast cancer or a suspicious breast lump, have a mammogram yearly. Mammography is now very safe and is performed with such a tiny amount of radiation that it poses an extraordinarily low risk.

Personal Safety Devices

If you are athletic and have few health problems, you will require little, if any, safety equipment either at home or outside the house. However, if you have serious osteoporosis, arthritis, or other debilitating disease, if you tend to fall, or even if your walking is a bit unsteady, simple precautions can make your life safer.

For example, be sure that there are secure handrails wherever you have stairs. If you must use stairs that don't have rails, ask someone to lend a hand. Don't stand on a stool or chair to reach for things stored up high; wait until you have help or get someone to move them permanently within easy reach.

The bathroom is a particularly dangerous place: there is little extra space, surfaces get wet and slippery, and bathing and using the toilet tend to lower your blood pressure, which can make you light-headed. If you can't get in and out of a tub or shower easily, have sturdy handrails installed to help you. Be sure that your tub has an antislip surface and that any bath mats have rubber backings so that they too will not slip.

Throughout your home, be sure that you have good lighting. As chapter 8 describes, most older people see better with indirect lighting. If you have rugs, be sure that you can see their edges and will not trip on them. Rugs can be beautiful, but if they cause you to trip, remove them.

If you have had problems with falling or balance, use a cane at least, or a walker if necessary. Your doctor and physical therapist will help you determine what's best for you. Canes can be elegant and, more important, can protect you from falling and thereby breaking a wrist or hip. Walkers are harder to dress up but can help keep you active and prevent a disastrous fall.

If you live alone and are afraid that you won't be able to get help quickly if anything happens, consider getting a medical alert system. According to your needs, these systems—often a small cartridge with a button to push—can be installed in your home or worn around your neck. If you fall or injure yourself, they allow you to summon help easily. Your doctor can help you decide whether a medical alert system makes sense for you.

If you have a serious medical condition or allergies to commonly used medications, wear a medical alert bracelet. Especially if you have diabetes, dementia, heart disease, or allergies to antibiotics, an alert bracelet can save your life by giving the emergency-room doctor vital information that you may be unable to provide.

There is an old saying: "The only way to prevent old age is to die young." The truth is, old age doesn't have to be a time of bad health. You can take steps to prevent some of the less desirable features of old age and many of its more common tribulations. It is never too late to give up bad habits, such as smoking, and it is never too late to start exercising. Your doctor can help you plan a more healthful lifestyle, provide vaccinations to prevent flu and pneumonia, and check your health periodically to discover and treat many illnesses before they become major problems. If your home is not safe for you, you can make it safer with the help of your family or a handyman. In short, you can take advantage of the present to preserve your future.

19

LEGAL ISSUES

In the play *King Henry VI,* Shakespeare's advice seems clear: "The first thing we do, let's kill all the lawyers." It's an attitude shared by many who have confronted the law—or lawyers. But it need not be your experience. There are two inevitabilities—death and taxes, and one possibility—serious illness or incapacity. By taking several simple steps now, you can put the legal system on your side, making it easier for you and your family to confront situations later when illness, disability, or death occurs. You can insure that at the time of your death, or earlier if you become ill or incapacitated, your wishes will control the management of your health care and the management and disposition of your property.

This chapter answers two important questions that you have probably asked yourself. First, who will make health-care decisions for you if you can't make them yourself; second, what will happen to your property—your home, savings, and investments—if you become incapable of managing it yourself and, later, at your death? It is neither ghoulish nor silly but, rather, quite natural to worry about these matters. With a small amount of attention now, you can reduce the anxiety, delays, costs, and loss of control that otherwise will occur if you become incapacitated or die without putting your affairs in the kind of good order you want. Also, you will enjoy the satisfaction of knowing that your wishes have been expressed, and that your desires—and not anyone else's—will control what happens to you and to your property.

In the first part of this chapter, "Your Health Care and the Law," I discuss how you can direct your own medical care if you should become incapacitated. In the second part, "Your Property and the Law," I discuss how you can arrange for the management of your property during any period when you may be incapacitated and for an orderly disposition of your property when you die.

Our legal system operates on federal, state, and local levels. Federal laws apply throughout the United States; state laws apply in a specific state; and local laws apply within a county, town, or city. Federal law affects how your property is taxed when you give it away, whether during your lifetime or at death, and controls the nation's Medicare system. State law determines how you can direct your health care if you are incapacitated and whether you qualify for Medicaid benefits. State law also controls how your property is distributed at your death, unless you make a will or create a living trust. Many states also tax transfers of property, but usually the state tax issues are secondary to the federal.

Although there is only one federal legal system, each of the fifty states (and the District of Columbia) has its own. The differences in law between one state and the next can be significant, making it impossible for me to give you specific advice. Rather, I intend to make you aware of the legal issues you will face and the general way in which the law approaches those issues, and to inform you sufficiently so that you can ask your own attorney the right questions. To make the most of the information in this chapter, you must take what you learn from it to an attorney in your state. If you have summer and winter residences in different states, talk to an attorney in each state, particularly about how each approaches the matter of living wills and health care powers of attorney, both described below.

Certainly there are steps you can take without an attorney. For example, if you live in a state where progressive legislation permits durable powers of attorney for health care and living wills, you may be able to find standardized forms for these documents in your doctor's office or in a stationery store. However, even in many states with new, helpful laws on these matters, you must comply carefully with very specific requirements. Some states require that these forms be notarized; others require that they be witnessed. There is no uniformity. The best advice is to seek out good legal counsel where you live. Seeing an attorney need not be expensive. In many cities there are senior advocacy groups, and your local bar associations may be able to refer you to an attorney who can handle these matters inexpensively.

Your Health Care and the Law

Advance Medical Directives

There are two ways to continue exercising control over your medical care if you become incapacitated. One is to complete a *living will;* the other is to prepare a *durable power of attorney for health care*. Both of these documents are called *advance medical directives,* meaning that they allow you to direct, in advance, aspects of your health care during any period when you can no longer effectively communicate your wishes yourself. An advance medical directive becomes effective only if and when you become incapacitated. As long as you are mentally competent and physically able to communicate, you will control your own health care. An advance medical directive comes into play only after you are no longer able to tell your doctor and your family what you want.

In the absence of an advance medical directive, many states vest control of your health care in a member of your family. If you have no family member who can act, the court may need to appoint a guardian or conservator to oversee your care.

Living Wills

The term *living will* is a bit odd, but is now in general use. The document is so called because it is effective prior to your death (thus, "living") and expresses your desires (thus, "will") for medical care. In some states, the document is referred to as a "directive to physicians" or by some other name. More than forty states now have specific laws authorizing the use of a living will. These state laws vary greatly. Some give effect to your statement of desires only if you are terminally ill. Others allow you to direct your health care if you are permanently incapacitated even if death is not imminent. If your state has a living will statute, you must comply with its requirements to be certain that your wishes will be carried out. That is the lesson of the tragic case of Nancy Cruzan, the young Missourian whose plight led to a landmark Supreme Court decision in 1990.

Nancy was terribly injured in a car accident and entered a permanent vegetative state. There was no reasonable hope that Nancy would ever recover. She was not, however, terminally ill; her death was not imminent. With continued artificial feeding and hydration, Nancy could have lived for another thirty years, bedridden, unconscious, her arms and legs disfigured and shrunken by lack of use. Without modern medical technology, Nancy would neither have survived the accident nor been kept alive thereafter. Her survival was the result of heroic medical intervention just after the accident and, subsequently, of life-prolonging medical technology.

Prior to her accident, Nancy had told a close friend that she feared being kept alive by medical technology under these kinds of circumstances. But Nancy never wrote out her preferences for health care.

Many people deeply believe that if there is any possible way to continue living, regardless of the degree of medical intervention required or the quality of one's life, heroic measures and aggressive technology should be used to extend life for as long as possible. Many other people feel just as strongly otherwise, preferring not to be kept alive if they are dependent on medical engineering or if there is no reasonable hope of a return to their former selves. Nancy was among the second group.

Although Missouri had a law permitting residents to state the kind of medical care they wish to receive if they became incapacitated, the law required clear and convincing evidence of its citizens' desires. The United States Supreme Court ruled that Missouri could require that high degree of evidence. Put another way, if Nancy had put her wishes into writing, they would have been carried out; her comment to her friend wasn't legally sufficient. Accordingly, if you have strong feelings that you don't want your life extended by artificial means, express that belief in writing in accordance with your state law. There is no other way to be certain that your wishes will be followed.

In some states, your wishes must fit into a prescribed statutory form—a standardized legal document. In other states, the law is more lenient. For example, in California, you can make an effective living will by writing your preferences in your own words, provided that you also comply with the other statutory formalities.

If you want to have very aggressive medical treatment, you might sign a statement that says:

> *I want my life to be prolonged to the greatest extent possible without regard to my condition, the chances I have for recovery, the burdens of the treatment, or the costs of the procedures.*

If you want to avoid attempts to extend your life with medical treatments, the statement might read:

> *I do not want my life to be prolonged and I do not want life-sustaining treatment (including artificial feeding and hydration) to be provided or continued if the burdens of the treatment outweigh the expected benefits. I want the relief of suffering and the quality of my life to be considered in determining whether life-sustaining treatment should be started or continued.*

An intermediate position might read:

> *I want my life to be prolonged and I want life-sustaining treatment to be provided unless I am in a coma that my doctors reasonably believe to be irreversible. After my doctors have reasonably concluded that I am in an irreversible coma, I*

do not want life-sustaining treatment (including artificial feed-
ing and hydration) to be provided or continued.

Even if your state does not have a law that permits you to
make a binding living will, expressing your wishes in writing
is still beneficial. The statement can guide your family and
doctors even if it is not legally enforceable.

Durable Powers of Attorney for Health Care

Many states have enacted laws that permit you to create a
Durable Power of Attorney for Health Care (DPAHC). Under
any power of attorney, one person (called the "principal")
designates another person (called the "agent" or the "attorney-in-fact") to act on the principal's behalf. A health care
power of attorney is a document in which you, as principal,
name another person, as your agent, to make your health care
decisions if you can't make them yourself. The power is "durable" because it endures throughout any period that you are
incapacitated. Other kinds of powers of attorney—permitting
someone to take business and other actions on your behalf—
are discussed later in this chapter.

A DPAHC differs from a living will. In a living will, you
express your wishes for the *kind* of medical treatment you
want; with a DPAHC, you designate *who* it is that you want to
have making health care decisions for you whenever you are
unable to make them for yourself. The living will states *what*
you want done and the DPAHC states *who* it is who will direct
your care. For example, if you are in an accident and are
temporarily unable to give direction to your doctors, the
person named in your DPAHC will discuss your medical
alternatives with your doctors and reach a decision on your
behalf. Some DPAHCs include a living will provision, allowing you not only to name an agent to make decisions for you
when you no longer can make them for yourself, but also
giving you the opportunity to express the kind of health care
choices you would make if you were able to communicate.

If your state recognizes DPAHCs, take advantage of the law
by completing the proper form, naming the person in whom

you have the greatest confidence as your agent for making health care decisions. None of us knows when we will be in an accident or suddenly fall ill. The DPAHC allows you to consider, while you are alert and healthy, in whom you place this great trust to carry out your wishes. Whom you should choose is not always obvious or logical, and it is something you need to consider very carefully.

For example, if you feel strongly that you want to avoid aggressive medical treatment, you wouldn't want to name as your agent a child who believes that every possible kind of medical intervention should be used to treat disease. Not everyone will want to name his or her spouse. If you are so ill or incapacitated that you can't make your own decisions, it's quite likely that your spouse will be in a period of enormous emotional stress. You may prefer to name a trusted business associate or longtime personal or family friend to serve as your agent.

Speak frankly with your spouse, children, or other family members before you name someone as your health care agent. Talk to them about your own preferences and listen to their opinions. That way, if the time comes when your health care agent must make a decision for you, you will have selected someone in whom you have confidence, and your family will recognize that your wishes—even if they don't match those of your family—are being carried out. By designating a person whom you trust and by having discussed the matter openly with your family, you minimize the chance that a family feud will develop over the issue of the kind of health care you should receive.

Finally, if you have any unusual circumstance, ask your attorney whether it should be addressed in your advance medical directives. For example, let's say that you are a widower who has been living for several years with a widow, whom you have never married. Let's also say that your own children are not on good terms with your companion. What would happen if you fall grievously ill and your doctors decide to limit your visitors? Under most circumstances, your family would have priority to visit. But in your case, you may prefer that your companion be the first in line. Discuss this kind of special situation—or any other—with your attorney to see whether a specific instruction in your advance medical directives can be helpful in making your desires clearly known and legally enforceable.

Give copies of your DPAHC and living will to each of your doctors. Request that they place the copies in your permanent medical record. If you have used a DPAHC, give a copy to the agent you have named. Place an additional copy or two with your other important papers, somewhere where they can be quickly located if needed. If your lawyer is willing to hold on to the original documents, you may want to keep them on file in that office. If not, file the original in a safe place with your other important papers. Regardless of where you keep the originals, be certain that family members and the agent named in the DPAHC know where they are.

YOUR PROPERTY AND THE LAW

Management of Your Property When You Are Incapacitated

As long as you're capable of managing your own affairs, and if you enjoy doing so, there's no reason not to continue. At any age, however, it's prudent to have contingency plans in the event that you are injured or become ill. Although many accidents and sicknesses will not reduce you to incapacity, it is often useful to have someone with the legal authority to take care of matters while you recover. If you are seriously injured or ill, circumstances may require that someone else step in to manage things. If you have made plans for such an event, the disruption it causes can be minimized and costs kept low. If you haven't, legal fees, court appearances, and a degree of unpredictability enter the scene, making the transition from your management to someone else's expensive, fraught with delays, and the results not necessarily to your liking.

The three principal mechanisms by which you can arrange in advance for someone else to take care of your property if you are unable to do so are: the power of attorney; the revocable trust, also known as a living trust; and joint tenancies.

Powers of Attorney

Recall the discussion earlier in this chapter about durable powers of attorney for health care. A power of attorney, again, is a document in which you appoint an agent to perform specified actions on your behalf. The agent is often called the "attorney-in-fact" (which distinguishes him or her from an attorney-at-law). The document in which you grant powers to act on your behalf to your attorney-in-fact is referred to as a "power of attorney."

A durable power of attorney for health care is a special power of attorney used to designate someone to make health care decisions for you if you cannot make them yourself. But if you become incapacitated—or merely no longer care to deal personally with your bank accounts, investments, or other property—you will also need someone to handle your business affairs. A power of attorney will permit you to designate an agent to do just that. Generally, I recommend using two powers of attorney: one for health care and another for business matters. The agent (that is, the attorney-in-fact) named in the two powers may be the same or may differ. This section discusses the business power of attorney; the health care power of attorney has already been discussed earlier in this chapter.

A power of attorney is effective only *until* you become incapacitated, unless the document is a *durable* power of attorney. There is a legal presumption that a power of attorney is automatically withdrawn if you become incapacitated. However, it is exactly at that moment—when you lose the capacity to act for yourself—that you most need to have an agent to act for you. To overcome this difficulty, almost every state has enacted laws authorizing durable powers of attorney, documents that give your agent the power to act for you during any period of your incapacity. To see the advantages of a durable power of attorney, let me give an example. Let's say that you name your sister to be your attorney-in-fact under a normal power of attorney. While you are away on a trip, your sister can manage your affairs because of the powers given to her under the document. But let's say that on your return home you take a fall, hit your head, and are hospitalized in a coma for a week. During that period of your incapacity, legally, the power of attorney is no longer valid. If, however, you had used a *durable* power of attorney, your sister's authority to act would have continued during the time that you were incapacitated.

A durable power of attorney can become effective either immediately or, if your state law permits, only if you become incapacitated. This second kind of document is known as a *springing power of attorney*—it "springs" into effect when you are incapacitated.

At first, it might seem that the springing power is ideal. After all, why should you give someone the power to buy and sell your home, open and close your bank accounts, buy and sell your stocks, C.D.s, and Treasury Bills, or renew or cancel your lease, until it is necessary to do so? The reason is simple. Demonstrating that a springing power has become effective may require a court hearing, and a court hearing always entails delays and legal costs. I will explain:

When your agent uses the power to perform an act for you, the person on the other side of the table will ask for evidence of the agent's authority to act. For example, a bank manager will ask to see the power of attorney. The manager will want to be certain that it complies with state law, is properly signed, and that the agent is the person named in the document. With a durable power of attorney effective at the moment you sign it, the bank manager may be satisfied by seeing the power and positive identification from the agent. But with a springing power of attorney, the bank manager may also ask for evidence that you are incapacitated—that is, he or she will ask your agent to prove that the power has actually come into effect. Often, the only evidence that the bank manager will accept is a court decree. To minimize this difficulty, some springing powers of attorney state that a third party, such as the bank manager, can rely on medical certificates signed by one or more doctors. However, this certification procedure is rarely satisfactory, and, in practice, it is often difficult to convince someone that your springing power of attorney has become legally effective.

Accordingly, I generally prefer to use a durable power of attorney that is effective when signed rather than a springing power. If you trust someone to handle your affairs when you are incapacitated, you should be able to trust him or her now, while you are well. If giving the power to the agent now causes you to worry, it may be that you have chosen the wrong agent. As long as you have the capacity to act for yourself, you can withdraw your agent's power to act under a durable power of attorney whenever you want. Thus, your choice of agent is not permanent; if circumstances change, you can always name another person to act.

Some lawyers suggest that their clients sign a durable power of attorney that is then kept in the lawyer's vault until needed. In this way, you avoid the problems of a springing power but have not yet delivered the power of attorney into the hands of your agent just yet. The idea is that your lawyer will deliver the power to your agent when you become ill so that the agent can then begin to act. This arrangement may be helpful. However, it also has pitfalls. What happens if you are in an accident when your lawyer is on vacation? What happens if you fall ill and your lawyer does not hear of your condition for several weeks? What happens if your lawyer moves or retires without contacting you? In fact, for these purposes many lawyers are not willing to hold a durable power of attorney. Nevertheless, if this alternative interests you, discuss it with your lawyer. Additionally, if you have known your lawyer for a long time, trust his or her judgment, and believe that he or she knows enough about your affairs to manage them effectively, you also may want to ask him or her to serve as your attorney-in-fact. However, many lawyers routinely prefer not to serve in that capacity and as a matter of course will decline the request.

Before you sign a power of attorney, speak to the person you will name as your agent. Usually this is a husband or wife, a child or other family member, or a close and trusted business associate or friend. Be certain that the person you would like to name is willing to serve. A person named in a power of attorney is not obligated to act and may refuse to do so. It is better to discover now that your selected agent is unwilling to serve. Also, name at least one alternate or successor agent.

Some people prefer to name two or more agents to act at the same time. Here, again, you have some choice. For example, you can require that all of the persons named must act together ("jointly"), or you may permit any one of the named persons to act alone ("severally"). There are advantages to each choice. A *jointly held power* has greater protection because both (or all, if you name more than two) of your agents must agree to act together. But in a world where people travel frequently, move away, or often can't be found quickly, a joint power may not always work: one of the agents may not be available when needed. A *severally held power* gives your agents greater flexibility because any one of your agents can act alone. It may be that you have one child who is particularly good at accounts and another who is especially effective at running your business. You may trust them both to help each other out. In that event, naming them to act severally will permit them to divide up the work and to act on their own, each taking responsibility for a certain portion of your affairs while still holding the power to act in all capacities if the other is out of town.

Whatever choice you make, be certain that you create a power of attorney in accordance with your state's law. For a power to be durable, most states require that it explicitly state something like, *"This power of attorney shall not be affected by my subsequent incapacity and shall remain effective after the incapacity occurs."* For a springing power, the required language may state something like, *"This power of attorney shall become effective upon my subsequent incapacity and remain effective during any such period of incapacity."* Some states require that you use specific wording; others require only that you use language that clearly expresses your intention. Almost everywhere, a durable power of attorney must carry not only your signature but the signature and seal of a notary public. If you sign the power in your lawyer's office, he or she may be a notary or will have a notary available. Also, if the power of attorney is to be used to transfer real estate (for example, if your agent may need to sell your house or a piece of commercial property that you own), the power generally must also be recorded with the recorder of deeds in the county where the house or land is located. Some lawyers record powers of attorney as a matter of course; others wait until it is necessary.

A power of attorney can be "general" or "special." If it is *general*, it gives your agent the power to do virtually anything on your behalf, from selling your home to negotiating a settlement with your business partners. It is possible that a general power of attorney will permit your agent even to make health care decisions for you. If you intend for the agent to have this power, however, you should use a separate durable power of attorney for health care, described earlier in this chapter. Alternatively, a power of attorney can be *special*—that is, limited to a specific purpose. A special power of attorney gives your agent only the specific powers you want to delegate. For example, if you own rental property—and want to give someone only the power to manage that one piece of property, that is, to collect rents from your tenants, to enter into leases, and to authorize repairs and renovations—you will want to use a special power.

Some institutions, particularly banks and brokerage houses, provide their own power of attorney forms for use with accounts at that institution. If they do, they will want you to use them. Do so. Banks are notorious for failing to recognize forms other than their own, even when a lawyer has prepared the other form. You will avoid delays by completing the forms that your financial institutions offer you as well as the power of attorney prepared by your lawyer.

If you live in more than one state—having summer and winter residences in different parts of the country—prepare powers of attorney in accordance with the laws of each of those states. Again, state laws can differ in important ways. You will want to be certain that your powers of attorney are effective under the law of any state in which you spend extended periods of time.

Durable powers of attorney can be extremely helpful if you are temporarily unable to handle your affairs. It is often difficult, however, to convince other people that your agent, your attorney-in-fact, actually has authority to act. Durable powers often are particularly appropriate if you are in good health now, are not suffering from a progressive illness, and do not have a history of potentially serious disease. However, if you have recently been diagnosed with a life-threatening cancer, heart disease, Alzheimer's disease, have had a stroke, or are otherwise at risk of becoming incapacitated, there are other ways to provide a more efficient handling of your affairs after you have become incapacitated. The most important such alternatives are the revocable trust, also known as a living trust, and the holding of property in joint tenancy form.

Revocable or "living" trusts (see also p. 321). A great deal has been written about the *revocable trust,* often called a *living trust* (because it is a trust that is created and effective during your lifetime) or an *inter vivos trust* (Latin for "between the living" or, put another way, "during life"). It is usually contrasted with a *testamentary trust* created by your will at the time of your death. It is called a *revocable* trust because you can revoke it whenever you want.

A trust places legal title to property in the hands of a person, called the *trustee,* who holds the property for the use and benefit of the *beneficiary.* The person who creates the trust is referred to as the *grantor* or the *settlor* of the trust. The grantor, trustee, and beneficiary can be the same person.

The trustee is bound by law to hold, administer, and distribute trust property strictly in accordance with the terms of the trust. (The written document itself is sometimes referred to as a *deed of trust, declaration of trust,* or *trust indenture.* I will refer here to the trust "document.") The trustee cannot legally use the trust property for any purpose not specifically authorized in the trust document or by state law.

The chief advantage of a living trust for someone who becomes incapacitated is this: because the trust creates a legal condition in which the grantor's property is transferred to the trustee as the true and legal owner, the trustee avoids the difficulties that an agent acting under a power of attorney often confronts in carrying out the wishes of the grantor. Remember, the agent under a power of attorney (that is, the attorney-in-fact) never takes title to your property; the agent merely acts on your behalf. By contrast, a trustee actually holds legal title to the trust property. There usually is no question about a trustee's authority to manage property held in the trust and thus no legal questions or delays from banks or brokerage houses or other institutions when property must be sold or transferred.

To take advantage of a living trust, you would first create one by signing a trust document and then transfer title to your property to the trustee. If you want, and for as long as you are able, you may serve as the only trustee or as one of two or more co-trustees. The other co-trustees might be your spouse, another family member, your lawyer or accountant, or a financial institution such as a local trust company or bank. All of the trust property would be used to benefit you. For example, when you transfer title to your house to the trust, you would continue to live there. When you transfer your bank accounts to the trust you would continue to make deposits and withdrawals as always. In short, as long as you are willing and able to act as a trustee, there is no real difference in how you buy, sell, and use the property that you transfer from yourself to your trust. However, if you should become incapacitated or decide that you no longer want to be bothered managing matters, the true advantage of having created the trust and having transferred property into it becomes immediately apparent.

At that moment, your co-trustee or your successor trustee will begin to manage the trust without you, stepping in to run the trust—according to its terms—for your benefit. There is no delay, no court appearance, and usually little, if any, cost involved. Thus, if you are suddenly stricken with a catastrophic illness or are injured in an accident, the successor or co-trustee continues to hold and administer the trust property for your benefit.

Trusts are nothing fancy, nor are they only for the rich. A nationally renowned attorney once described a revocable trust as nothing more than a shoe box, a place to put all your property for safekeeping. While you are healthy, you hold on to the shoe box and use everything you place into it as you wish. However, if you become incapacitated or simply tire of dealing with business matters, the shoe box automatically gets handed over to someone else, the successor or co-trustee. That trustee then holds on to the shoe box and uses all the property in it for your benefit either until you are well enough again to manage it or until your death, if you should fail to recover. At the time of your death, the trustee then distributes the property in the shoe box to the people you have named in the trust document. (The matter is discussed in greater detail later in this chapter.)

You will need a lawyer's help to prepare a living trust. There are three steps in the process. The first is to plan the trust—that is, to determine what you want done with your property during your lifetime and after you die. Your plans will depend on the kind of assets you have and your wishes. The second is for your lawyer to prepare the trust document and for you to review and sign it. The third step is to transfer your property from your own name to the name of the trust, a process often called "funding" the trust.

At the first meeting with your lawyer, discuss what the cost will be for the lawyer's services in planning and drafting the trust and for assistance in funding the trust. You can often save money by taking care of the funding process yourself. For example, bank and brokerage accounts can be changed from your own name to the name of the trust by completing forms that the financial institutions will provide. Generally, however, you will need the lawyer's help to transfer your home and other realty to the trust, because those transfers require that new deeds be prepared and recorded.

If the idea of a revocable trust is attractive to you, and particularly if you suffer from a progressive illness, act promptly. Don't put off another day the discussion you could have now. Remember, you will not become locked in to the plan set out in your revocable trust. If you change your mind later, as long as you have the capacity to act, you can revoke the trust or change its terms. A revocable trust gives you great flexibility and provides a safety net for managing your affairs.

As you will see later in this chapter, the revocable trust also eliminates the need for a probate proceeding at your death, which is often a significant advantage. Thus, the revocable trust is often a very important and useful tool to plan for the management of your property during your life *and* for the orderly distribution of your property at the time of your death.

Joint tenancies. Many people hold their bank accounts and homes in joint tenancies, relying on this form of ownership to provide for management of their affairs if they become incapacitated and for disposition of their property at the time of death. Unfortunately, in many instances, reliance on joint tenancies is misplaced.

Joint tenancy is a form of ownership that allows every person named as an owner the right to manage the property and, importantly, that automatically gives to the surviving joint tenants a deceased joint tenant's share of the property when he or she dies. The hallmark of a joint tenancy is that a joint tenant's interest passes automatically, by operation of law, to the surviving joint tenants at the time of his or her death.

Thus, if you have a bank account in joint tenancy with your two children, either of them—in addition to yourself—can write checks from the account, which is often a great convenience. When you die, your children will receive all the money in the account as the surviving joint tenants. If you own your house in joint tenancy with your husband or wife, at the time of your death your spouse will automatically take your share of the property. You don't need a will or trust to be certain that your children—in these examples—receive your bank account or that your widow or widower takes your interest in your house. Indeed, if you hold property in joint tenancy form, the surviving joint tenant will take your share of the property *regardless* of what your will says, because the joint tenancy form of ownership automatically passes your interest to the surviving joint tenant when you die, without regard to other documents you may have signed.

Joint tenancies can play a role in estate planning. For example, if you have a son or daughter who is willing to handle the chore of paying your bills for you, naming him or her as a joint tenant on your checking account can be quite helpful. However, reliance on this form of ownership as the sole means of managing your affairs can prove dangerous. For example, if you and the child whom you have named as your joint tenant on your checking account are both seriously injured in an accident, who will take care of your expenses while you are both incapacitated? Because we never know when we or anyone else will die, unexpected results can occur. For example, let's say that you own your home in joint tenancy with your two grown children, with the idea that at your death each of them will own one-half of the house. If you and one of your children die together in an accident, your one surviving child will inherit the entire house. That result means that your grandchildren by the child who died with you will never receive their parent's share of your house.

Accordingly, I tend to use joint tenancies only as one element in a comprehensive plan that also makes use of powers of attorney and a will or living trust. As part of a coordinated plan, joint tenancies can be helpful. As the sole means of planning for your incapacity and death, however, they present risk and do not assure the wanted results.

Guardianship and Conservatorship. If you don't name an agent under a durable power of attorney for health care and if you don't establish a trust and transfer your property to it, matters become quite a bit more complicated if you become incapacitated. Although there is great variety in the way each state addresses this problem in its laws, generally speaking, in every jurisdiction, the law provides a mechanism for the court to appoint someone to oversee your affairs. The person who oversees your property is often called the *guardian* or *conservator of your estate*. If necessary, the court may also appoint someone to oversee how you are cared for, and that individual is referred to as the *guardian* or *conservator of your person*. "Guardian" is the more common term and is the one I will use here.

With careful planning you shouldn't need to have a court-appointed guardian of your estate. For example, if you have created and funded a revocable trust, the successor trustee will automatically take charge of your property if you are incapacitated. If you have named an agent under a durable power of attorney, the agent should be able to manage your affairs for you. If you don't know someone to name as a successor trustee under a living trust, trust companies and the trust departments of banks can serve in that capacity. Often, however, these professional trustees will not accept an appointment as trustee unless the trust property is in excess of a minimum amount, often as high as $250,000. Generally, the financial institution charges a minimum annual fee—say, 1.5 percent of the value of the investment assets in the trust per year—for its services. These costs, however, are often less than the amounts you will incur if a court must appoint a guardian, because both the guardian and your attorney will be paid their fees from your property.

In selecting someone to be your guardian, most states give preference to your spouse, if you have one, and then to other family members. If you do not have family and if no one comes forward as a friend, the court will appoint a guardian for you. Obviously, it is better if you have the choice. In some states—California, for example—you can express your preference in a durable power of attorney for health care.

Distribution of Your Property at Your Death

It has been said that the perfect estate plan is to die on the day you spend your last dollar. None of us knows which day will be our last, and sensibly, we want to have more than a dollar to our name just in case we live to see tomorrow. Thus, most of us prudently conserve our property and make plans to distribute it to our loved ones when we die. Unfortunately, many people—out of simple procrastination, superstition, or other reasons—put off this important responsibility.

It may surprise you to learn that you already have an estate plan even though you may never have written a will. The estate plan you now have is the one that your state legislature wrote for you. If you die before you make your own plan, your property will be distributed to the persons (and in the shares) that your state legislators have decreed. In some situations, that plan will get your property to the right people and in the right amounts. For example, in every state, if you die without a will and if your spouse survives you, part or all of your property will go to your widow or widower. But if you are also survived by children, part of your property may also pass to them, possibly leaving your spouse without sufficient assets to maintain his or her current lifestyle.

The statues that provide for the passing of property from a decedent to his or her heirs are called the *intestacy laws*. The word *intestate* means "without a testament," that is, without a will. These statutes apply to your property unless you take steps to provide alternate instructions in a will or other legal document. Everyone is free to say where his or her property will go. But if you don't take advantage of that right, you forfeit it. How then do you avoid having your property distributed according to the intestacy statutes? The answer is simple: by making your own estate plan. There are three basic mechanisms by which you can arrange for the disposition of your property after you are gone. The first is a will; the second is the revocable, or living, trust; and the third is joint tenancy.

Wills

A will is a writing in which you state your directions for the distribution of your property at the time of your death. There are rare circumstances in which an oral will is valid, but for our purposes here it is critical to understand that your will must be written and signed in accordance with your state's law. If you make an invalid will, the court will not be bound to honor it and may determine that you died intestate.

Some states permit you to make a valid will by writing it yourself. A will that you yourself write is known as a *holographic will*. If you prepare a holographic will, be careful: state laws vary greatly in this area and are strictly enforced. For example, California will recognize your will if you write it out entirely in your own hand and sign and date it. But California will not recognize the will if you type it out and sign and date it—unless the will is witnessed. If your holographic will is not prepared completely in accordance with your state's laws, the court may fail to recognize it and may instead distribute your property according to the intestacy statutes. If you want to make a holographic will, be certain that you know what your state's rules are and comply with them in every detail. One way to learn the requirements is to go to a local law library (often housed in or close to your local courthouse), or to a nearby law-school library, if it is open to the public. However, be aware that a holographic will can be dangerous. If you slip up in preparing it, and if the document fails to meet the statutory requirements, the court won't recognize it as your will, and your property will instead be distributed according to your state's intestacy statutes. In short, use a holographic will only if you must.

The surest way to make a valid will is to find a lawyer who will prepare it for you. If your assets are modest, so that tax planning is not necessary, the time and money involved will probably be very low. Your state bar association should have a referral service that can put you in touch with a lawyer who does this kind of work. When you call the attorney to set up an appointment, don't hesitate to ask whether he or she will charge you for the initial consultation and what the expected fees and costs will be to prepare a simple will. If you have more substantial assets (under current federal tax law, that means if you have assets of more than $600,000), you will also want to discuss how to reduce estate taxes. That discussion, along with the more sophisticated will, may result in higher legal costs—but those fees may well result in enormous estate-tax savings later and thus be worth the cost now.

Living Trusts

The living or revocable trust discussed earlier as a mechanism for managing your property during your lifetime can also be used to distribute your property at the time of your death. The trust document will have separate provisions for how trust property is to be managed and distributed during your lifetime and after your death. If you have transferred all your property to the trust during your lifetime, at your death you will not need a probate proceeding.

Probate is the process by which the court oversees the

gathering of a decedent's assets, the payment of a decedent's debts and taxes, and the distribution of a decedent's property in accordance with his or her will or, if there is no will, in accordance with the state's intestacy laws.

In this process, the court will appoint the individual or financial institution named in the will to serve as the decedent's *executor.* If there is no will, the court will appoint an *administrator* to administer the decedent's affairs according to the state's intestacy laws. An executor or administrator is charged by the court with overseeing the entire probate process. Although some states have enacted new laws to streamline the probate process, in many states probate remains a time-consuming and expensive proposition.

Recall that with a living trust, you transfer title to your property from yourself to your trustee. If you are serving as your own trustee, title passes from your own name, individually, to yourself in your capacity as trustee. Accordingly, at your death you do not legally own your property, your trustee does. (It makes no difference for probate purposes if you are your own trustee.) At the time of your death, the successor trustee automatically takes title to the trust property. Thus, there will be no need for a probate proceeding because during your lifetime you already have given your property away—to the trust. At your death, your trustee will, of course, be obligated to pay all your debts—including taxes—from assets held in the trust. Your trustee will then distribute your property to your beneficiaries named in the trust. All of this will occur without a court proceeding—without probate.

Placing your property in a living trust does not in and of itself save taxes. It can, however, save the costs and delay of a probate proceeding. On the other hand, if you use a living trust to avoid probate, you must transfer all of your assets to the trust during your lifetime. Making those transfers can be costly (for example, you will need to execute new deeds to your house and other real estate) and time-consuming. Some assets, in fact, may not be transferrable to the trust. For example, the terms of a partnership agreement may restrict you from transferring a partnership interest to a trust. If you don't transfer all your property to the trust, you may still need a probate proceeding to transfer the assets outside the trust.

Whether a living trust makes sense for you depends on your circumstances. There is no one easy answer for everybody. A good estate-planning lawyer will advise you if a living trust is an appropriate alternative for you.

Joint Tenancies

The use of joint tenancies to distribute property at the time of your death has been discussed earlier in this chapter. Please refer to that section.

It's not pleasant to contemplate the possibility of our own incapacity or certain mortality. Nevertheless, if we confront these ideas now and plan for them, we can help ourselves and those we love to avoid additional difficulties in the future. The law in this area can become quite complex, but its basic features are really very simple. There is no mystery here. By coming to an elementary understanding, you can talk intelligently and meaningfully with a lawyer who can then be certain that your wishes will be heeded later. Although consulting a lawyer will cost you money and time, it will save you both many times over in the long run. Moreover, you will have the satisfaction of knowing that you have done everything you can to put your wishes and desires into a form that will be legally effective, a satisfaction that usually outweighs the initial frustration the law may cause you. With a few simple steps taken now, neither you nor your family should have to join Shakespeare's character who denounced the lawyers. Instead, you may well discover that the law can offer you protection and assurance and that lawyers can indeed play a helpful role at this time in your life.

GLOSSARY

Achalasia A malfunction of the normal, rhythmic muscular action of swallowing.

Advance Medical Directive A written document stating your instructions to your doctors in the event that you can't communicate at some later time.

Ageism Bigotry against older people.

Alzheimer's Disease The disease that is the leading cause of dementia.

Anemia A condition in which the number of red blood cells in the blood is too low.

Angina A synonym for pain. The most common use of the word is as angina pectoris—chest pain caused by coronary artery disease.

Angiogram—Arteriogram Two names for a test that uses dye and x-rays to examine the arteries of the body, such as those to the heart and brain.

Angioplasty A procedure in which blocked arteries, such as those to the heart and kidney, are opened using a catheter and a balloon.

Antibody A chemical made by the body that helps fight infections.

Anticholinergic   The property of some medications that blocks the function of part of your nervous sytem (the parasympathetic nervous system), leading to confusion, urinary retention, blurred vision, dizziness, or constipation.

Anticoagulant   A medication given to prevent blood clots from forming.

Antigen   Anything, usually a virus or bacterium, that your body recognizes as foreign and that stimulates your body to produce antibodies.

Aphakia   The change in vision after the eye's lens is removed in a cataract operation. Aphakia can be corrected with glasses, a contact lens, or a lens implant.

Arcus   A gray ring around the colored part of the eye that normally appears with aging.

Arrhythmia   An abnormal beating of the heart.

Artery   The kind of blood vessel that carries blood away from the heart to the rest of the body.

Arthritis   Inflammation of joints leading to pain and deformity. Arthritis can be caused by rheumatoid arthritis, degenerative arthritis, and less common diseases such as gout.

Atherosclerosis   The buildup of fat (plaque) in arteries, which blocks the flow of blood. The condition is also called arteriosclerosis.

Atrial Fibrillation   One kind of abnormal heartbeat in which one of the two chambers of the heart (the atrium) does not contract properly.

Atrium   One of the chambers of the heart, which works like a prepump, filling the ventricle with blood.

Atrophic   A synonym for *thinned*. Atrophic urethritis, for example, means that the tissue of the urethra is thinned.

Attorney-in-fact   Someone, appointed by you, to act in your behalf as your agent. He or she may make decisions about your health care or transact your business affairs, depending on kind of power of attorney you use.

Audiologist   A specialist in evaluating hearing problems and advising on the use of hearing aids.

Bed Sores   A breakdown of the skin caused by prolonged pressure. They are also called *pressure sores* and *decubitus ulcers.*

Benign   Noncancerous

Benign Prostatic Hypertrophy   A noncancerous enlargement of the prostate gland. It is often called BPH.

Biopsy   A procedure in which a piece of tissue is removed so that it can be examined.

Brady   A prefix meaning *slow.* For example, bradykinesia means *slow movements* and bradycardia means *slow heart.*

Bruit   A noise in a blood vessel, heard by a doctor through a stethoscope, sometimes indicating a partial blockage of blood flow. *Bruit* rhymes with *phooey.*

Bypass   See CABG.

CABG   Coronary Artery Bypass Graft—an operation performed to treat coronary artery disease.

Carcinogen   Any substance—a chemical or virus, for example—that can cause cancer.

Carcinoma   A cancer arising on the skin, glands, and other tissues. (*also* Sarcoma)

Cardiologist   A doctor who specializes in heart problems.

CAT Scan   Abbreviation for Computerized Axial Tomography, a special kind of x-ray that shows a three-dimensional picture of parts of the body.

Cataract   Clouding of the lens of the eye.

Catheter   A tube. Catheters can be inserted into many parts of the body, including the bladder, a vein, or an artery.

Cellulitis   A bacterial infection of the skin.

Cerebro-Vascular Accident (CVA)   A synonym for *stroke*.

Chemotherapy   Medications used to treat cancer.

Cholesterol   A fatty substance found in some foods but also made in the liver. It can build up in arteries and block blood flow.

Claudication   Pain in the legs when walking, caused by inadequate blood flow.

Congestive Heart Failure   A backup of blood caused by inadequate heart function, leading to congestion in the lungs and swelling.

Conservator   A person appointed by the court to oversee your health care and property.

Coronary Artery Disease (CAD)   Blockage in the arteries to the heart. CAD can lead to angina and heart attacks.

Debriding   Removing dead tissue from around a wound or bed sore.

Decubitus Ulcer   Skin breakdown caused by prolonged pressure. They are also called *bed sores* and *pressure sores.*

Delirium   The sudden onset of confusion, usually caused by a serious medical illness.

Dementia   The slow onset of memory problems and progressive deterioration of the functions of the brain. Dementia is caused by several diseases, most commonly Alzheimer's disease.

Dermatitis   Irritation to the skin.

Dermatologist   A doctor who specializes in skin problems.

Diuretic A medication that causes your kidneys to make more urine—a "water pill."

Diverticulitis An infection in one of the small pockets (diverticula) that form in the intestinal wall in persons who have diverticulosis. It can lead to pain, fever, and other serious complications.

Diverticulosis A condition in which small pockets (diverticula) form in the intestinal wall, often leading to abdominal pain.

Durable Power of Attorney for Health Care The kind of advance medical directive in which you name someone to make health care decisions for you if you are unable to do so yourself.

Dyspareunia Pain during sexual intercourse.

Echocardiogram A test that uses sound waves to examine the heart.

Edema A synonym for *swelling*.

Electrocardiogram (EKG or ECG) A recording of the electrical activity of the heart, useful in determining whether you have coronary artery disease or have suffered a heart attack.

Embolism A blood clot that blocks blood flow. If it blocks blood in the lung, it causes a pulmonary embolism; if it blocks blood flow in the brain, it causes an embolic stroke.

Eschar A scab.

Executor The person, named in your will, who administers your estate according to state laws and the instructions you give in your will. When an executor is a woman, she is sometimes called an *executrix*.

Gastritis Irritation of the lining of the stomach causing loss of appetite, pain, and internal bleeding.

Gastroenterologist   A medical doctor who specializes in stomach and intestinal problems.

Geriatrician   A medical doctor who specializes in caring for older people.

Gerontologist   A person, not a medical doctor, who studies aging.

Glaucoma   An elevation of the pressure in the eye that can lead to blindness if not treated.

Guardian   Someone appointed by a court to oversee your health care or your property.

Hematocrit   A blood test used to determine whether you are anemic.

Hemorrhage   A synonym for *bleeding*.

Hemorrhoids   Engorged veins at the anus, causing pain, itching, and bleeding.

Herpes Zoster   A viral infection causing a painful skin rash.

Impaction   An accumulation of stool in the last part of the colon, causing severe constipation.

Impotence   The inability to have sexual intercourse.

Incontinence   The inability to control urination (or bowel movements).

Infarction   The death of tissue. When heart tissue dies, it is called *myocardial infarction;* when brain tissue dies, it is called *cerebral infarction*.

Keratoses   Noncancerous growths that form on the skin, often with a light brown color and a wrinkled surface.

Leukoplakia   A white patch in the mouth that can be an early form of cancer.

Libido   Sexual desire.

Living Will   One kind of advance medical directive—a way to give written instructions to your doctors.

Macula   The small part of the eye's retina where the highest number of light-sensing cells are concentrated. Disease in this area, called *macular degeneration,* is a leading cause of blindness.

Malignant   Cancerous.

Mammogram   X-rays of the breast, used to detect breast cancer.

Medicaid   The federally mandated but state-run program to cover the cost of health care for poor Americans.

Medicare   The federal program subsidizing health care costs for older Americans.

Melena   Black, tarry stools caused by bleeding in the stomach from ulcers, gastritis, or cancer.

Metastasize   The ability of most cancers to spread to distant parts of the body and grow there. Each of these distant growths is called a *metastasis.*

Mohs Surgery   A special technique for removing skin cancers.

MRI Scan   Magnetic Resonance Imaging—a test that uses magnets to produce three-dimensional pictures of internal parts of the body.

Neurosurgeon   A doctor who specializes in surgery of the brain.

Occult Blood   Blood from bleeding in the gastrointestinal system, which you cannot see but which your doctor can find with a simple test.

Oncologist   A doctor who specializes in the treatment of cancer.

Ophthalmologist A doctor who specializes in eye problems.

ORIF Open Reduction and Internal Fixation—a surgical procedure to fix a fractured bone using screws, pins, and plates rather than a cast.

Orthopnea Difficulty in breathing when you lie down due to an accumulation of fluid in the lungs.

Osteoporosis Decreased amounts of calcium and the other components of bone causing bones to become weaker and break more easily.

Otolaryngologist A surgeon who specializes in problems of the ears, nose, and throat.

Pacemaker An electronic device that stimulates the beating of the heart.

Palliation Treatment, usually for cancer, that will not cure the disease but may help keep it in control for some time.

Parkinsonism The symptoms of Parkinson's disease such as stiffness, slow movement, and tremor.

Peristalsis The rhythmic contraction of the muscles of the gastrointestinal system that keeps food and waste moving.

Physiatrist A doctor who specializes in rehabilitation.

Physiology The way an organ functions.

Polypharmacy The use of many medications.

Postherpetic Neuralgia A painful skin condition that can persist after an eruption of herpes zoster.

Power of Attorney A legal document in which a person empowers someone else to act as his or her agent.

Presbyopia The normal age-related visual change making it difficult to focus on objects that are close.

Primary-Care Physician   The one doctor who oversees all of your medical care.

Psychosis   A kind of abnormal thinking that includes unreasonable fears (paranoia) and seeing or hearing things that aren't there (hallucinations).

Ptosis   A droopy eyelid.

Pulmonary Edema   The accumulation of fluid in the lungs caused by congestive heart failure.

Pulmonary Embolism   A blood clot, formed in the legs or other parts of the body, which gets trapped in the lungs.

Pulmonologist   A doctor who specializes in lung problems.

Radiologist   A doctor who performs and evaluates x-ray studies, CAT scans, and MRI scans.

Radiotherapist   A doctor who treats cancer using x-ray treatments.

Retinopathy   Disease in the eye's retina, often caused by diabetes, that can lead to blindness.

Sarcoma   A cancer arising in muscles, bones, cartilage, and several other tissues. *See also* Carcinoma.

Senescence   A synonym for *aging*.

Senile   A synonym for *old*. It does **not** mean "demented."

Sign   Something your doctor discovers that may indicate you are ill.

Stress Test   A test for coronary artery disease performed by recording an EKG while you run on a treadmill. Often the radioactive material thallium is used to make the test more accurate.

Symptom   A change in your health that you bring to your doctor's attention.

Syncope   A synonym for *fainting*. (It rhymes with *recipe*.)

Transient Ischemic Attack (TIA)   The symptoms of a stroke that completely resolve within one day, caused by inadequate blood flow to the brain.

Tremor   A synonym for *shaking*.

TURP   Transurethral Resection of the Prostate—an operation in which a doctor removes part of the prostate gland using a scope inserted into the penis.

Urinary Retention   The inability to urinate.

Urologist   A surgeon specializing in problems of the urinary tract, including prostate conditions, incontinence, and impotence.

Veins   The blood vessels through which blood flows back to the heart.

Ventricle   The main pumping chamber of the heart.

Xerosis   Dry skin.

Xerostomia   Dry mouth.

INDEX

Abnormal (term), 14
Abnormal aging, 13–14
Abscess, abdominal, 175–76
Accommodation, 135
Acetaminophen (Tylenol), 29*t*, 40,
    59, 80, 106
Acetylcholine, 16, 17, 25–26, 127;
    see also Anticholinergic
Achalasia, 178, 325
Acoustic neuroma, 154
Acute myelogenous leukemia
    (AML), 79
Adaptation to light, 134, 135
Adrenal glands, 16, 241
Adrenaline, 48
Adult onset (Type II) diabetes, 205,
    207
Advance medical directives, 194–95,
    226, 303–08; defined, 325
Advil, 80, 106, 179
Aerobic exercise, 54, 292
Ageism, 6, 10, 325
Aging, 1; and body's changing re-
    sponse to medication, 24–31; as
    continuous process, 10–11; nor-
    mal changes of, 2, 18–19*t*; normal
    versus abnormal, 13–14; term, 4;
    theories of, 11–13
AIDS, 77, 250*t*
Air pollution, 290–91
Akinesia, 237

Alcohol use: and impotence, 280;
    and osteoporosis, 93, 96; and
    tremor, 233, 235
Alcoholism, 92, 279; and dementia,
    249, 250*t*
Aldomet, 64, 279*t*
Alka-Seltzer, 180
Alkeran, 86
Allergies, 39, 115–16, 224, 300
Alpraxolam (Xanax), 38*t*
Aluminum, 180, 248
Alupent, 235
Alzheimer's disease, 26, 243–59,
    314; as cause of dementia, 247–48,
    250*t*, 253, 256, 259; defined, 325
Amantadine, 240
Amiodarone, 67
Amitriptyline (Elavil), 28*t*, 34*t*, 39
Amputation, 205, 209
Amyloid, 16
Anal sphincter, 164
Analgesics, 40–41
Anaprox, 106
Anemia, 74–77, 79, 91, 170, 325
Anemia of chronic disease, 75
Angina, 44, 52, 58, 59, 69, 73; de-
    fined, 325; *see also* Heart disease
Angiogram (arteriogram), 57–58,
    224, 325
Angioplasty, 56, 57, 58, 61–63, 62*f*,
    70; defined 325

Antacids, 180, 181, 182, 189
Antianxiety medications, 27t, 38t, 38–39, 269t
Antiarrhythmics, 66–67
Antibiotics, 78, 117, 123, 154, 156, 175; allergies to, 300
Antibodies, 16, 81, 82–83, 325
Anticholinergic: defined, 326
Anticholinergic effects, 25–26, 27t, 39, 40, 42, 126–27, 240, 257, 286
Anticholinergic medications, 26, 27–28t, 41–42, 126–27, 144, 178; and constipation, 166–67; in treatment of incontinence, 265, 267–68, 269t
Anticoagulants, 66, 81–82, 102, 219, 222–23, 224; defined, 326
Antidepressants, 28, 28t, 34t, 39, 127, 167, 246
Antifungal agents, 117
Antigens, 82, 326
Antihistamines, 27t, 34t, 39, 127, 167; as cause of incontinence, 269t
Antipsychotic medications, 28t, 29t, 34t, 41–42, 167, 247; causing Parkinson's syndrome, 242; in treatment of dementia, 256
Antispasmodics, 167
Anusol-HC, 176
Anxiety pills. See Antianxiety medications
Aorta, 48
Aortic valve, 69
Aphakia, 141, 326
Appetite loss, 166, 202
Arachnoid, 221
Arcus (arcus senilis), 133f, 134, 135, 326
Arrythmias, 44, 50, 52, 63–67, 69, 70, 223; defined, 326
Artery(ies), 80, 326
Arthralgia, 105
Arthritis, 87, 104–07, 108, 121, 292, 299; defined, 326; degenerative, 105–07; rheumatoid, 105
Artificial Tears, 135
Aspirin, 29t, 35t, 40, 106, 154, 223–24; and bleeding, 80, 82; effect on stomach, 179; in treatment of CAD, 58, 60–61

Asterixes, 235
Asthma, 60
Atenolol (Tenormin), 34t, 35t, 60, 233, 279t
Atherosclerosis, 50, 53, 56, 63, 74, 80; defined, 326; and diabetes, 209–10; diet and, 294; and erectile impotence, 280, 281; and stroke, 219, 249
Ativan, 38t
Atrial fibrillation, 64–66, 326; and stroke, 219, 222
Atrium (heart), 47, 64, 326
Atrophic: defined, 326
Atrophic urethritis, 263, 266, 275
Atrophic vaginitis, 275, 277, 281–82
Attorney-in-fact, 309, 314, 315, 326–27; see also Lawyer
Audiologist, 153, 156–57, 159, 327
Audiometry, 156–57
Audioscope, 156
Auditory canal, 152
Auditory threshold, 151, 157
Autoimmune disease, 76, 105

Background retinopathy, 146; see also Retinopathy
Bacteria, 12, 77, 83, 116–17, 163, 208; "good," 163, 165
Barbiturates, 279t
Barium enema, 170–71, 181, 202
Basal cell cancer, 119
Bed rest, 94, 100, 121, 168
Bed sores (decubitus ulcer), 73, 94, 100, 120–24, 227, 327, 328; defined, 327; with diabetes, 210; dressings for, 122–23
Belladonna, 28t, 40
Benadryl, 27t, 32, 34t, 38t, 167, 240
Beneficiary, 314
Benign prostatic hypertrophy (BPH), 267, 285–86, 327
Bentyl, 28t, 40
Benztropine (Cogentin), 240
Beta-blockers, 34t, 35t, 58, 60, 64, 144; and impotence, 279t; in treatment of tremor, 233, 236
Betadine, 123
Betaxolol (Betoptic), 144

Bethanechol (Urecholine), 265
Betoptic, 144
Bicarbonate, 164, 180
Bicycle riding, 292
Bile, 164
Biological old age, 10
Biopsy(ies): bone marrow, 76, 85; breast, 196; colon, 170, 171, 202; defined, 327; lung, 200, 201; prostate, 198; skin, 113, 188; stomach lining, 182
Birthmarks, 114–15
Bisacodyl (Dulcolax), 173, 174t
Bladder, 19t, 26, 261f, 262–63, 264, 265, 266, 267–68, 286; see also Urinary incontinence
Bladder infections, 208, 263, 271
Bleeding, 79, 80, 81–82, 224, 330; anticoagulants and, 82
Blindness, 136, 137, 147; with diabetes, 205, 209; from glaucoma, 141, 142; legal blindness, 136; from macular degeneration, 136–37, 139, 146–47, 331
Blood, 72–86; functions of, 72–73; in sputum, 200; in stool, 74, 169, 175, 179, 182, 187, 189, 202, 298; transfusions, 76–77, 91
Blood clot(s), 65–66, 94, 100, 102, 219, 223–24, 227; see also Clotting system
Blood flow, 17; to brain, 20, 30, 63, 64, 217, 218, 222; through liver, 20, 165; to vagina, 276; lack of, 210, 211; smoking and, 289
Blood pressure, 17, 20, 30, 40, 48–49, 64, 144, 298; high/low, 223; and stroke, 219; see also High blood pressure (hypertension)
Blood proteins, 81–83; abnormal, 85–86
Blood sugar: checking, 206, 207; controlling, 145, 146, 209, 212–13, 214–16; monitoring at home, 213; normal age-related changes in, 205–06
Blood sugar levels, 41, 53, 295; in diabetes, 204, 205, 207, 208, 209–10, 211

Blood tests, 66, 76, 81, 82, 93, 102, 169–70, 211, 223, 248, 298; in detection of cancer, 186, 189, 198
Blood vessels, 26, 219; in skin, 110, 111f
Blood volume: water and, 83–85
Bone, 185; density, 90, 91, 93; loss of, 91–92, 96–98; see also Osteoporosis; Fractures
Bone marrow, 72, 73–74, 75–76, 78, 87, 201; decrease in, 91; effect of medications on, 78–79; function of, 89; biopsy, 76, 85
Bone scan, 198
Bones, 87–108; age-related changes in, 89–90; changes in shape and activity of, 90–91; composition and structure of, 87–88, 90; functions of, 89–90; healing, 99; see also Osteoporosis; Fractures
Bowel movement, 161–63, 164, 166; straining at, 49, 166; see also Constipation; Laxatives
Braces, 228, 241
Bradycardia, 64
Bradykinesia, 237, 239
Brain, 18t, 20, 26, 109, 201; blood to, 63, 64, 217, 218, 222
Brain function, 20, 244, 255
Brain tumor, 147, 235, 248; as cause of dementia, 249, 251t
Bran, 174t, 294
Breast cancer, 75, 97, 99, 185, 187, 188, 189, 194, 196–98, 275, 298, 299
Breast exam, 298; self, 187, 197–98
Breasts, 275
Breathing problems, 34t, 60, 77, 234–35
Briosche, 180
Bromocriptine (Parlodil), 241
Bronchitis, 289; chronic, 289, 290
Bronchoscopy, 200–01
Bronkosol, 235
Bruit, 224, 327
Bulk (in diet), 168, 172, 176, 174t
Bumetanide (Bumex), 264

CABG. *See* Coronary artery bypass surgery (CABG)
CAD. *See* Coronary artery disease (CAD)
Caffeine, 233, 234
Calan, 34*t*, 35*t*, 59, 64
Calcitonin, 98
Calcium, 88, 89–90, 91, 95–96, 97, 98, 110; abnormalities of, as cause of dementia, 252*t*, 255; supplements, 95
Calcium channel blockers, 58, 59, 60
Calcium level, 108, 169
Cancer(s), 4, 75, 85, 89, 184–203, 314; common in later life, 196–203; defined, 184–85; early detection, 120, 129, 185–86, 196, 197, 198, 203, 283; early warning signs, 189; frequency of, in older people, 185; gynecological, 283–84; incurable, 194–95; pain control, 194–95, 203; screening for, 186–89; treatment of, 189–95; *see also* under specific type, *e.g.*, Colon cancer
Canes, 228–29, 300
Capoten, 35*t*, 69
Captopril (Capoten), 35*t*, 69
Carafate, 181
Carbamazepine (Tegretol), 211
Carbohydrates (diet), 214, 293
Carcinogens, 185, 289, 327
Carcinoma, 185, 327
Cardiac arrest, 66, 77
Cardiazem, 59
Cardiologist(s), 57, 58, 64, 70; defined, 327
Cardiovascular surgeons, 57, 61
Carisoprodol (Soma), 40
Carotid arteries, 218; blockage in, 224–25
Carotid echo, 224
Carotid endarterectomy, 225
Cascara, 25, 41, 173, 174*t*
Castor oil (Neoloid), 173, 174*t*
Castration, 199
CAT scan, 93, 198, 200, 223, 236, 248, 255, 284; defined, 327
Catapres, 279*t*

Cataracts, 4, 136, 137–41, 143; defined, 327; treatment of, 138–41
Cathartics. *See* Laxatives
Catheters, 268, 271, 328; foley catheter, 268, 271
CBC (complete blood count), 298
Cells, 12, 15–16; blood, 72–73, 83, 91; cancerous, 83, 184, 185, 192
Cellular changes, 15–16
Cellulitis, 116–17, 328
Cerebellum, 235
Cerebral hemorrhage, 220–21; *see also* CVA
Cerebral infarction, 220, 330; *see also* CVA
Ceruminex, 155
Cervical cancer, 187, 282, 283–84
Cervix, 261*f*
Checkups. *See* Physical examination(s)
Chemotherapy, 79, 130, 178, 192, 193–94; with breast cancer, 197; with colon cancer, 203; defined, 328; with lung cancer, 201; with ovarian cancer, 284
Chest pain, 52, 65, 74, 76, 177
Chest x-rays, 188–89, 200
Chloral hydrate, 38*t*
Chlordiazepoxide (Librium), 27*t*, 38*t*
Chlorpheniramine (Chlor-Trimeton), 27*t*
Chlorpromazine (Thorazine), 28*t*, 29*t*, 41
Chlorpropamide (Diabenese), 29*t*, 41, 215
Chlor-Trimeton, 27*t*
Cholesterol, 53, 209, 210, 293–94, 298; and CAD, 53, 54–56, 70; defined, 328; serum, 54–56
Cholestyramine (Questran), 55
Cholinergic nervous system, 40
Chronic lymphocytic leukemia (CLL), 79
Cimetidine (Tagamet), 180, 279*t*
Citrate of magnesia (Mag Citrate), 172
Claudication (leg cramps when walking), 35*t*, 36, 60, 74, 210; defined, 328

Clinidium (Librax), 28*t*
Clonidine (Catapres), 279*t*
Clotting system, 79, 80, 81–83, 89, 164, 219
Cochlea, 152
Codeine (Tylenol #3, Hicodan), 25, 41, 167, 279*t*
Cogentin, 240
Colace, 172, 174*t*
Collagen, 16
Colon, 4, 26, 163, 166, 173; growths in, 167; *see also* Gastrointestinal system
Colon cancer, 74–75, 167, 168, 169, 185, 187, 188, 189, 192, 201–03
Colonoscopy, 171, 202
Compression fractures, 93, 94–95
Confusion, 17, 20, 23, 25, 27*t*, 28*t*, 29*t*, 39, 41, 76, 84, 102, 181, 209, 265; in hypoglycemia, 212; medications causing, 17, 20, 23, 25, 27–29*t*, 39, 41, 180–181, 265; postoperative, 103; in stroke, 218, 221; sudden, 246
Congestive heart failure, 32, 35*t*, 44, 50, 60, 67–69, 70, 85, 126; defined, 67, 328; diet and, 293, 295; evaluation of, 68; treating, 68–69; *see also* Heart disease
Conservatorship, 318–19, 328
Constipation, 24, 26, 27*t*, 39, 41, 102, 166–77, 180, 202, 265; diet and, 294; evaluation of, 169–71; exercise and, 291; and incontinence, 267; medicine-induced, 173, 174*t*, 177, 181; problems related to, 175–77; as side effect, 25, 28*t*, 29*t*, 55; *see also* Laxatives
Contact dermatitis, 116
Corgard, 233
Cornea (eye), 133*f*, 134, 136
Coronary arteries, 48, 50, 51*f*, 56, 58, 59, 60; repairing blocked, 61–63; *see also* Heart
Coronary artery bypass surgery (CABG), 56, 57, 58, 61–63, 70; defined, 327
Coronary artery disease (CAD), 44, 50–63, 51*f*, 70–71; defined, 50–52,

328; evaluation of, 56–63; diet and, 294; medications in treatment of, 58–61; risk factors for, 51–56; treatment of, 59–63; *see also* Heart disease
Cortex (bone), 87–88
Coumadin (warfarin), 66, 81–82, 102, 219, 222–23, 224
Counseling, 280, 282
Cramps, cramping, 166, 174, 175, 202
Creutzfeld-Jacob disease, 249, 250*t*
Curvature of the spine, 93, 94
Cushing's disease, 92
CVA (cerebro-vascular accident), 217, 218; defined, 328; *see also* Stroke
Cyclobenzaprine (Flexeril), 28*t*, 40
Cyclospasmol, 256
Cytotec, 181

Dalmane, 25, 27*t*, 38*t*
Darvocet, Darvon. *See* Propoxyphene
Deafness, 151
Debriding, 122, 328
Debrox, 155
Decubitus ulcers. *See* Bed sores (decubitus ulcers)
Deep vein thrombosis (DVT), 81
Degenerative arthritis (osteoarthritis; degenerative joint disease [DJD]), 105–07, 186
Dehydration, 20, 68, 83–85, 126, 127
Delirium, 255, 328; versus dementia, 245–46
Dementia, 4, 28*t*, 32, 34*t*, 39, 41, 42, 103, 120, 159, 243–59, 300; Alzheimer's disease as cause of, 247–48, 250*t*, 253, 256, 259; care of person with, 256–59; causes of, 247–49, 250–52*t*; characteristics of, 252–53; defined, 328; versus delirium, 245–46; and depression, psychosis, 246–47; evaluation of, 253–55; with Parkinson's disease, 238; in stroke, 218, 221–22; treatment of, 255–59
Dentures, 125, 127, 128–29, 187

Deprenyl, 241
Depression, 35*t*, 43, 60, 199; dementia and, 246–47, 251*t*; and libido, 279; and sexual function, 281; in stroke, 218
Dermatitis, 328
Dermatologist, 113, 119, 120, 188; defined, 328
Dermis, 110, 111*f*
DES. *See* Diethylstylbesterol (DES)
Diabenese, 29*t*, 41, 215
Diabeta, 214
Diabetes, 4, 53, 120, 126, 204–16, 255, 298, 300; avoiding problems from, 211–14; complications of, 209–11; control of, 217; and dementia, 248–49; diabetic retinopathy, 139, 144–46, 211; diet and, 293, 295; and impotence, 280; medication for, 29*t*, 41, 43; risk factors for developing, 206–07; and stroke, 219, 222, 229; symptoms of, 207–09; treatment for, 214–16; and urinary incontinence, 263, 268; and vision loss/blindness, 136, 137, 144–46; what it is, 205–06
Diamox, 144
Diarrhea, 106, 180, 181, 202
Diazepam (Valium), 27*t*, 38
Dicyclomine (Bentyl), 28*t*
Diet, 15, 55, 75, 81, 92, 122, 183, 234, 288, 293–96; and CAD, 56; and colon cancer, 201–02; and constipation, 166; with diabetes, 214; fiber in, 168; and GI system, 165; and heart disease, 48; high-fiber, 176; and osteoporosis, 96, 97, 98
Diethylstylbesterol (DES), 199–200, 279*t*
Dietitian, 96, 168, 214
Digestion. *See* Gastrointestinal system
Digoxin (Lanoxin), 64, 65, 68–69
Diltiazem (Cardiazem), 59
Diphenhydramine (Benadryl), 27*t*, 32, 34*t*, 38*t*, 167, 240
Dipivefrin (Propine), 144

Discrimination (hearing), 151, 153, 157; *see also* Hearing
Disopyramide (Norpace), 34*t*, 35*t*
Diuretics ("water pills"), 34*t*, 68, 69, 127; as cause of urinary incontinence, 264, 269*t*; and constipation, 167; defined, 329; and dehydration, 85
Diverticula, 175
Diverticulitis, 175–76, 329
Diverticulosis, 166, 168, 175, 176; defined, 329; diet and, 294
Donnatal, 28*t*
Dopamine, 16, 236, 237, 239–40, 241, 242
Doppler study, 224
Drug interactions, 32; *see also* Medications
Drugs. *See* Medications
Dry eyes, 134, 135–36
Dry mouth, 23, 26, 27*t*, 28*t*, 39, 126–28, 208
Dry skin, 112, 113–14, 334
Dual photon absorption, 93
"Dukes stages," 202–03
Dulcolax, 25, 41, 173, 174*t*
Dulcosate (Colace), 172, 174*t*
Duoderm, 122
Dura, 221
Durable power of attorney for health care (DPAHC), 194, 258, 302–03, 306–08, 309, 318; defined, 329; *see also* Powers of attorney
Durable powers of attorney, 309–10, 311, 312–13, 319
Dyazide, 264
Dyspareunia, 276, 280, 281, 282; defined, 329
Dysphagia, 178

Ear, 18*t*, 150–60; canal, 155, 156; drum, 152, 153, 155, 156, 157; lobe, 152; view of, 152*f*; wax, 155, 156, 157; *see also* Hearing
Echocardiogram, 68, 69, 329
Edecrin, 264
Edema, 67, 200, 320
Editronate, 98
Ejaculation, 282

Elavil, 28*t*, 34*t*, 39
Electrocardiogram (EKG, ECG), 56, 65, 223, 329
Electrolyte abnormalities, 29*t*, 252*t*
Embolic stroke, 219
Embolism, 219, 220, 329
Emphysema, 60, 289, 290
Enalaporil (Vasotec), 35*t*, 69
Endocrinologist, 146
Enemas, 171, 174–75, 174*t*; barium, 202
Environment, 15, 17, 21, 48, 112; *see also* Pollution
Enzymes, 16, 20, 125, 163, 164
Epidermis, 110, 111*f*, 120
Ephedrine, 265, 266
Epinephrine (Epitrate), 16, 144
Epiphora, 136
Epitrate, 144
Erectile impotence, 280–81
Erections, 278, 279, 280–81, 282
Eschar, 122, 329
Esophageal cancer, 178
Esophagus, 162*f*, 163, 177–78
Estate plan, 317–18, 319–23
Estrogen, 16, 53, 91, 92, 197, 266, 274–75; use by men, 279*t*
Estrogen replacement therapy, 96–97, 98, 275–76, 277, 281–82
Ethacrynic acid (Edecrin), 264
Eustachian tube, 152*f*
Exactech (monitor), 213
Executor, 322, 329
Exercise, 15, 53, 183, 288, 291–93, 300; and CAD, 53–54, 55, 56, 70; and constipation, 166, 168; and diabetes, 206–07; and osteoporosis, 92, 96, 98
Exercise tolerance test (stress test), 56–57, 333
Ex-Lax, 41, 174*t*
Eye, 18*t*, 26, 132–49; cross-sectional view, 133*f*; frontal view, 133*f*; eye drops, 32, 34*t*, 35*t*, 135–36, 143–44; eyelids, 133*f*

Fainting, 17, 20, 24, 26, 30, 49, 65, 66, 69, 76; in hypoglycemia, 212; *see also* Syncope

Falls, 24, 25, 59, 132, 300; and hip fracture, 99–100
Familial tremor, 232
Family practitioner, 2, 4
Famotadine (Pepsid), 180
Fat (in diet), 214, 293–94
Fatigue, 208–09
Feces. *See* Stool
Femur, 100, 101*f*, 102
Fiber (in diet), 167, 183, 294
Fibermed, 172, 294
5-fluorouracil (5 FU), 118–19
Flat bones (compact bones), 88, 93–94
Flavoxate (Urispas), 265
Flexeril, 28*t*, 40
"Floaters," 148
Flu vaccine, 43, 83, 288, 297
Fluorescein angiography, 145
Fluoride, 97–98
Flurazepam (Dalmane), 25, 27*t*, 38*t*
Folate, 75, 251*t*, 255
Foley catheter, 268, 271
Food and Drug Administration (FDA), 30
Fractures, 24, 87, 98–104, 107, 132; causes of, 98–99; healing, 99; hip, 99–104; from osteoporosis, 93–95; wrist, 94–95
Fungal infections, 116, 117, 208
Furosemide (Lasix), 68, 85, 264

Gallbladder, 164
Gastric ulcers. *See* Ulcers
Gastritis, 179–80, 329; treatment of, 180–82
Gastroenterologist, 4, 170, 181, 202; defined, 330
Gastrointestinal antispasmodics, 28*t*, 34*t*, 39–40; as cause of urinary incontinence, 269*t*, 270
Gastrointestinal problems, 163, 177–82; *see also* Constipation
Gastrointestinal (GI) system, 40, 76, 125, 161–83, 162*f*; functions of, 161; normal age-related changes in, 164–66; what it is, 161–64
Gastroscopy, 179, 182
Genetics, 12, 15, 21, 53, 92

Gentamicin, 154
Geriatric medicine, 1, 2–3
Geriatricians, 2–3, 4, 146, 256, 270, 272; defined, 330
Gerontologists, 10, 14, 330
Gibbus, 94
Glaucoma, 32, 34t, 39, 43, 136, 137, 139, 141–44; angle-closure, 142, 144; defined, 330; screening for, 142–43; open-angle, 142, 144; treatment of, 143–44; what it is, 141–42
Glucose monitors, 213
Glucotrol, 215
Glyburide (Micronase, Diabeta), 214
Glypizide (Glucotrol), 215
Grantor (settlor), 314, 315
Guanethidine (Ismelin), 279t
Guardianship, 318–19, 330
Gynecological cancers, 282, 283–84
Gynecological examination, 283; see also Pelvic examination
Gynecology, 273–87

Hair, 109, 110, 111f
Halcion, 38t
Haldol, 29t, 41, 242, 256
Hallucinations, 41–42, 246
Haloperidol (Haldol), 29t, 41, 242, 256
Hardened arteries to the brain, 245, 249
HCTZ, 264
Health-care decisions, 4, 301–02; see also Treatment decisions
Health care team, 4–5
Hearing, 150–60; vs. understanding, 151–52
Hearing aids, 151, 153, 155, 157–59, 160
Hearing loss, 108, 150–51, 153; evaluating, 156–57; noise-induced, 153–54; sensorineuronal, 154–55; sudden, 155–56, 160
Heart, 16, 26, 44–71, 298; chambers of, 45f; functions and anatomy of, 47–48, 67, 70; normal age-related changes in, 18t, 48–50; output, 49–50; surface of, 46f

Heart attack (infarction), 44, 48, 65, 66, 73, 80, 81; defined, 330; exercise and, 54, 291; preventing, 60; see also Coronary artery disease
Heart disease, 43, 44, 50–70, 126, 144, 233, 300, 314; diabetes and, 209; diet and, 294; exercise and, 291; see also Heart attack; Coronary artery disease
Heart rate, 64; and sinus node, 47, 48–49
Heart valves, 47; artificial, 219, 222; problems with, 44, 50, 69–70; repairing faulty, 70
Hematocrit, 74, 76, 330
Hematologist, 76
Hemoglobin, 73, 74
Hemolytic anemia, 76
Hemorrhage, 140, 330; eye, 145, 147
Hemorrhoids, 166, 169, 175, 176–77; defined, 330
Heparin, 224
Hernias, 284–85
Herpes zoster, 20–21, 78, 117–18; defined, 330
Hicodan, 167
Hidden blood. See Occult blood
High blood pressure (hypertension), 43, 53, 85, 126, 264, 280; and CAD, 70; control of, 217; and dementia, 248–49; diet and, 293, 295; medications in treatment of, 35t; and stroke, 219, 222, 229
Hip, 89, 101f, 106, 107
Hip fractures, 94–95, 99–104; rehabilitation for, 103–04; surgery for, 102, 107; types of, 101f
Hip replacement, 102, 107
Histamine, 16, 180
Histamine-2 blockers, 180–81
Holographic will, 320–21
Holter Monitor, 65, 223
Home care: with cancer, 195; of person with dementia, 257, 258, 259; physical therapy, 104; stroke rehabilitation, 226, 227–28
Homeostasis, 26–30
Hormonal therapy: breast cancer, 197; prostate cancer, 199–200

Hormones, 16; female, 274–75; male, 199, 277–78
Hospice, 195
Human insulin, 215
Huntington's chorea, 250*t*
Hyalin cartilage, 105–06
Hydergine, 256
Hydralazine, 34*t*, 69
Hydrocephalus, 249, 251*t*
Hydrochlorothiazide (HCTZ and Dyazide), 264)
Hydrocortisone, 116, 176
Hyoscyamine (Donnatal), 28*t*
Hyperosmolar coma, 209
Hyperparathyroidism, 92, 93
Hypertension. *See* High blood pressure (hypertension)
Hyperthyroidism, 167, 169–70
Hypoglycemia, 212
Hypothyroidism, 169
Hysterectomy, 283

Ibuprofen (Motrin, Advil), 80, 106, 179
Imipramine, 265, 266
Immune system, 19*t*, 20–21, 78, 83, 117; and cancer, 185
Impaction, 166, 174–75, 330
Impotence, 23, 35*t*, 199, 205, 210, 277, 278–82; defined, 330; medications causing, 279*t*, 280, 282
Incapacitation, 301, 314, 318–19; medical care in, 302, 303–08; property management in, 308–09
Incontinence. *See* Urinary incontinence
Incontinence pads, 271–72
Inderal, 60, 64, 233
Indocin, 106
Indomethacin (Indocin), 106
Industrial pollution, 290–91
Infarction. *See* Heart attack (infarction, cerebral infarction)
Infection(s), 20, 21, 43, 79; antibodies fighting, 82–83; bed sores, 120, 123; bladder, 208, 263, 271; with cataract surgery, 140; with diabetes, 208, 209, 210; ear, 155, 156, 157; and hearing loss, 154; in

mouth, 127; skin, 109, 110, 115, 116–17; vaginal, 281, 282; white blood cells in fighting, 77, 78
Inflammatory bowel disease, 201
Influenza (flu), 20, 33–36, 83; *see also* Flu vaccine
Inguinal hernia, 284–85
Insomnia, 39; *see also* Sleeping medications
Insulin, 41, 81, 164, 204, 205, 212, 214; injected, 215–16
Internist, 2, 4, 146
Intestacy laws, 320, 321, 322
Intracerebral hemorrhage, 221
Intraocular pressure, 141–42, 143, 144
Iris, 133*f*
Iron, 73, 75, 167
Iron-deficiency anemia, 74–75
Irritable colon, 168
Ischemia, 52, 56, 58, 59; control of, 60, 61
Ismelin, 279*t*
Isoethrane (Bronkosol), 235
Isordil, 59

Jogging, 292
Joint tenancies, 314, 317–18, 323
Joints, 105–07, 108; replacing, 107

Keratin, 110, 111*f*
Keratoses, 114–15, 330
Kidney failure. *See* Renal failure
Kidneys, 17–20, 19*t*, 24, 67, 68, 84, 85, 261*f*, 262; diabetes and, 209; function of, 106, 255; problems, 93, 295
Konsyl, 172, 174*t*, 294

L-dopa, 239, 240
Laboratory tests, 13–14, 298; in detection of cancer, 186–87, 188–89; in diagnosis of dementia, 254–55
Lactulose, 172, 174*t*
Lacunar infarcts, 210, 221–22, 248, 249
Lanoxin, 64, 68–69
Large intestines, 163–64; *see also* Gastrointestinal system

Laser irridectomy, 144
Laser therapy, 148; diabetic retinopathy, 145–46; macular degneration, 147
Lasix, 68, 85, 264
Lawyer, 308, 311, 316, 321, 323
Laxatives, 167, 171–73, 174t; abuse of, 173; osmotic, 172–73, 174t; stimulant, 25, 28t, 41, 172, 173, 174t, 177; stool softeners, 172, 174t, 176
Lead-pipe stiffness, 237
Lecithin, 256
Leg cramps. See Claudication (leg cramps when walking)
Legal counsel, 302, 303; in care of person with dementia, 257–58; see also Lawyer, Legal issues
Legal issues, 4, 301–23
Lens (eye), 133f, 134, 135, 137, 140, 141
Lens implant, 141
Leukemia, 75, 78–79, 194; AML (acute myelogenous), 79; CLL (chronic lymphocytic), 79
Leukoplakia, 129, 330
Leuprolide, 199
Libido, 278–80, 282
Lidocaine, 67
Life span, average, 11; maximum, 11
Light-headedness, 23, 24, 26, 27t, 28t, 29t, 64, 84, 278–80, 282
Lithium, 235
Liver, 19t, 20, 24, 67, 81, 161, 164, 165, 203
Liver diseases, 20, 92, 235, 279, 295
"Liver spots," 114–15
Living trust, 302, 314–17, 318, 319, 321–23
Living wills, 194, 258, 302–06, 308; defined, 331
Long bones (cortical bones), 88; fractures of, 93, 94
Lopid, 55
Lopressor, 60, 279t
Lorazepan (Ativan), 38t
Losec, 181
Lower GI series, 170–71
Lumbar puncture (spinal tap), 255

Lumen, 50
Lumpectomy, 197
Lung cancer, 99, 188–89, 194, 200–01, 290
Lung disease, 62, 76, 234–35, 292; smoking and, 289, 290
Lungs, 16, 18t, 54, 192
Lymphatics, 185, 196
Lymphocytes, 79
Lymphoma, 185

Maalox, 180
Macroglobulinemia, 85, 86
Macula, 133f, 145, 146–47; defined, 331
Macular degeneration, 136–37, 139, 146–47, 331
Magnesium citrate, 174t
Mammography (mammogram), 188, 189, 196, 197–98, 288, 299; defined, 331
Mastectomy, 197
Medicaid, 302, 331
Medical alert bracelet, 216, 300
Medical alert system, 300
Medical examinations. See Physical examination(s)
Medicare, 188, 257, 302, 331
Medications, 17, 20, 23–43, 64; body's changing responses to, 24–31; causing impotence, 279t, 280, 282; causing Parkinson's syndrome, 241–42; causing tremor, 234–35; causing urinary incontinence, 263, 264, 269t, 270; and constipation, 166–67; for diabetes, 41, 214–15; dosage, 43; effect on bone marrow, 78–79; effect on stomach, 179; exacerbating medical conditions, 32–33, 34–35t; and GI system, 165; for hemorrhoids, 176–77; to lower cholesterol, 55; metabolization and excretion of, 24–25; for muscle spasms, 40; newly released, 30–31; and osteoporosis, 92, 93; over-the-counter, 4, 5, 23, 26, 32, 37, 143, 270; overuse of, 24, 31–33; polypharmacy, 31–33; with special risk for el-

derly, 27–29, 38–42; for stomach cramps, 39–40; in treatment of arrhythmias, 66–67; in treatment of arthritis, 106; in treatment of bone loss, 98; in treatment of CAD, 58–61; in treatment of colds and allergies, 39; in treatment of congestive heart failure, 68–69; in treatment of dementia, 256; in treatment of gastritis and ulcers, 180–81; in treatment of glaucoma, 143–44; in treatment of incontinence, 265, 266–67, 268; in treatment of Parkinson's disease, 239–41; in treatment of tremor, 236; underuse of, 33–36; that worsen dementia, 257; *see also* Anticholinergic medications; Antipsychotic medications; Pain medications (analgesics)
Melanomas, 118, 119–20
Melena, 179, 331
Mellaril, 28*t*, 29*t*, 41, 242, 256
Melphalan (Alkeran), 86
Memory loss, 28*t*, 36, 243–45; in dementia, 252, 254, 255
Meningiomas, 251*t*
Menopause, 91, 92, 95, 96, 266, 274
Menstruation, 274, 275
Mental function: change in, 248, 249, 255; change in, in dementia, 243, 244, 245; effect of stroke on, 221–22
Metabolism, 19*t*
Metamucil, 172, 174*t*, 294
Metaproterenol (Alupent), 235
Metastasize, 118, 120, 186, 192, 196–97, 198, 199, 201, 202–03; defined, 331
Methocarbamol (Robaxin), 40
Methyldopa (Aldomet), 64, 279*t*
Metoprolol (Lopressor), 34*t*, 35*t*, 60, 279*t*
Mevaclor (Lopid), 55
Mexilitine, 67
Microaneurysms, 145
Micrographia, 238
Micronase, 214
Micturition, 262

Milk of magnesia, 172, 174*t*, 182
Mineral oil, 173
Misoprostal (Cytotec), 181
Mitral valve, 69
Moderil, 279*t*
Mohs Surgery, 119, 331
Mononeuropathy, 211
Morphine 25, 167
Motrin, 106, 179
Mouth, 18*t*, 26, 125–31, 187
Mouth cancer. *See* Oral cancer
MRI (magnetic resonance imaging) scan, 223, 236, 248, 255; defined, 331
Multiinfarct dementia, 221–22, 248–49, 250*t*, 254
Multiple myeloma, 75, 85–86, 92
Murmur, 69
Muscle relaxants, 28*t*, 167
Muscle spasms, 40
Muscles, 89, 94, 185, 227, 231, 235
Myelocytes, 79
Mylanta, 180
Myocardial infarction (MI). *See* Heart attack (infarction)
Myeloma, multiple, 75, 85–86, 92

Nadolol (Corgard), 34*t*. 35*t*, 233, 279*t*
Naprosyn, 106
Naproxyn (Naprosyn, Anaprox), 106
Narcotic painkillers, 28–29*t*, 34*t*, 102–03, 167, 173, 175, 177, 269; as cause of confusion, 25, 28–29*t*, 41, 102–03; as cause of urinary incontinence, 267–68, 269*t*; and constipation, 167; and impotence, 279*t*; sensitivity to, 25
Nasogastric tube, 225, 226
Nausea, 166, 181, 195
Navane, 28*t*, 29*t*, 41, 242
Neoloid, 173, 174*t*
Nerve damage, 107–08; with diabetes, 209, 211
Neurological examination, 223, 254, 255
Neurological system, 25, 254
Neurologist, 225, 236
Neurosurgeon, 331

Neurotransmitters, 20, 236
Niacin, 55
Nifedipine (Procardia), 59
Nitroglycerin, 34*t*, 58–59, 60
Noise-induced hearing loss, 153–54
Nolvadex, 197
Nonsteroidal antiinflammatories (NSAIDS), 35*t*, 80, 106; effect of stomach, 179, 181
Normal (term), 4, 13–14, 21–22
Normal age-related changes, 15–22, 18–19*t*; in blood sugar, 205–06; in GI system, 164–66; in heart, 48–50
Normal aging, 7–22; versus abnormal, 13–14; defined, 21–22
Norpace, 34*t*, 35*t*
Nursing home, 104, 195, 260; stroke rehabilitation, 226, 227, 228
Nutrition, 17, 121; *see also* Diet

Oat cell cancer, 194, 201
Obesity, 53, 266; and CAD, 53, 54, 55, 56; and diabetes, 206
Occult blood, 169, 170, 179; defined, 331
Occupational therapy, 5, 227, 228, 234, 241
Ocular plethysmography, 224
Oil glands (skin), 111*f*
Old age: defined, 4, 9–11
Omeprazole (Losec), 181
Oncologist, 4, 130, 190–91, 194, 203; defined, 331
Open-heart surgery, 63, 70; *see also* Coronary artery bypass surgery (CABG)
Open reduction and internal fixation. *See* ORIF
Opsite, 122
Ophthalmologist, 4, 136, 138, 140, 141, 142, 144, 145, 146, 147, 148, 149; defined, 332
Ophthalmoscope, 138, 142, 145
Optic nerve, 133*f*, 134, 142
Oral cancer, 129–30, 187, 189
Oral hypoglycemic agents, 41, 214–15
Orgasm, 282

ORIF (Open Reduction and Internal Fixation), 99, 100–03, 332
Orinase, 215
Orthopaedic surgeon, 99, 100, 103
Orthopnea, 67, 332
Oscal-D, 95, 97
Ossicles, 108, 152, 153, 154, 157
Osteoporosis, 87, 88, 90, 91–98, 108, 276, 299; defined, 91–92, 332; evaluation of, 93; exercise and, 291; prevention and treatment of, 95–98; risk factors in, 92, 93
Otic nerve, 108, 152, 154
Otitis externa, 155
Otitis media, 156
Otolaryngologist, 154, 332
Otoscope, 156
Ovarian cancer, 282, 284
Ovary(ies), 261*f*, 274
Overflow incontinence. *See* Urinary incontinence
Overhydration, 67, 84–85
Over-the-counter drugs. *See* Medications
Oxazepam (Serax), 38*t*
Oxycodone, 25
Oxycodone (Percocet, Percodan), 25, 41, 167, 279*t*
Oxygen, 73, 74

Pacemaker(s), 64, 332
Paget's disease, 107–08, 154
Pain control, 25; in cancer, 194–95, 203
Pain medications (analgesics), 40–41, 80, 233; narcotic, 28–29*t*, 102–03, 167, 173, 175, 177, 269
Palate, 162*f*, 163
Palliation, 190, 193, 332
Palpitations, 65, 69
Pancreas, 81, 161, 164, 204, 205
Pap smear, 187, 283–84, 298–99
Paranoia, 42, 246, 256
Parasympathetic nervous system, 164, 165, 166–67
Parkinsonism, 332
Parkinson's disease, 43, 230, 236–42; causes of, 236–37; and dementia, 249, 250*t*; diagnosing, 239;

symptoms of, 236–37; treatment for, 239–41

Parkinson's syndrome, 29*t*, 241–42

Parlodil, 241

Pathological fracture, 99

Pelvic examination, 187, 270, 277, 298–99

Pentazocine (Talwin), 25, 28*t*

Pentoxifylline (Trentyl), 36

Pepsid, 180

Peptic ulcer. *See* Ulcers

Percocet, 25, 41, 167, 279*t*

Percodan, 25, 41, 167, 279*t*

Perdiem, 172, 174*t*, 294

Perforated ulcer, 179

Pergolide, 241

Pericolace, 174*t*

Peripheral neuropathy, 211

Peripheral vision, 141, 142

Peristalsis, 163–64, 166, 167, 173; defined, 332

Personality change, 218; in dementia, 244–45, 252–53

Pessary, 266

Phacoemulsification, 140

Pharmacist(s), 5, 37–38

Phenobarbital, 279*t*

Phenophthalene (in Ex-Lax), 41, 174*t*

Photocoagulation, 146

Physiatrists, 227, 332

Physical examination(s), 68, 93, 186, 270, 288, 295, 297–99; checking for cancer in, 187–88; in diagnosis of dementia, 254; for tremor, 235–36

Physical therapy, 104, 106, 211, 228, 241; therapists, 5, 103–04, 227, 228

Physiology, 4, 17–21, 18–19*t*, 217–18, 332; medications, 24–31; of men, 277–78; of women, 274–77

Pigmentation, 110, 111*f*, 120

Pilocar, 144

Pilocarpine (Pilocar), 144

Pinna, 152

Plaque, 50, 219

Plasmacyte, 85

Platelets, 50–52, 60, 72, 79–80, 89, 106, 220, 223–24, 298

Pneumonia, 21, 78, 83, 94, 100, 102, 189, 289, 296

Pneumonia vaccine, 35, 43, 296

Pollution, 15, 289–91

Polydipsia, 208

Polyphagia, 208

Polypharmacy, 31–33, 332

Polyps (colon), 167, 171, 188, 201, 202

Polyuria, 207–08

Postherpetic neuralgia, 118, 332

Postvoid residual, 270

Potassium, 68, 295

Powers of attorney, 309–19; defined, 332; general/special, 313; *see also* Durable powers of attorney

Prazocin, 34*t*

Prednisone, 35*t*, 78, 86, 92, 93, 118, 137, 138, 179

Premature ventricular contraction (PVC), 66

Presbycusis, 152–53, 157

Presbyesophagus, 178

Presbyopia, 134–35, 332

Pressure sores. *See* Bed sores

Prevention, 4, 288–300; of constipation, 172, 174*t*, 176; of coronary artery disease, 53–56; of osteoporosis, 95–97; of strokes, 222–24

Primary-care physician, 4, 5, 99, 113, 138, 191; communication with, 141, 144, 194, 203, 225, 258; defined, 333; review of medications with, 33, 37, 43, 270

Pro-Banthine, 28*t*

Probate, 321–22

Procaine, 67

Procardia, 59

Proctoscopes, 170

Progesterone, 16, 97, 274–75, 276

Propantheline (Pro-Banthine), 28*t*

Propine, 144

Propoxyphene (Darvon, Darvocet, Wygesic), 25, 29*t*, 40–41, 167, 279*t*

Propranolol (Inderal), 34*t*, 35*t*, 60, 64, 233, 279*t*

Prostaglandin inhibitor, 181

Prostate, 19*t*, 198, 261*f*, 284, 285–87; enlarged, 28*t*, 34*t*, 267, 284, 285–86; examination of, 298
Prostate cancer, 75, 99, 185, 187, 194, 198–200, 284, 286–87
Prostatectomy, 198–99; *see also* Transurethral resection of the prostate
Proteins, 16; in blood, 72, 73, 81–83, 84, 85–86; in diet, 96, 214, 293
Pseudephedrine, 265, 266
Psychological illness, 278, 279, 280, 281, 282
Psychosis, 42, 333; dementia and, 246–47
Psyllium (in Metamucil, Konsyl), 172, 174*t*
Ptosis, 134, 136, 333
Pulmonary edema, 67, 333
Pulmonary embolism, 81, 102, 333
Pulmonologist, 201, 333
Pupil (eye), 133*f*, 134, 144

Questron, 55
Quinidine, 67

Radiation, 75, 99, 188
Radiation therapy, 130, 281, 282; radioactive implants, 193, 199; in treatment of cancer, 178, 191, 192–93, 197, 199
Radical mastectomy, 197
Radiologist, 181, 200, 333
Radiotherapist, 333
Rantitidine (Zantac), 180
Rashes, 115–18; viral, 116, 117–18
Rauwiloid, 279*t*
Rectal examination, 169, 187, 198, 202, 270, 285, 298
Rectal (fecal) impaction, 166, 174–75, 330
Rectum, 164, 165–66, 170, 267
Red blood cells (RBCs), 72, 73–77, 89, 298
Reflux (regurgitation), 69, 177
Regurgitation, 69, 177
Rehabilitation, 5, 63; with hip fractures, 103–04; with stroke, 226–29

Rehabilitation hospitals, 226, 227, 228
Renal failure, 35*t*, 89, 205, 209, 210, 224, 255; *see also* Kidneys
Reproductive organs, 273–87
Reserpine, 35*t*, 279*t*
Restoril, 38*t*
Reticulocytes, 75
Retin A, 112
Retina (eye), 133*f*, 134, 137, 142, 143, 145, 148
Retinal detachment, 147–48
Retinopathy, 146, 211, 333
Revocable trust. *See* Living trust
Rheumatoid arthritis, 105
Risk factors: for CAD, 52–56; for developing diabetes, 206–07; in osteoporosis, 92, 93; in stroke, 217, 219–20
Robaxin, 40

Safety devices, 241, 299–300
Saliva, 125, 126–27, 128, 163
Salt (in diet), 126, 165, 295
Sandril, 279*t*
Sarcoma, 185, 333
Schatski's ring, 178
Scoliosis, 94
Screening tests, 186–87, 188–89, 198, 298; for cancer, 186–89; for glaucoma, 142–43
Scrotum, 284–85
Sedation, 28*t*, 39, 102, 257
Sedatives. *See* Antianxiety drugs; Sleeping medications
Sedimentation rate, 255
Seligiline (Deprenyl), 241
Senescence, 333
Senile, 245; defined, 333
Senile Dementia of the Alzheimer's Type (SDAT). *See* Alzheimer's disease
Senility, 245
Senna, 173, 174*t*
Serax, 38*t*
Serpasil, 279*t*
Sexual intercourse, 275, 276–77, 278, 280–82

Sexuality, 273–87
Shingles, 118
Shortness of breath, 65, 69, 74, 76, 200, 290
Sick-sinus syndrome, 32
Sigmoid colon, 164, 170
Sigmoidoscopy, 170, 188
Sinemet, 239–40
Sinus node (heart), 47; and heart rate, 47, 48–49
Sitz bath, 176
Skin, 19*t*, 73, 109–24, 298; age-related changes in, 110–13; cancer, 96, 112, 118–20, 123, 185, 187–88, 196, 283; functions of, 109; growths, 112, 114–15, 283; infections, 78, 208, 210; parts of, 110, 111*f*; *see also* Bed sores; Rashes
Skull, 107, 108
Sleeping medications/sleeping pills, 25, 27*t*, 32, 34*t*, 38–39, 167; better and worse, 38*t*; as cause of urinary incontinence, 269*t*, 270
Small cell carcinoma, 201
Small intestines, 163–64
Smell, 18*t*, 126, 165
Smog, 290
Smoking, 53, 289–90; and CAD, 53, 54, 55, 56, 70; and lung cancer, 200, 201; and oral cancer, 129; and stroke, 219, 222, 229
Social workers, 5, 180, 195, 221, 226, 257, 259
Soma, 40
Sorbitol, 172, 174*t*
Speech, 125, 128
Sphincter muscle, 261*f*, 262, 265, 266, 267
Spinal column (vertebrae), 88, 89
Spinal cord, 94
Spinal-cord injuries, 120
Spontaneous bladder contractions, 263, 268
Springing power of attorney, 310–11, 312
Squamous cell carcinoma, 118–19, 201

Stenosis, 69
Steroids, 78, 92, 93, 118, 137, 138; effect on stomach, 179; topical, 114, 116, 176
Stomach, 23, 162*f*, 163, 178–82, 189
Stomach acid, 16, 164, 165, 180–81
Stomach cramps: medicines for, 39–40
Stool, 164; blood in, 74, 169, 175, 179, 182, 187, 189, 202, 298; straining at, 165–66, 167, 172, 176; *see also* Constipation; Laxatives
Stool softeners. *See* Laxatives
Stress incontinence, 263, 265–67, 272; cause and treatment of, 266–67; *see also* Urinary incontinence
Stress test. *See* Exercise tolerance test
Stroke(s), 65–66, 73, 74, 76, 80, 81, 147, 217–29, 248, 314; defined, 217–18; diabetes and, 209; kinds of, 220–22; prevention of, 222–24; rehabilitation, 226–29; risk factors for, 217, 219–20; treatment of, 225–26
Subcutaneous fat (skin), 110–12, 111*f*
Subdural hematoma, 221, 248; as cause of dementia, 249, 251*t*, 255
Sucralfate (Carafte), 181
Sugar (in diet), 126, 165, 214, 295
Sun exposure, 95–96, 98, 110, 137, 138; avoiding, 112, 123; and skin cancer, 118, 119, 120
Surgery, 36; for blocked carotid arteries, 225; with breast cancer, 197; with cataracts, 139–41; with colon cancer, 202; with degenerative arthritis, 107; for ears, 154–55; with esophageal cancer, 178; eye, 136; with glaucoma, 144; with gynecological cancer, 283; with hemorrhoids, 176–77; with oral cancer, 129–30; prostate, 198–99, 267, 287; and risk of stroke, 219–20; with skin cancer, 119; in treatment of cancer, 191, 192; in treatment of erectile impotence, 281; in

Surgery (*cont.*)
  treatment of Parkinson's disease, 241
Swallowing, 163, 238
Sweat glands (skin), 109, 111*f*
"Swimmer's ear," 155–56
Swimming, 292–93
Syncope, 34*t*, 49, 334; *see also* Fainting
Syphilis, 249, 251*t*, 255

Tagamet, 180, 279*t*
Talwin, 25, 28*t*
Tamoxifen (Nolvadex), 197
Taste, 125, 126, 165
Tears, 133*f*, 136
Teeth, 125–31; care of, 128–29, 130
Temazepam (Restoril), 38*t*
Temporal arteritis, 147
Tenormin, 34*t*, 35*t*, 60, 233, 279*t*
Tegretol, 211
Testamentary trust, 314
Testicles, 284–85
Testosterone, 16, 53, 199, 277
Thallium, 56–57
Theodure, 235
Theophylline (Theodure), 235
Theories of aging, 11–13
Thiazide, 85
Thioridazine (Mellaril), 28*t*, 29*t*, 41, 242, 256
Thiothixene (Navane), 28*t*, 29*t*, 41, 242
Thorazine, 28*t*, 29*t*, 41
Throat, 187
Throat cancer, 129–30
Thyroid gland, 169–70; abnormal, 249; disease as cause of dementia, 249, 252*t*; hormone replacement, 255; overactive, 65; underactive, 169
Timolol, 32, 34*t*, 35*t*, 64, 144
Timoptic, 32, 34*t*, 35*t*, 64, 144
Tinnitus, 154
Tobramicin, 154
Tolbutamide (Orinase), 215
Tongue, 125, 162*f*, 163, 165
Trabecular bones, 88, 93–94

Tranquilizers: as cause of urinary incontinence, 269*t*; *see also* Antianxiety drugs
Transfusion(s), 76–77, 91; reaction, 77
Transient ischemic attacks (TIAs), 222, 223, 224; defined, 334
Transurethral prostatectomy (TURP), 199, 286, 334
Tremor, 230, 231–36, 242; defined, 231–32, 334; essential, 232, 234; evaluation of, 235–36; kinds of, 234–35; with Parkinson's disease, 236, 237, 238, 239; pill-rolling, 238; senile, 232–34
Trentyl, 36
Triazolam (Halcion), 38*t*
Trustee, 314–15, 322
Tumors, 185–86, 192; benign, 186; brain, 235; malignant, 186; rectal, 169
Tums, 95
TURP. *See* Transurethral resection of the prostate
Tylenol. *See* Acetaminophen
Tylenol #3, 25, 41, 167

Ulcers, 106, 179–80; bleeding, 74–75; treatment of, 180–82; *see also* Bed sores
Ultrasound, 198, 284
Upper GI series, 179, 181–82
Urecholine, 265
Ureter, 261*f*, 262
Urethra, 261*f*, 262, 266, 275, 276, 285, 286
Urge incontinence. *See* Urinary incontinence
Urinary incontinence, 35, 260–72, 282; caused by medications, 263, 264, 267–68, 269*t*, 270; overflow incontinence, 263, 267–68, 270; stress, 263, 265–67, 272; types of, 263–68; urge in, 263–65, 270, 272
Urinary retention, 24, 26, 28*t*, 29*t*, 41; defined, 334
Urinary tract: female, 261*f*; male, 261*f*

Urination, 49, 262–63, 282; difficulty with, 27*t*, 28*t*, 39; prostate enlargement and, 285–86; in diabetes, 207–08, 209
Urine tests, 213–14, 270
Urispas, 265
Urodynamics, 271
Urologist, 198, 199, 266, 270, 271, 272, 281; defined, 334
Uterus, 261*f*, 274; cancer, 97, 275; prolapse, 282–83

Vaccinations, 33–36, 43, 82, 288, 296–97, 300
Vagina, 261*f*, 275, 276, 281, 283; atrophic vaginitis, 275, 277, 281–82; lining of, 275; lubrication and engorgement of, 276–77
Vaginal cancer, 283
Vaginal examination, 266
Vaginal infections, 281, 282
Valium, 27*t*, 38*t*
Valvuloplasty, 70
Vancomycin, 154
Vasotec, 35*t*, 69
VDRL (test), 255
Veins, 334
Ventricle (heart), 47, 64, 65, 334
Ventricular arrhythmias, 66–67
Ventricular fibrillation, 66
Ventricular tachycardia, 66
Verapamil (Calan, Isoptin), 34*t*, 35*t*, 59, 64
Vertebrae. *See* Spinal column
Vertebral compression fractures, 93–95

Viruses, 77, 78, 82,–83, 237
Vision, 132–49; age-related changes in, 134–36; blurred, 23–24, 26; 27*t*, 28*t*, 29*t*, 39, 146, 265; symptoms of, in diabetes, 208
Vision loss, 132, 136–137, 149; aids for, 147–49; causes of, 147–48; with diabetes, 144–46, 211
Visiting-nurse services, 258
Vitamin deficiency: B_{12}, 251*t*; as cause of dementia, 249, 251*t*
Vitamins, 256, 295–96; A, 296; B, 296; B_{12}, 75, 255, 256, 296; C, 122, 296; D, 95–96, 98, 109, 110, 296; E, 296; K, 81

Walkers, 229, 241, 300
Weight control. *See* Obesity
White blood cells (WBCs), 16, 72, 77–79, 89, 298; problems with, 78–79
Will(s), 302, 318, 319–21; *see also* Living will
Wrinkles, 112, 275; smoking and, 289
Wrist fracture, 94–95
Wygesic, 25, 29*t*, 40–41, 167

Xanax, 38*t*
Xerosis. *See* Dry skin
Xerostomia. *See* Dry mouth

Zantac, 180
Zenker's diverticulum, 178